Du Bois on Religion

Du Bois on Religion

Edited by
Phil Zuckerman

ALTAMIRA
PRESS

A Division of
ROWMAN & LITTLEFIELD PUBLISHERS, INC.
Walnut Creek • Lanham • New York • Oxford

ALTAMIRA PRESS

A Division of Rowman & Littlefield Publishers, Inc.
1630 North Main Street, Suite 367
Walnut Creek, CA 94596
http://www.altamirapress.com

Rowman & Littlefield Publishers, Inc.
4720 Boston Way
Lanham, MD 20706

12 Hid's Copse Road
Cumnor Hill, Oxford OX2 9JJ, England

Copyright © 2000 by AltaMira Press

British Cataloguing in Publication Information Available

Library of Congress Cataloging-in-Publication Data

Du Bois, W. E. B. (William Edward Burghardt), 1868-1963.
    Du Bois on religion / [edited by] Phil Zuckerman.
        p. cm.
    Includes bibliographical references and index.
    ISBN 0-7425-0420-4 (hardcover : alk. paper)—ISBN 0-7425-0421-2 (pbk. : alk. paper)
        1. Du Bois, W. E. B. (William Edward Burghardt), 1868-1963—Religion. 2.
Afro-Americans—Religion. 3. United States—Race relations. 4. Race relations—Religious
aspects—Christianity. I. Zuckerman, Phil. II. Title.

E185.97.D73 A322 2000
306.6—dc21

00-038044

Printed in the United States of America

∞™ The paper used in this publication meets the minimum requirements of American
National Standard for Information Sciences—Permanence of Paper for Printed Library
Materials, ANSI/NISO Z.39.48-1992.

Contents

vi   *Contents*

Acknowledgments

First, I would like to acknowledge W. E. B. Du Bois himself, whose humanity, insight, and love of justice were so courageously pronounced in a world sadly lacking all three.

I would like to thank professors Peter Nardi, Benton Johnson, Richard Newman, Linda Seidman, and David Levering Lewis for their help and encouragement. I would also like to thank Erik Hanson, Mitch Allen, and everyone else at wonderful AltaMira Press. I would especially like to thank Tonya Lindsey, my research assistant, for her invaluable help and patience, and Joanne Zhang, who came through so many times in helping me with the technical traumas of this project. I must also thank my father for his encouragement, love, and work, and my mother and brother for their love. Finally, thanks, love, and awe to my wife, Stacy, and my daughter, Ruby Pandora Natya.

Introduction

PHIL ZUCKERMAN

Who should be named "Person of the Twentieth Century"?
As the year 2000 approached, *Time* magazine wanted to know. So the editors of *Time* polled various world leaders, ranking politicians, famous entertainers, leading intellectuals, and other such figures, soliciting their nominations. Responding to the poll, renowned Harvard professor Henry Louis Gates Jr. put forth this name: W. E. B. Du Bois. Gates wrote:

> W. E. B. Du Bois, the great African-American intellectual, is the Person of the Century for me. Du Bois was the first black Ph.D. from Harvard; he was one of the founding fathers of sociology. He helped establish the N.A.A.C.P. and edited its journal, *The Crisis*, for 24 years. He was an architect of the Harlem Renaissance and the civil rights movement, and throughout his life brilliantly fought against racial discrimination and for the full participation of blacks in American society. He conceived of the *Encyclopedia Africana*, a comprehensive history of the African diaspora. He was a staunch opponent (with Bertrand Russell) of the use of nuclear weapons. Who could possibly have done more than he to redefine American democracy over 60 years of the 20th century? (*Time*, May 10, 1999)

Du Bois was a national as well as an international leading figure of the twentieth century and "one of the greatest intellectuals America ever produced," as Meyer Weinberg (1970, xiii) has declared. His legacy remains strong; Du Bois is well respected as a distinguished scholar of race relations, African and American history, and culture and politics. His reputation as both a powerful man of letters (Gates 1989) and founding sociologist is secure (Collins and Makowsky 1998; Lemert 1993; Green and Driver 1978).

1

Du Bois also delved into religion. However, his insights, critiques, praises, beliefs, and theories concerning religion have not received the attention they deserve from academics. What Du Bois had to say concerning religion was quite powerful and insightful, and yet scholars of religion have failed to acknowledge or draw from his foundational work. Indeed, as a sociologist of religion, Du Bois remains virtually unknown. Take, for instance, the *Encyclopedia of Religion and Society* (Swatos 1998). In this impressive volume we find four pages devoted to Emile Durkheim, five pages devoted to Max Weber, two and a half pages to Talcott Parsons, two and half pages to Karl Marx—and four sentences to Du Bois. Four sentences! Despite such monumental, seminal works as *The Philadelphia Negro* (which presented the first social survey of black congregations in an urban setting; Baer 1998) and the classic edited volume *The Negro Church*, as well as numerous essays, articles, chapters, letters, speeches, and short stories concerning religion, Du Bois's work in the area of religion has been left unexplored. For example, nearly all recently published major survey texts on social theory and religion fail to even mention his name; the ones that do, mention it only in passing (Turner 1991; Kurtz 1995; Hamilton 1995; Thrower 1999; Johnstone 1997; McGuire 1997; Chalfant, Beckley, and Palmer 1994).

It is quite baffling that scholars have ignored Du Bois's contributions to religion. Is it because he was at times overtly critical of religious institutions, thereby rankling the religiously sympathetic? Or conversely, is it because he at times approached religion with a faithful adoration, thereby rankling scholars of the more skeptical persuasion? Or is it because he was so well known as a "race theorist" that his significant contributions in others areas have been neglected by default? I am not sure—more research is necessary to address that question. But I am sure that there is a need for a volume that explores his writings on religion.

Hence this book.

Through this collection I hope to place Du Bois where he deserves to be: squarely in the firmament of founding sociologists of religion. If "classical" refers to the quality of enduring over time, then Du Bois should be considered a classical theorist of religion in his own right, for his insights are as relevant today as they were in his own time.

A LIFE

William Edward Burghardt Du Bois (pronounced Doo-Boyss) was born on a Sunday, February 23, 1868, on Church Street in Great Barrington, Massachusetts. It was the year of President Andrew Johnson's impeachment. Du Bois died in

Accra, Ghana, on August 27, 1963, on the night before the famous Civil Rights March on Washington.

He married Nina Gomer in 1896 and they had two children: a son, Burghardt (who died at the age of three), and a daughter, Yolande. A year after Nina's death in 1950, he married his second wife, Shirley Graham.

He was a "tireless explorer and a gifted discoverer of social truths," eulogized Martin Luther King Jr. (1968). He received a B.A. in 1888 from Fisk University, a second B.A. from Harvard in 1890, and an M.A. from Harvard in 1892. After studying for two years at the University of Berlin, he received his Ph.D. from Harvard in 1895. He studied under such notables as Max Weber, George Santayana, and William James. He was professor of Greek and Latin at Wilberforce University from 1894 to 1896 and assistant instructor of sociology at the University of Pennsylvania from 1896 to 1897. At Atlanta University he was professor of economics and history from 1897 to 1910 and chairman of the Sociology Department from 1934 to 1944.

He wrote over twenty books and was a prolific journalist, writing hundreds of essays and articles throughout the course of his life. He wrote regularly for the New York *Age*, the New York *Globe*, and the Springfield *Republican*. He was editor of *The Moon* in 1906, editor of *The Horizon* from 1907 to 1910, editor of *The Crisis* from 1910 to 1934, and editor of *Phylon* magazine from 1940 to 1944.

In addition to writing, he worked as an activist for social and racial justice. He was the principal founder of the Niagara Movement (forerunner of the NAACP) and served as its general secretary. He was a prominent founder of the National Association for the Advancement of Colored People (NAACP) and waged a sustained battle against lynchings and discrimination. He was a world leader of the Pan-African Movement, serving as secretary of the first Pan-African Congress and leading many subsequent congresses.

And he was much more: world traveler, labor rights supporter, novelist, poet, women's suffrage proponent, antiwar activist, Communist Party member, world peace advocate, statesman, lecturer, and so on. In the words of Philip S. Foner (1970, 8), he was a man "who was throughout his life passionately devoted to freedom, peace, and human dignity."

THE RELIGIOUS IDENTITY OF W. E. B. DU BOIS

In 1906, following the outbreak of violence against blacks in the infamous Atlanta Pogrom, Du Bois wrote the poem "A Litany at Atlanta," in which he directly beseeches God as the "good Lord," "Judge of men," "great God," "heavenly Father," and "Christ of all the Pities." He also refers to "miserable sinners." In 1920 Du Bois published *Darkwater: Voices from within the Veil*, a collection of his writings. The first piece, entitled "Credo," begins with an affirmation of faith ("I believe in God") and continues to expound distinctly religious sentiments: "knowing that men be brothers in Christ" and "I believe in the Devil and his angels."

Some forty years later, however, in his last autobiography, he would write:

> The Soviet Union does not allow any church of any kind to interfere with education, and religion is not taught in the public schools. It seems to me that this is the greatest gift of the Russian Revolution to the modern world. Most educated men no longer believe in religious dogma. If questioned they will usually resort to double-talk before admitting the fact. But who today actually believes that this world is ruled and directed by a benevolent person of great power who, on humble appeal, will change the course of events at our request? Who believes in miracles? Many folk follow religious ceremonies and services; and allow their children to learn fairy tales and so-called religious truth, which in time the children come to recognize as conventional lies told by their parents and teachers for the children's good. One can hardly exaggerate the moral disaster of this custom. We have to thank the Soviet Union for the courage to stop it. (1968, 42)

And furthermore,

> It is our great debt to the Soviet Union that it alone of nations dared stop that lying to children. . . . we filled little minds with fairy tales of religious dogma which we ourselves never believed. We filled their thoughts with pictures of barbarous revenge called God which contradicted all their inner sense of decency. We repeated folk tales of children without fathers, of death which was life, of sacrifice which was shrewd investment and ridiculous pictures of an endless future. The Soviets have stopped this. They allow a child to grow up without religious lies and . . . without scaring him into Hell or rewarding him with a silly Heaven. (1968, 412)

From speaking passionately of God, Christ, and sinners—from expressing a fiery faith in "God . . . Christ . . . [and the] Devil and his angels"—to offering a stinging critique of religious belief and unabashed praise for the Soviet Union's antireligious policies, Du Bois's religious identity was a long and meandering but essentially direct path from faithful Christian to skeptical agnostic (Lewis 1993). Though religion permeated his writings and perpetually infused his life, he died critical of organized religion and unaccepting of traditional religious doctrines.

Du Bois writes that there were four leading Protestant churches in Great Barrington while he was growing up. He recalls that "because we lived near the Congregational church, and because my mother had many acquaintances there, and because the minister, Scudder, was especially friendly, my mother early joined this church. I think we were the only colored communicants" (Du Bois 1968, 88).

It was in this congregation that Du Bois received most of his religious training, but there was also a Negro Methodist Zion church in Great Barrington, which he "sometimes attended" in his adolescent years.

As a child, Du Bois loved his church. According to biographer Herbert Aptheker (1982, 6), "outside of his school his major contact with the people of his town was through the church." He enjoyed its festivals throughout the year, its Sunday school, the Hebrew and Greek instruction, and the weekly sermons. He was inspired by the altar's biblical inscription: "The Truth Shall Make You Free." At this church, according to biographer Arnold Rampersad (1976, 5), Du Bois was "directly exposed to the fundamental doctrines of New England Puritanism"—an exposure that staunchly tutored him in the "seriousness and combativeness" of "severe Calvinism." He describes the period he spent at this church as "very happy." And yet, though he felt himself to be "in his element" during Sunday school discussions, he also acknowledged later in life that even as a child his beliefs were never quite solid: "in the weekly Sunday School, we studied the bible with its tales of the impossible but I remember distinctly that I questioned the validity of some of them, like the story of Jonah" (Du Bois 1968, 413).

Du Bois drew from his Christian upbringing throughout his life. Religious themes, religious metaphors, and references to God and Jesus permeate the body of his work. He knew the Bible well and wouldn't hesitate to draw from its literature to add weight to a plea, expound upon a point, or drive home an argument. The fact that he could write such faith-filled pieces as "A Litany in Atlanta" and "Credo" speaks of the enormous significance religion held for Du Bois. It was a source of personal and professional inspiration.

Du Bois could even be considered—to use the words of Max Weber— "religiously musical." The greatest evidence for such a characterization comes from the cache of prayers he wrote that were found among his papers entrusted to the care of Herbert Aptheker and posthumously published under the title *Prayers for Dark People* (1980). Aptheker dates the prayers—which were written on "scraps of paper of varying sizes" and stored "helter-skelter" in a brown manila envelope—as having been written around 1909 or 1910. Their content overflows with spiritual expression and reverence. Nearly every prayer begins with an entreaty to God for strength, hope, or protection; faith and grace are constant themes. The following untitled prayer is emblematic of the others and is quoted in its entirety:

In the solemn silence of this Thy Holy night, O Heavenly Father, let the Christ spirit be born anew in this our home and in this land of ours. Out of the depths of

selfishness and languor and envy, let spring the spirit of humility and poverty, of gen-
tleness and sacrifice—the eternal dawn of Peace, good-will toward men. Let the
birth-bells of God call our vain imaginings back from pomp and glory and wealth—
back from the wasteful warships searching the seas—back to the lowly barn-yard and
the homely cradle of a yellow and despised Jew, whom the world has not yet learned
to call Wonderful, Counselor, the Mighty God, the Everlasting Father, and the
Prince of Peace. Amen. (Du Bois 1980, 15)

Despite his religiously musical writings and despite the preponderance of religious metaphors and references to God that pervade his work, his religious beliefs
gave way to skepticism and criticism—in regard to religious institutions as well
as religious beliefs. His own discussion of his religious development attests to the
accuracy of this description.

In his autobiographies (the first was published in 1940 and the second in
1968), Du Bois details his steady withdrawal and final cleavage from religion.
Upon arriving to study at Fisk University, he quickly joined the college Congregational church. Soon after his enrollment at the school he wrote a letter to the
pastor of his church back home in Great Barrington, in which he declared that
"I am glad to tell you that I have united with the Church here and hope that the
prayers of my Sunday School may help guide me in the path of Christian duty"
(Du Bois 1968, 110).

Yet his union with the Congregationalists at Fisk was short-lived. He soon
"became critical of religion and resentful of its practice" (1940, 33). One incident mentioned in both autobiographies was decisive in his break with religion:
a controversy concerning dancing. As he recalls (1968, 110–111),

"Pop" Miller did not allow my church membership to progress as placidly as I
planned. He was an official of the church and a fundamentalist in religion. He
soon had me and others accused before the church for dancing. I was astonished.
I had danced all my life quite as naturally as I sang and ran. . . . at the homes of
colored friends in the city, we nearly always danced and a more innocent pastime
I could not imagine. But Miller was outraged. . . . in his mind dancing figured as a
particularly heinous form of sin. I resented this and said so in very plain terms. The
teachers intervened and tried to reconcile matters in a way which for years afterward made me resentful and led to my eventual refusal to join a religious organization. They admitted that my dancing might well be quite innocent, but said that
my example might lead others astray. They quoted Paul: "If meat maketh my
brother to offend, I will eat no meat while the world standeth." I tried to accept
this for years, and for years I wrestled with this problem. Then I resented this kind

of sophistry. I began again to dance and I have never since had much respect for
Paul. (1968, 110–111)

While a student in Germany, he "turned still further from religious dogma"
(Du Bois 1940, 50). During his time abroad he became even more skeptical of
religious teachings, a position that deepened while he was at Harvard and per-
sisted for the rest of his life. According to Rampersad, Du Bois's college years
marked the onset of his loss of faith:

> The omniscient God of Du Bois' Congregational youth was slowly but surely dis-
> placed by the Unknowable of Herbert Spencer. Paradoxically, the search for truth
> was also the gospel of those who acknowledged this unknowable. For them, man
> scrutinized the universe unclouded by religious dogma: secular learning was religion
> enough. To those faithful to the old God, the new learning led almost inevitably to
> amorality and eventually to fatalism. As in his religion, so in his formal education,
> Du Bois would make a significant but unsteady transition between the old and new
> orders. (1976, 19–20)

And as Du Bois himself recounts his religious journey,

> My religious development has been slow and uncertain. . . . At 17 I was in a mis-
> sionary college where religious orthodoxy was stressed; but I was more developed to
> meet it with argument, which I did. . . . by the time of graduation I was still a
> "believer" in orthodox religion, but had strong questions which were encouraged at
> Harvard. In Germany I became a freethinker and when I came to teach at an ortho-
> dox Methodist negro school I was soon regarded with suspicion, especially when I
> refused to lead the students in public prayer. When I became head of a department
> in Atlanta, the engagement was held up because I balked at leading in prayer. . . .
> From my 30th year on I have increasingly regarded the church as an institution
> which defended such evils as slavery, color caste, exploitation of labor and war. I
> think the greatest gift of the Soviet Union to modern civilization was the
> dethronement of the clergy and the refusal to let religion be taught in public
> schools. (1968, 285)

Despite his ultimate withdrawal from religion and his pronounced criticisms
of religious teachings, it would be erroneous to label Du Bois an out-and-out
atheist. As Aptheker (1982, 5) argues,

> while Du Bois was an agnostic in his last years, he never was an atheist. Though
> the record shows a diminution as time passed in the confidence with which he held

some religious concepts . . . he never quite rejected a belief in some creative and persistent force.

Indeed, just such a self-characterization is found in Du Bois's correspondence. In 1948 a priest wrote to Du Bois asking him whether or not he believed in God. Du Bois replied:

> Answering your letter of October 3, may I say: If by "a believer in God," you mean a belief in a person of vast power who consciously rules the universe for the good of mankind, I answer No; I cannot disprove this assumption, but I certainly see no proof to sustain such a belief, neither in History nor in my personal experience.
>
> If on the other hand you mean by "God" a vague Force which, in some uncomprehensible way, dominates all life and change, then I answer, Yes; I recognize such Force, and if you wish to call it God, I do not object. (1978, 223)

ON RELIGION: THE GOOD AND THE BAD

In September 1999, I fell off my bike while riding home from campus and ended up in the emergency room. Dr. Bock, the physician who stitched up my chin and set my displaced pinkie, noticed the book by Du Bois that I had with me. I explained to him that I was a sociologist of religion and that I was reading what Du Bois had to say on the subject.

"So," began the doctor, "is religion just the opiate of the masses, a mere tool for oppression and exploitation, a bastion of hypocrisy—or is religion a positive force in the world, a source of human betterment that can help uplift people and nurture their spirits?"

"Both," I replied. It was a response that rose out of my recent immersion into the writing of Du Bois.

One of the most striking aspects of Du Bois's treatment of religion is that he saw—and noted—both potentials of religion: the good and the bad, to put it simply. One minute he could praise religious institutions and speak of religion sympathetically and in the next minute denounce religious institutions and speak of religion in unrelentingly harsh terms. Such a position could be characterized as contradictory or schizophrenic. Or it might be characterized as simply realistic. Astute. Accurate. The truth is that religion is neither good nor bad but has the potential for both. Contemporary sociologist Meredith McGuire expresses this notion in her succinct discussion of black religion and politics in the United States:

One recurring question is whether U.S. minority religions, such as African-American churches, serve to support the status quo or to promote social change for their people. The answer is "yes": Religion *both* supports the status quo *and* promotes active social change, often simultaneously. (1997, 257)

Du Bois's writings on religion attest to, and illustrate, McGuire's insight. As a social construction and a human projection, religion encapsulates both the wonders and the warts of humanity and has the potential to exemplify one, the other, or both. Few scholars of religious life have recognized this to the degree that Du Bois did, and few have expounded upon and illustrated the potential dual nature of religion as aptly and honestly.

To be sure, Du Bois was often more skeptical of religion than sympathetic, and his reputation as a harsh critic above all else runs deep. For instance, when I mentioned this book project to a highly respected professor (who wishes to remain anonymous), his immediate reaction was: "Du Bois on religion? Why, that's like doing Hitler on democracy." Such an analogy, albeit made in jest, is clearly unfair. Yes, Du Bois was an outspoken critic of religion. But he was also sympathetic at times, and his belief in religion's potential for goodness and human betterment is well documented.

In his book on John Brown (1962), Du Bois draws an unambiguously sympathetic portrayal of the role that religion played in the great abolitionist's movement and struggle, and he stresses the enormously positive and pervasive impact religion had on him throughout his life. Du Bois (1899, 21) spoke respectfully of the African Methodist Episcopal Church of America as "the most remarkable product of American Negro civilization." He characterized the black church as a site for potential political awakening (Du Bois 1963, 117), as well as a center for "social betterment" and racial consciousness. He spoke highly of religious black women and the role they played in uplifting their race during the dark days of slavery (Du Bois 1920, 174). On occasion he spoke well of black preachers, as in his chapter on Alexander Crummell in *The Souls of Black Folk*. He wrote with great pride of black religious music, dubbing it "the most original and beautiful expression of human life and longing yet born on American soil" (Du Bois 1989, 134), and he lauded the essentially democratic nature of black churches (Du Bois 1985, 84). He definitely acknowledged the achievements of organized black religion, declaring that

it has accomplished much. It has instilled and conserved morals, it has helped family life, it has taught and developed ability and given the colored man his best business training. It has planted in every city and town of the Union, with few exemptions, meeting places for colored folk which vary from shelters to luxurious and beautiful edifices. (Du Bois 1972, 332)

As Aptheker (1980, viii) has written of Du Bois, "he viewed the Black church as, at best, the 'basic rock' of his people, their shield and sword, their solace and goad; an indispensable source of their persistence and historical confidence despite all oppression."

In addition to characterizing the black church as a positive institution on occasion, Du Bois also approached the specific religious doctrines of Christianity as having potential social and psychological value for black people. One of the most pervasive metaphors throughout Du Bois's writings is that of the black man as suffering Jesus Christ. In such powerful pieces as "Jesus Christ in Texas," "The Gospel according to Mary Brown," "Pontius Pilate," and "The Son of God," Du Bois goes to great socioliterary lengths to illustrate the similarities between the suffering of blacks and that of Jesus: "Jesus Christ was a laborer and black men are laborers; He was poor and we are poor; He was despised; He was persecuted and crucified, and we are mobbed and lynched" (Du Bois 1972, 334). Such writings project a clear and definite sense that Du Bois understood how powerful a symbol Jesus Christ was to suffering black Americans: they could relate their agony to his and in such relation feel a sense of worth, comfort, and even godliness.

Although much of what Du Bois had to say about religion was positive, without a doubt, his negative sentiments are more well-known. His positive characterizations of it are certainly not typical and often appear on the fringes of his analyses. Not so his negative characterizations. They ring and tinker throughout his writings and speeches like persistent wind chimes of condemnation and rebuke.

In a commencement speech delivered to the graduating class of Fisk University in 1938, Du Bois (1970, 110) openly criticized the black organized religious community:

> Behold . . . the Black Churches of America. . . .
>   Their five millions of members in 40,000 groups, holding $200,000,000 in their hands, are the most strongly organized body among us. . . . what is this church doing today toward its primary task of teaching men right and wrong, and the duty of doing right?
>   The flat answer is nothing if not less than nothing. Like other churches and other religions of other peoples and ages, our church has veered off on every conceivable side path, which interferes with and nullifies its chief duty of character building.
>   It has built up a body of dogma and fairy tale, fantastic fables of sin and salvation, impossible creeds and impossible demands for unquestioning belief and obedience.

He criticized black urban churches for catering to the better-off and betraying the "working man" (Du Bois 1972, 330). He spoke disrespectfully of black preachers throughout his edited volume *The Negro Church*, often including multiple portraits of them as ignorant, unlearned, dishonest, and immoral. He faulted the black church for taking too great a portion of poor families' income, money that would be better used for more pressing needs such as better housing (Du Bois, 1899, xiii, 185).

Du Bois displayed a particular hostility toward the disturbing curiosity of white Americans who professed Christianity while upholding and participating in the racist systems of slavery and Jim Crowism. This is perhaps his most consistent lament: that the so-called Christianity of white America was nothing more than venomous hypocrisy writ large.

"A nation's religion is its life," he declared, "and as such white Christianity is a miserable failure" (Du Bois 1970, 309). He declared:

> It is painfully true that White Christianity has in the twentieth century been curiously discredited. . . . the leading nations representing His [Jesus'] religion have been murdering, maiming and hurting each other on a scale unprecedented in the history of Mankind. . . . into the White Church of Christ race prejudice has crept to such an extent it is openly recognized . . . and is considered the natural and normal thing. . . . These facts do not impugn Christianity but they do make terrible comment upon the failure of its white followers. (Du Bois 1985, 84)

In his first autobiography he noted that religious organizations are "segregated racially more completely than any other human activity; a curious and eloquent commentary upon modern Christianity" (Du Bois 1940, 201). He rebuked American Christianity, a system that "theoretically opens the doors to all men and yet closes it forcibly and insultingly in the face of black men" (Washington and Du Bois 1907, 178). He argued that religion in America was essentially "Jim Crowed from top to bottom" and that "no other institution in America is built so thoroughly or absolutely on the color line" (Du Bois 1970, 216–217). Furthermore,

> When the church meets the Negro problem, it writes itself down as a deliberate hypocrite and systematic liar. It does not say "Come unto me all ye that labor": it does not say "love its neighbor as itself"; it does not welcome "Jew and Gentile, barbarian, Scythian, bond and free"; and yet it openly and blatantly professes all this. . . . the church has opposed every great modern social reform; it opposed the spread of democracy, universal education, trade unionism, the abolition of poverty, the emancipation of women . . . and the emancipation of the Negro slave.

Again on church hypocrisy:

The church aided and abetted the Negro slave trade; the church was the bulwark of American slavery; and the church today is the strongest seat of racial and color prejudice. If one hundred of the best and purest colored folk of the United States should seek to apply for membership in any white church in this land tomorrow, 999 out of every 1,000 ministers would lie to keep them out. They would not only do this, but would openly and brazenly defend their action as worthy of followers of Jesus Christ. (Du Bois 1972, 334)

He regularly leveled criticisms at specific denominations—Episcopalians, Methodists, Baptists, and so on—for their apathy toward racial injustice.[1] As for the Catholic Church in particular, it "never champions the political or economic rights of subject peoples" (Du Bois 1978, 299). It "stands for color separation and discrimination to a degree equaled by no other church in America" (Du Bois 1973, 311). And furthermore,

In over 400 years the Catholic Church has ordained less than half a dozen black Catholic priests either because they have sent us poor teachers or because American Catholics do not want to work beside black priests and sisters or because they think Negroes have neither brains nor morals enough to occupy positions open freely to Poles, Irishmen, and Italians. (Du Bois 1973, 309)

He wrote disparagingly of Christian missionaries, speaking of "all their evil" wrought upon the native peoples of Africa (Du Bois 1920, 64); Christian missionaries "represent the oldest invasion of whites" and their purported religious activity was essentially a "cloak for conquest" (Du Bois 1915, 89). He chastised Christian missionary work for its underbelly of "ruthless economic exploitation and political downfall of less developed nations" (Du Bois 1963, 22). He implored the people of Africa to "reject the weakness of missionaries who teach neither love nor brotherhood, but chiefly the virtues of private profit from capital, stolen from your land and labor" (Du Bois 1971, 661).

In sum, while he recognized the positive possibilities of religion, especially among black Americans, Du Bois never hesitated to call attention to and condemn the hypocrisies and injustices that marred American religious institutions, both black and—more obviously—white.

CONTRIBUTIONS TO THE SOCIOLOGICAL STUDY OF RELIGION

Up to now I have explored Du Bois's personal religiosity (at times a believer but ultimately a skeptic) as well as his general perspective on religion and religious institutions (at times sympathetic but ultimately critical). I would like to conclude by summarizing what I believe are his greatest contributions to the sociological study of religion in general.

First, as already noted, *Du Bois reminds us of the dual capacity of religion for human good and/or ill.* There are those who are quick to laud religion as humanity's balm, and there are those who are equally quick to condemn religion as humanity's bane. Du Bois, through illustration and argumentation, shows us that religion is at various times neither, either, and both—it has the capacity for human betterment and detriment. The social setting Du Bois generally wrote about and focused on was nineteenth- and early twentieth-century America. Within this setting he shows how religion served as a source of organizational strength and pride for black Americans as well as a wellspring of hope and comfort. And yet, simultaneously, he describes how religion also served to uphold the status quo, specifically in terms of racial injustice and class disparity. And Du Bois's insight—that religion is neither good nor bad but has the potential for both—transcends the specific historical circumstances of which he wrote. While we may choose to focus on one (the potential for good) or the other (the potential for ill) for any given investigative or theoretical purpose, we must always bear in mind that religion is seldom an either/or phenomenon when it comes to benefiting or harming humanity.

Second, it is without question that *the sociological study of black American religion begins with the work of Du Bois.* His scholarship represents the starting point for any serious consideration of the role of religion in the black American experience. His investigations were thorough and unprecedented in scope. He analyzed rural black religiosity as well as urban. He relied on quantitative as well as qualitative data. From his detailed analyses of church membership and budget information to his rich descriptions of black southern revival meetings, Du Bois took seriously the role of religion in African-American life and devoted a considerable amount of scholarship to the phenomenon; his contributions are seminal.

Finally, and most important, Du Bois rightly emphasizes *religious institutions as social/communal centers and the specifically social rewards that religious affiliation affords*. In *The Philadelphia Negro* Du Bois argued that the black church "is, to be sure, a social institution first, and religious afterwards" (1899, 205). What is the distinction? While the dividing line between that which constitutes "social" and that which constitutes "religious" is admittedly ambiguous and evanescent, Du Bois's meaning is that the "social" entails the profane elements of communal living and human bonding, while the "religious" entails the sacred elements of spiritual/divine communion and devotion. Though Du Bois acknowledged the spiritual aspects of black religious institutions, he stressed their social aspects above all else. Indeed, the central communal importance of the church in black American life is a pervasive theme in his treatment of religion. The black church is repeatedly characterized not by its doctrinal, spiritual, or theological significance, but by its communal/social import: the black church is the "center of social life," the "center of social intercourse," the "central clubhouse," a "social institution." Such characterizations are repeated often and are not merely stated but are thoroughly illustrated and documented. Du Bois reveals the ways in which the church is more than just a house of worship and prayer—it is a hub for communal activities and social bonding. This insight is not limited to black American churches but is generalizable to all religious institutions. Du Bois reminds us to recognize the ways in which *all* religious institutions are not merely houses of God but are also houses of people—friends, families, peers, colleagues, lovers, partners—who come together not merely for spiritual communion but for social communion as well.

When reading Du Bois on religion, I am frequently reminded of the theme song of the enormously popular 1980s television show *Cheers*. The show was about a group of friends who hung out in a bar. Why? The theme song was quite clear; people like to go where "everybody knows their name," where everyone's troubles are all the same, and everyone is "always glad you came."

As far as what went on in the bar depicted in *Cheers*, the beer was secondary—the social bonding was primary. Although the ostensible purpose of a bar is to serve alcohol, its deeper function may be to provide community. So it is with religious institutions: their ostensible purpose is to provide spiritual rewards, but their deeper function may be to provide social rewards. And Du Bois illustrates this fact: for blacks in America, the church was ostensibly a place to worship God, but its deeper function was to provide community. The church was a place where people could feel a sense of social solidarity, a place "where everybody knows your name."

I like to call it a *Cheers* theory of religiosity: people are religiously involved for the social rewards, the sense of community that belonging to a religious institution provides. No classical sociologists of religion stressed this aspect of religious life to the degree that Du Bois did. Of course, Emile Durkheim in his classic treatise on religion, *The Elementary Forms of the Religious Life* (1915), argued that the source of religion was society itself. His imaginative theory, simply put, is that when ancient tribal people physically came together in great numbers, a "collective effervescence" arose that was the ultimate source of religious feeling. But Durkheim's is a theory of *genesis*, of *origin*, of "elementary forms"—not sustenance and continuity per se. Durkheim is addressing the birth of the religious impulse, as opposed to the matter of why individual people continue to choose to be religiously active. While Durkheim may be right—that social gathering was what spawned the religious impulse in the first place—he does not address the way sociocommunal needs and rewards remain at the heart of contemporary religious organizational life, as Du Bois does.

Max Weber (1946) argued that religion provides explanations for the good or terrible things people experience in life ("theodicy of good fortune"/"theodicy of suffering") as well as addressing issues of salvation ("soteriology"). Sigmund Freud (1961) argued that people were religious because they needed a personal/psychological sense of comfort, consolation, and security in a hostile world; religion was the wish or "illusion" that everything is going to be okay and we are all loved by a supernatural and benevolent parental figure. Karl Marx (1974, 35) similarly characterized religion as an (albeit alienating) source of comfort in the face of oppressive social circumstances: "religion is the sign of the oppressed creature, the heart of a heartless world . . . the spirit of spiritless conditions . . . the opium of the people." In sum, Durkheim, Weber, Freud, and Marx—all classic theorists of religion—contributed enormous insights to our understanding of the subject, but none paid attention to the simple, basic socially/communally rewarding aspects of everyday religious involvement. Yes, religion provides cosmic meaning and psychological comfort—but it also provides clubhouses. It is this basic and yet incredibly important insight concerning the nature of religious life that Du Bois clearly asserts.

Modern social theorists of religion (Berger 1967; Stark and Bainbridge 1985) have continued to ignore the social/communal aspects of religious involvement and, like the classical theorists, have stressed other matters: religion provides ultimate meaning, religion helps people make sense of the universe, religion provides spiritual compensation and offers unverifiable rewards that cannot be readily obtained in this world, and so on. While these speculations may all hold their fair share of validity, it is important to understand that not all rewards and comforts people reap from religious involvement are otherworldly, spiritual, or cosmic. Sometimes the ultimate heart of involvement in religion is to find and maintain that social connection, that place of belonging. Du Bois explained that the black church provides

> social intercourse, it provides amusements of various kinds, it serves as a newspaper and intelligence bureau, it supplants the theater, it directs the picnic and excursion, it furnishes the music, it introduces the stranger to the community, it serves as a lyceum, library, and lecture bureau—it is, in fine, the central organ of the organized life of the American Negro. ([1897] 1978, 228)

To be sure, not all religious institutions can be characterized thus, and perhaps the black church of nineteenth- and early twentieth-century America was unique in is social/communal breadth. But the sociological point to be derived from Du Bois's discussion of the black church is that while religious institutions may be ostensibly about God, they are intrinsically about people, and we have Du Bois to thank for stressing the social/communal heart of religious life.

NOTE

1. It is interesting to note, however, that throughout his life Du Bois wrote sympathetically of the Jewish people. Aside from a couple of disparaging remarks concerning "shrewd and unscrupulous Jews" written as a young man (Du Bois 1978, 257), he wrote empathetically of the subjugation of Jews in Europe, he condemned the pogroms of Eastern Europe and the anti-Semitism of Nazi Germany, he equated the Pan-African Movement with Zionism, he regularly emphasized the similar oppresion of blacks and Jews, and he worked closely with Jews throughout his life (most notably while with the NAACP).

REFERENCES

Aptheker, Herbert. 1982. "W. E. B. Du Bois and Religion: A Brief Reassessment." *Journal of Religious Thought* 39 (Spring-Summer): 5–11.

Aptheker, Herbert, ed. 1980. *Prayers for Dark People.* Amherst: University of Massachusetts Press.

Baer, Hans. 1998. "Du Bois." In *Encyclopedia of Religion and Society.* Edited by William Swatos. Walnut Creek, Calif.: AltaMira.

Berger, Peter. 1967. *The Sacred Canopy.* New York: Anchor.

Chalfant, H. Paul, Robert Beckley, and Eddie Palmer. 1994. *Religion in Contemporary Society.* Itasca, Ill.: Peacock.

Collins, Randall, and Michael Makowsky. 1998. *The Discovery of Society*. Boston: McGraw-Hill.

Du Bois, W. E. B. 1899. *The Philadelphia Negro: A Social Study*. New York: Benjamin Blom.

———. 1915. *The Negro*. New York: Holt.

———. 1920. *Darkwater: Voices from within the Veil*. New York: Harcourt, Brace, and Howe.

———. 1940. *Dusk of Dawn: An Essay toward and Autobiography of a Race Concept*. New York: Schocken.

———. 1962. *John Brown*. New York: International.

———. 1963. *An ABC of Color*. New York: International.

———. 1968. *The Autobiography of W. E. B. Du Bois: A Soliloquy on Viewing My Life from the Last Decade of Its First Century*. New York: International.

———. 1970, *W. E. B. Du Bois: A Reader*. Edited by Meyer Weinberg. New York: Harper & Row.

———. 1970. *W. E. B. Du Bois Speaks: Speeches and Addresses, 1920–1963*. Edited by Philip S. Foner. New York: Pathfinder.

———. 1971. *The Seventh Son: The Thought and Writings of W. E. B. Du Bois*. Vol 2. Edited by Julius Lester. New York: Vintage.

———. 1972. *The Crisis Writings*. Edited by Daniel Walden. Greenwich, Conn.: Fawcett.

———. 1973. *The Correspondence of W. E .B. Du Bois*. Vol. 1, *Selections, 1877–1934*. Edited by Herbert Aptheker. Amherst: University of Massachusetts Press.

———. 1978. *The Correspondence of W. E. B. Du Bois*. Vol. 3, *Selections, 1944–1963*. Edited by Herbert Aptheker. Amherst: University of Massachusetts Press.

———. 1978. *On Sociology and the Black Community*. Edited by Dan Green and Edwin Driver. Chicago: University of Chicago Press.

———. 1980. *Prayers for Dark People*. Edited by Herbert Aptheker. Amherst: University of Massachusetts Press.

———. 1985. *Against Racism: Unpublished Essays, Papers, Addresses, 1887–1961*. Edited by Herbert Aptheker. Amherst: University of Massachusetts Press.

———. [1903] 1989. *The Souls of Black Folk*. New York: Bantam.

Durkheim, Emile. 1915. *The Elementary Forms of the Religious Life*. New York: Free Press.

Foner, Philip S. 1970. *W. E. B. Du Bois Speaks: Speeches and Addresses, 1890–1919*. New York: Pathfinder.

Freud, Sigmund. 1961. *The Future of an Illusion*. New York: Norton.

Gates, Henry Louis, Jr. 1989. *Introduction: The Souls of Black Folk*. New York: Bantam.

Green, Dan, and Edwin Driver. 1978. *W. E. B. Du Bois on Sociology and the Black Community*. Chicago: University of Chicago Press.

Hamilton, Malcolm. 1995. *The Sociology of Religion*. London: Routledge.

Johnstone, Ronald. 1997. *Religion in Society*. Upper Saddle River, N.J.: Prentice Hall.

King, Martin Luther, Jr. 1968. "Honoring Dr. Du Bois." *Freedomways*, Spring, pp. 104–111.

Kurtz, Lester. 1995. *Gods in the Global Village*. Thousand Oaks, Calif.: Pine Forge.

Lemert, Charles. 1993. *Social Theory*. Boulder: Westview.

Lewis, David Levering. 1993. *W. E. B. Du Bois: Biography of a Race, 1868–1919*. New York: Holt.

Marx, Karl. 1974. *Karl Marx on Religion*. Edited by Saul Padover. New York: McGraw-Hill.

McGuire, Meredith. 1997. *Religion: The Social Context*. Belmont, Calif.: Wadsworth.

Rampersad, Arnold. 1976. *The Art and Imagination of W. E. B. Du Bois*. Cambridge: Harvard University Press.

Stark, Rodney, and William Simms Bainbridge. 1985. *The Future of Religion*. Berkeley: University of California Press.

Swatos, William, ed. 1998. *Encyclopedia of Religion and Society*. Walnut Creek, Ca.: Alta Mira Press.

Thrower, James. 1999. *Religion: The Classical Theories*. Georgetown University Press.

Turner, Bryan. 1991. *Religion and Social Theory*. London: Sage.

Washington, Booker T., and W. E. B. Du Bois. 1907. *The Negro in the South*. New York: Citadel.

Weber, Max. 1946. *From Max Weber: Essays in Sociology*. Edited by Hans Gerth and C. Wright Mills. New York: Oxford University Press.

Weinberg, Meyer. 1970. *W. E. B. Du Bois: A Reader*. New York: Harper & Row.

CHAPTER ONE

The Problem of Amusement

This essay, written in 1897, illustrates Du Bois's ability to understand and analyze religious organizations as catering not merely to the limited spiritual or otherworldly needs of their members but to their social, this-worldly needs as well. Du Bois is specifically concerned with the problem of amusement for young black adults and in what ways the Black Church can or cannot address the matter.

I wish to discuss with you somewhat superficially a phase of development in the organized life of American Negroes which has hitherto received scant notice. It is the question of the amusements of Negroes—what their attitude toward them is, what institutions among them conduct the recreations, and what the tendency of indulgence is in amusements of various sorts. I do not pretend that this is one of the more pressing of the Negro problems, but nevertheless it is destined as time goes on to become more and more so; and at all times and in all places, the manner, method, and extent of a people's recreation is of vast importance to their welfare.

I have been in this case especially spurred to take under consideration this particular one of the many problems affecting the Negroes in cities and in the country because I have long noted with silent apprehension a distinct tendency among us to depreciate and belittle and sneer at means of recreation, to consider amusement as the peculiar property of the devil, and to look upon even its legitimate pursuit as time wasted and energy misspent. I have heard sermon after sermon and essay after essay thunder warnings against the terrible results of pleasure and the awful end of those who are depraved enough to seek pleasure. I have heard such a fusillade of "don'ts" thrown at our young people: don't dance, don't play cards, don't go to the theatre, don't drink, don't smoke, don't sing songs, don't play kissing games, don't play billiards, don't play foot-ball, don't go on excursions—that I have not been surprised, gentlemen and ladies, to find in the feverish life of a great city, hundreds of Negro boys and girls who have listened for a life-time to the warning, "Don't do this or you'll go to hell," and then have taken the bit between their teeth and said, "Well, let's go to hell."

If you go out through the country side of Virginia, to the little towns and hamlets, the first thing you will note is the scarcity of young men and women. There are babies aplenty, and boys and girls up to fifteen, sixteen, and seventeen—then suddenly the supply seems to stop, and from eighteen to thirty there is a great gap. Where are these young people? They are in Norfolk, Richmond, Baltimore, Washington, Philadelphia and New York. In one ward of Philadelphia young people between the ages of sixteen and thirty form over a third of the population; the Negro population of the whole city of Philadelphia, which has increased fully one hundred per cent since 1860, has received its main element of increase from these young boys and girls. Why have they gone? Primarily, their migration is, of course, but a belated ripple of that great wave city-ward which is redistributing the population of England, France, Italy, Germany, and the United States, and draining the country districts of those lands of their bone and sinew. The whole movement is caused by that industrial revolution which has transferred the seat of human labor from agriculture to manufacturing and concentrated manufacturing in cities, thus by higher wages attracting the young people. This is the primary motive, but back of this is a powerful and in some cases even more deciding motive; and that is the thirst for amusement. You, who were born and reared amid the kaleidoscopic life of a great city, scarcely realize what an irresistible attraction city life has for one who has long experienced the dull, lifeless monotony of the country. When now that country life has been further shorn of the few pleasures usually associated with it, when the public opinion of the best class of Negroes in the country districts distinctly frowns, not only upon most of the historical kinds of amusements usual in a peasant community, but also to some extent upon the very idea of amusement as a necessary, legitimate pursuit, then it is inevitable that you should have what we are seeing to-day, a perfect stampede of young Negroes to the city.

When now a young man has grown up feeling the trammels of precept, religion, or custom too irksome for him, and then at the most impressionable and reckless age of life, is suddenly transplanted to an atmosphere of excess, the result is apt to be disastrous. In the case of young colored men or women, it is disastrous, and the story is daily repeated in every great city of our land, of young men and women who have been reared in an atmosphere of restricted amusement, throwing off when they enter city life, not one restriction, not some restrictions, but almost all, and plunging into dissipation and vice. This tendency is rendered stronger by two circumstances peculiar to the condition of the American Negro: the first is his express or tacit exclusion from the public amusements of most great cities; and second, the little thought of fact that the chief purveyor of amusement to the colored people is the Negro church, which in theory is opposed to most modern amusements. Let me make this second point clear, for much of the past and future development of the race is misunderstood from igno-rance of certain fundamental historic facts. Among most people the primitive sociological group was the family or at least the clan. Not so among American Negroes: every vestige of primitive organization among the Negro slaves was destroyed by the slave ship; in this country the first distinct voluntary organiza-tion of Negroes was the Negro church. The Negro church came before the Negro home, it antedates their social life, and in every respect it stands to-day as the fullest, broadest expression of organized Negro life.

We are so familiar with churches, and church work is so near to us, that we have scarce time to view it in perspective and to realize that in origin and func-tions the Negro church is a broader, deeper, and more comprehensive social organism than the churches of white Americans. The Negro church is not sim-ply an organism for the propagation of religion; it is the centre of the social, intellectual, and religious life of an organized group of individuals. It provides social intercourse, it provides amusements of various kinds, it serves as a news-paper and intelligence bureau, it supplants the theatre, it directs the picnic and excursion, it furnishes the music, it introduces the stranger to the community, it serves as a lyceum, library, and lecture bureau—it is, in fine, the central organ of the organized life of the American Negro for amusement, relaxation, instruction, and religion. To maintain its preeminence the Negro church has been forced to compete with the dance hall, the theatre, and the home as an amusement-giving agency; aided by color proscription in public amusements, aided by the fact mentioned before, that the church among us is older than the home, the church has been peculiarly successful, so that of the ten thousand Philadelphia Negroes whom I asked, "Where do you get your amusements?" fully three-fourths could only answer, "From the churches."

The minister who directs this peculiar and anomalous institution must not be criticised with full knowledge of his difficult role. He is in reality the mayor, the chief magistrate of a community, ruling to be sure, but ruling according to the dictates of a not over-intelligent town council, according to time-honored cus-tom and law; and above all, hampered by the necessities of his budget; he may be a spiritual guide, he must be a social organizer, a leader of actual men; he may desire to enrich and reform the spiritual life of his flock, but above all he must have church members; he may desire to revolutionize church methods, to elevate the ideals of the people, to tell the hard, honest truth to a people who need a little more truth and a little less flattery—but how can he do this when the people of this social organism demand that he shall take from the purely spiritual activities of his flock, time to minister to their amusement, diversion, and physical comfort; when he sees the picnic masquerading as a camp-meeting, the revival becoming the social event of the season, the day of worship turned into a day of general reception and dining out, the rival church organizations plunging into debt to furnish their houses of worship with an elegance that far outruns the financial ability of a poverty stricken people; when the church door becomes the trysting place for all the lovers and Lotharios of the community; when a ceaseless round of entertainments, socials, and necktie parties chase the week through—what minister can be more than most ministers are coming to be, the business managers of a picnic ground?

This is the situation of the Negro church today—I do not say of all Negro churches, but I mean the average church. It is rather the misfortune than the fault of the church. With the peculiar development we have had in this country, I doubt if the Negro church could have more nobly fulfilled its huge and multiform task; if it totters beneath its burden, it nevertheless demands respect as the first demonstrator of the ability of the civilized Negro to govern himself. Notwithstanding all this, the situation remains, and demands—peremptorily demands—reform. On the one hand we have an increasingly restless crowd of young people who are always demanding ways and means of recreation; and every moment it is denied them is a moment that goes to increase that growth of a distinct class of Negro libertines, criminals, and prostitutes which is growing among us day by day, which fills our jails and hospitals, which tempts and taints our brothers, our sisters, and our children, and which does more in a day to tarnish our good name than Hampton can do in a year to restore it. On the other hand we have the Negro church seeking to supply this demand for amusement—and doing so to the detriment and death of its true, divine mission of human inspiration.

Under such circumstances two questions immediately arise: first, Is this growing demand for amusement legitimate? and second, Can the church continue to be the centre of amusements?

Let us consider the first question; and ask, What is amusement? All life is rhythm—the right swing of the pendulum makes the pointer go round, but the left swing must follow it; the down stroke of the hammer welds the iron, and yet the hammer must be lifted between each blow; the heart must beat and yet between each beat comes a pause; the day is the period of fulfilling the functions of life and yet the prelude and end of day is night. Thus throughout nature, from the restless beating of yonder waves to the rhythm of the seasons and the whirl of comets, we see one mighty law of work and rest, of activity and relaxation, of inspiration and amusement. We might imagine a short sighted philosopher arguing strongly against the loss of time involved in the intermittent activities of the world—arguing against the time spent by the hammer in raising itself for the second blow, against the unnecessary alternate swing of the pendulum, against sleep that knits up the ravelled sleeve of care, against amusements that reinvigorate and recreate and divert. With such a philosophy the world has never agreed, the whole world today is organized for work and recreation. Where the balance between the two is best maintained we have the best civilization, the best culture; and that civilization declines toward barbarism where, on the one hand, work and drudgery so predominate as to destroy the very vigor which stands behind them, or on the other hand, where relaxation and amusement become dissipation instead of recreation.

I dwell on these simple facts because I fear that even a proverbially joyous people like the American Negroes are forgetting to recognize for their children the God-given right to play; to recognize that there is a perfectly natural and legitimate demand for amusement on the part of the young people, and that no people can afford to laugh at, sneer at, or forcibly repress the natural joyousness and pleasure-seeking propensity of young womanhood and young manhood. Go into a great city today and see how thoroughly and wonderfully organized its avenues of amusements are; its parks and play grounds, its theatres and galleries, its music and dancing, its excursions and trolley rides represent an enormous proportion of the expenditure of every great municipality. That the matter of amusement may often be overdone in such centres is too true, but of all the agencies that contribute to its overdoing none are more potent than undue repression. Proper amusement must always be a matter of careful reasoning and ceaseless investigation, of nice adjustment between repression and excess; there is not a single means of amusement from church socials to public balls, or from checkers to horse racing that may not be carried to harmful excess; on the other hand it would be difficult to name a single amusement which if properly limited and directed would not be a positive gain to any society; take, for instance, in our modern American society, the game of billiards; I suppose, taken in itself, a more innocent, interesting, and gentlemanly game of skill could scarcely be thought of, and yet, because it is today coupled with gambling, excessive drinking, lewd companionship, and late hours, you can hear it damned from every pulpit from San Francisco to New York as the straight road to perdition; so far as present conditions are concerned the pulpit may be right, but the social reformer must ask himself: Are these conditions necessary? Was it not far sighted prudence for the University of Pennsylvania to put billiard tables in its students' club room? Is there any valid reason why the Y.M.C.A. at Norfolk should not have a billiard table among its amusements? In other words, is it wise policy to surrender a charming amusement wholly to the devil and then call it devilish?

If now there is among rational, healthy, earnest people a legitimate demand for amusement, and if from its peculiar history and constitution the Negro church has undertaken to furnish this amusement to American Negroes, is it fairly to be supposed that the church can be successful in its attempt? Of the answer to this question there is one unfailing sign: if the young people are flocking into the church then the church has accomplished its double task; but as matter of fact the young people are leaving the church; in the forty Negro churches of Philadelphia I doubt if there are two hundred young men who are effective, active church members; there are to be sure, two thousand young men who meet their sweethearts there Sunday nights—but they are not pillars of the church. The young women are more faithful but they too are dropping away; in the country, this tendency is less manifest because the young people have no other place to go, but even there it is found increasingly difficult to reach the young people. This simply means that the younger generation of Negroes are tired of the limited and hackneyed amusements the church offers, and that the spiritual message of the church has been dulled by too indistinct and inopportune reiteration.

And then there is another reason, deeper and more subtle, and therefore more dangerous than these; and that is, the recoil of young, honest souls against a distinct tendency toward hypocrisy in the apparent doctrine and the practice of the Negro church. The Methodist and Baptist and nearly all the churches which the slaves joined, had at the time of their introduction into America, felt the full impulse of a spiritual recoil against excessive amusement. The dissipations of an age of debauchery, of display, of license, had led those churches to preach the earnestness of life, and the disgrace of mere pleasure-seeking as a life work. Transported to America this religion of protest became a wholesale condemnation of amusements, and a glorification of the ascetic ideal of self-inflicted misery. In this tongue the Negro church first began to lisp; its earliest teaching was that the Christian stood apart from and utterly opposed to a world filled with pleasures, and that to partake of those pleasures was sinful. When now in these days the church speaks in those same tones and invites healthy and joyous young people from the back seats to renounce the amusements of this world for a diet of fasting and prayer, those same young people in increasing numbers are positively, deliberately, and decisively declining to do any such thing; and they are pointing to the obvious fact that the very church that is preaching against amusement is straining every nerve to amuse them; they feel that there is an essential hypocrisy in this position of the church and they refuse to be hypocrites.

As a matter of fact you and I know that our church is not really hypocritical on this point; she errs only in using antiquated and unfortunate phraseology. What the Negro church is trying to impress upon young people is that Work and

Sacrifice is the true destiny of humanity—the Negro church is dimly groping for that divine word of Faust:

"Embehren sallst du, sollst entbehren."

"Thou shalt forego, shalt do without."

But in this truth, properly conceived, properly enunciated, there is nothing incompatible with wholesome amusement, with true recreation—for what is true amusement, true diversion, but the re-creation of energy which we may sacrifice to noble ends, to higher ideals, while without proper amusement we waste or dissipate our mightiest powers? If the Negro church could have the time and the opportunity to announce this spiritual message clearly and truly; if it could concentrate its energy and emphasis on an encouragement of proper amusement instead of on its wholesale denunciation; if it could cease to dissipate and cheapen religion by incessant semi-religious activity then we would, starting with a sound religious foundation, be able to approach the real question of proper amusement. For believe me, my hearers, the great danger of the best class of Negro youth today is not that they will hesitate to sacrifice their lives, their money, and their energy on the altar of their race, but the danger is lest under continuous and persistent proscription, under the thousand little annoyances and petty insults and disappointments of a caste system, they lose the divine faith of their fathers in the fruitfulness of sacrifice; for surely no son of the nineteenth century has heard more plainly the mocking words of "Sorrow, cruel fellowship!"

There has been no time in the history of American Negroes when they had a more pressing need of spiritual guidance of the highest type; when amid the petty cares of social reform and moral reaction, there was wider place for a divine faith in the high destiny and marvelous might of that vast historic Negro race whose promise and first-fruits we of America are. There are creeping in among us low ideals of petty hatred, of sordid gain, of political theft, of place hunting and immodest self-praise, that must be stifled lest they sting to death our loftier and nobler sentiments.

Thus far I have sought to show: first, that the problem of proper amusement for our young people is rapidly coming to be a pressing one; second, that the Negro church, from its historic development has become the chief center of our amusements, and has been forced into the untenable position of seeming to deny the propriety of worldly amusements and dissipating at the same time its spiritual energy in furnishing them for its members.

I now wish to insist that the time has come when the activities of the Negro church must become differentiated and when it must surrender to the school and the home, and social organizations, those functions which in a day of organic poverty it so heroically sought to bear. The next social organism that followed the church among the Negroes was the school, and with the slow but

certain upbuilding of the Negro home, we shall at last become a healthy society. Upon the school and the home must rest the burden of furnishing amusements for Negro youth. This duty must not be shirked—it must not be an after-
thought—it must not be a spasmodic activity but a careful, rational plan. Take
the boys and girls of the primary schools: I want to impress the fact upon every
school teacher here who has children from six to thirteen under her care that
oversight over the amusements of those children is just as important as oversight over their studies. And first of all, let the children sing, and sing songs, not
hymns; it is bad enough on Sunday to bear the rude vigor and mighty music of
the slave songs replaced by that combination of flippant music and mediocre
poetry which we call gospel hymns. But for heaven's sake, let us not further
tempt Providence by using these not only for hymns but for day-school purposes. Buy good song books—books that sing of earth and air and sky and sea,
of lovers, birds, and trees, of every thing that makes God's world beautiful. Set
the Southland to singing Annie Laurie, the Lorelei, Santa Lucia, and "My
Heart's in the Hielands" let the children yodel, whistle, and clap their hands—
they will get more real religion out of one healthy, wholesome folk-song than
out of an endless repetition of hymns on all occasions, with sour faces, and
forced reverence. Again, make the observance of recess as compulsory as that of
work. In work time make the pupils work and work hard and continuously, and
at recess time make them play and play hard and joyously; join in and direct
their games, their "I Spy," and "King Consello" and "Grey Wolf" and the thousand and one good old games which are known from England to China. Watch
that boy who after a morning's work will not play; he is not built right. Watch
that girl who can mope and sleep at recess time; she needs a physician. In these
schools of primary grade especial attention should be paid to athletic sports;
boys and girls should be encouraged if not compelled to run, jump, walk, row,
swim, throw and vault. The school picnic with a long walk over hill and dale
and a romp under the trees in close communion with Mother Nature is sadly
needed. In fine, here should be developed a capacity for pure, open-hearted
enjoyment of the beautiful world about us, and woe to the teacher who is so big-
oted and empty-headed as to suggest to innocent laughing hearts that play is not
a divine institution which ever has and ever will, go hand in hand with work.

When the child grows up, in the momentous years from fourteen to eighteen,
the problem of amusements becomes graver, and because it is graver it demands
not less attention but more; generally the last thing that is thought of in the
organization of a great school is: How are we to furnish proper amusement of
these two or three hundred young people of all ages, tastes, and temperaments?
And yet, unless that school does amuse, as well as instruct those boys and girls,
and teach them how to amuse themselves, it fails of half its duty and it sends into

the world men and women who can never stand up successfully in the awful moral battle which Negro blood is today waging for humanity. Here again athletic sports must in the future play a larger part in the normal and mission schools of the South, and we must rapidly come to the place where the man all brain and no muscle is looked upon as almost as big a fool as the man all muscle and no brain; and when the young woman who cannot walk a couple of good country miles will have few proposals of marriage. The crucial consideration at this age of life, between fourteen and eighteen, is really the proper social intercourse of the sexes; it is a grave question because its mistaken answer today coupled with an awful social history compels us to plead guilty to the shameful fact that sexual impurity among Negro men and Negro women of America is the crying disgrace of the American republic. The Southern school which can so train its sons and daughters that they can mingle in pure and chaste conversation, and thoroughly enjoy the natural love they have for each other's companionship; which can amuse and interest them and at the same time protect them with a high sense of honor and chastity—that school will be the greatest of Negro schools and the mightiest of American institutions. On the other hand, the school which seeks to build iron walls between the sexes, which discourages honest, open intercourse, which makes it a business to set the seal of disapproval upon sensible and joyous amusement, that school is filling the bawdy houses and gambling halls of our great cities with its most hopeless inmates.

I wish to take but one illustration to make clear my meaning in this crucial question; and I take two common amusements which bring the sexes together—dancing and accompanying young ladies home from church Sunday night. I never shall forget a dance I attended in Eisenach, Germany; contrary to my very elaborate expectation the young men did not accompany the girls to the dance; the girls went with their fathers and mothers; the boys went alone. In the pretty, airy hall the mothers seated themselves in a circle about the sides of the room and drew up their daughters beside them; fathers and elder brothers looked on from the doorway. Then we danced under the eyes of mothers and fathers, and we got permission to dance from those parents; we felt ourselves to be trusted guests in the bosom of families; three hours glided by in pure joyousness until, finally, long tables were brought in; we sat down, and cooled off and drank coffee and sang. Then the mothers took their daughters home, and the young men took themselves. I have had many good times in life, but not one to which I look back with more genuine pleasure and satisfaction. When now we compare the amusement thus conducted with the universal custom among us of allowing our daughters, unattended and unwatched, to be escorted at night, through great cities or country districts by chance acquaintances unknown to parents, with no rational diversion, but frivolous conversation and aimless nonsense, I have no hesitancy in saying I would rather have a daughter of mine dance her head off under her mother's eye, than to throw her unguarded and uncared for into the hands of unwatched strangers. The cases I have cited are of course extreme—all escorting of girls from church is not improper, and all dancing is not carried on as at Eisenach, but I wish to leave this one query with you. Is it not possible for us to rescue from its evil associations and conditions, so pleasant, innocent, and natural an amusement as dancing?

I have already talked too long and have but half exhausted a fertile and peculiarly interesting subject; the whole question of home pleasures and of diversions for older people remains untouched. I wish to leave you with a reiteration of what I desire to be the central thought of this paper, it is not a defense of particular amusements or a criticism of particular prohibitions, but an insistence on the fact that amusement is right, that pleasure is God-given, and that the people that seek to deny it and to shut the door upon it, simply open wide the door to dissipation and vice. I beg you to strive to change the mental attitude of the race toward amusement for the young, from a wholesale negative to an emphatic positive. Instead of warning young people so constantly against excess of pleasure, let us rather inspire them to unselfish work, and show them that amusement and recreation are the legitimate and necessary accompaniments of work, and that we get the maximum of enjoyment from them when they strengthen and inspire us for renewed effort in a great cause; and above all, let us teach them that there can be no greater cause than the development of Negro character to its highest and holiest possibilities.

CHAPTER TWO

The Philadelphia Negro:
A Social Study

The following selections come from Du Bois's classic book *The Philadelphia Negro: A Social Study*, published in 1899. This brilliant work represents not only the first systematic sociological study of urban African Americans but quite possibly the first sociological study of its kind undertaken in the United States. Du Bois interviewed over 5,000 people in this exhaustive investigation of the historical, social, educational, political, racial, economic, religious, health, conjugal, criminal, environmental, employment, and demographic conditions of the black population of Philadelphia at the end of the nineteenth century. Du Bois describes the Black Church as "a social institution first, and religious afterwards," a theme that pervades his sociological work on religious institutions.

History of the Negro Church in Philadelphia—We have already followed the history of the rise of the Free African Society, which was the beginning of the Negro Church in the North. We often forget that the rise of a church organization among Negroes was a curious phenomenon. The church really represented all that was left of African tribal life, and was the sole expression of the organized efforts of the slaves. It was natural that any movement among freedmen should centre about their religious life, the sole remaining element of their former tribal system. Consequently when, led by two strong men, they left the white Methodist Church, they were naturally unable to form any democratic moral reform association; they must be led and guided, and this guidance must have the religious sanction that tribal government always has. Consequently Jones and Allen, the leaders of the Free African Society, as early as 1791 began regular religious exercises, and at the close of the eighteenth century there were three Negro churches in the city, two of which were independent.[2]

29

St. Thomas' Church has had a most interesting history. It early declared its purpose "of advancing our friends in a true knowledge of God, of true religion, and of the ways and means to restore our long lost race to the dignity of men and of Christians." The church offered itself to the Protestant Episcopal Church and was accepted on condition that they take no part in the government of the general church. Their leader, Absalom Jones, was ordained deacon and priest, and took charge of the church. In 1804 the church established a day school which lasted until 1816. In 1849 St. Thomas' began a series of attempts to gain full recognition in the Church by a demand for delegates to the Church gatherings. The Assembly first declared that it was not expedient to allow Negroes to take part. To this the vestry returned a dignified answer, asserting that "expediency is no plea against the violation of the great principles of charity, mercy, justice and truth." Not until 1864 was the Negro body received into full fellowship with the Church. In the century and more of its existence St. Thomas' has always represented a high grade of intelligence, and today it still represents the most cultured and wealthiest of the Negro population and the Philadelphia born residents. Its membership has consequently always been small, being 246 in 1794, 427 in 1795, 105 in 1860, and 391 in 1897.

The growth of Bethel Church, founded by Richard Allen, on South Sixth Street, has been so phenomenal that it belongs to the history of the nation rather than to any one city. From a weekly gathering which met in Allen's blacksmith shop on Sixth near Lombard, grew a large church edifice; other churches were formed under the same general plan, and Allen, as overseer of them, finally took the title of bishop and ordained other bishops. The Church, under the name of African Methodist Episcopal, grew and spread until in 1890 the organization had 452,725 members, 2,481 churches and $6,468,280 worth of property.

By 1813 there were in Philadelphia six Negro churches with the following membership:

St. Thomas', P. E	560
Bethel, A. M. E	1272
Zoar, M. E.	80
Union, A. M. E	74
Baptist, Race and Vine Streets	80
Presbyterian	300
	2,366

The Presbyterian Church had been founded by two Negro missionaries, father and son, named Gloucester, in 1807. The Baptist Church was founded in 1809.

Denomination	No. Churches	Members	Annual Expenses	Value of Property	Incumbrance
Episcopalian	1	100	$1,000	$36,000	. . .
Lutheran	1	10	120	3,000	$1,000
Methodist	8	2,860	2,100	50,800	5,100
Presbyterian	2	325	1,500	20,000	1,000
Baptist	4	700	1,300	4,200	. . .
Total	16	3,995	$6,020	$114,000	$7,100

Three more churches were added in the next ten years, and then a reaction followed. By 1867 there were in all probability nearly twenty churches. . . .

Statistics of Negro Churches, 1867.

Name	Founded	Number of Members	Value of Property	Pastors' Salary
P. E.—				
St. Thomas'	1792	. . .	. . .	. . .
Methodist—				
Bethel	1794	1,100	$50,000	$600
Union	1827	467	40,000	850
Wesley	1817	464	21,000	700
Zoar	1794	400	12,000	. . .
John Wesley	1844	42	3,000	No regular salary
Little Wesley	1821	310	11,000	500
Pisgah	1831	116	4,600	430
Zion City Mission	1858	90	4,500	. . .
Little Union	1837	200	. . .	. . .
Baptist—				
First Baptist	1809	360	5,000	. . .
Union Baptist	. . .	400	7,000	600
Shiloh	1842	405	16,000	600
Oak Street	1827	137	. . .	. . .
Presbyterian—				
First Presbyterian	1807	200	8,000	. . .
Second Presbyterian	1824	. . .	. . .	. . .
Central Presbyterian	1844	240	16,000	. . .

Since the war the growth of Negro churches has been by bounds, there being twenty-five churches and missions in 1880, and fifty-five in 1897.

So phenomenal a growth as this here outlined means more than the establishment of many places of worship. The Negro is, to be sure, a religious creature—
most primitive folk are—but his rapid and even extraordinary founding of
churches is not due to this fact alone, but is rather a measure of his development,
an indication of the increasing intricacy of his social life and the consequent mul-
tiplication of the organ which is the function of his group life—the church. To
understand this let us inquire into the function of the Negro church.

The Function of the Negro Church—The Negro church is the peculiar and characteristic product of the transplanted African, and deserves especial study. As a
social group the Negro church may be said to have antedated the Negro family
on American soil; as such it has preserved, on the one hand, many functions of
tribal organization, and on the other hand, many of the family functions. Its
tribal functions are shown in its religious activity, its social authority and general
guiding and co-ordinating work; its family functions are shown by the fact that
the church is a centre of social life and intercourse; acts as newspaper and intelligence bureau, is the centre of amusements—indeed, is the world in which the
Negro moves and acts. So far-reaching are these functions of the church that its
organization is almost political. In Bethel Church, for instance, the mother
African Methodist Episcopal Church of America, we have the following officials
and organizations:

The Bishop of the District	
The Presiding Elder	Executive.
The Pastor	
The Board of Trustees	Executive Council.
General Church Meeting	Legislative.
The Board of Stewards	
The Board of Stewardesses	Financial Board.
The Junior Stewardesses	
The Sunday School Organization	Educational System.
Ladies' Auxiliary, Volunteer Guild, etc.	Tax Collectors
Ushers' Association	Police.
Class Leaders	
Local Preachers	Sheriffs and Magistrates.
Choir	Music and Amusement.
Allen Guards	Militia.
Missionary Societies	Social Reformers.
Beneficial and Semi-Secret Societies, etc.	Corporations.

Or to put it differently, here we have a mayor, appointed from without, with
great administrative and legislative powers, although well limited by long and

zealously cherished customs; he acts conjointly with a select council, the trustees, a board of finance, composed of stewards and stewardesses, a common council of committees and, occasionally, of all church members. The various functions of the church are carried out by societies and organizations. The form of government varies, but is generally some form of democracy closely guarded by custom and tempered by possible and not infrequent secession.

The functions of such churches in order of present emphasis are:

1. The raising of the annual budget.
2. The maintenance of membership.
3. Social intercourse and amusements.
4. The setting of moral standards.
5. Promotion of general intelligence.
6. Efforts for social betterment.

1. The annual budget is of first importance, because the life of the organization depends upon it. The amount of expenditure is not very accurately determined beforehand, although its main items do not vary much. There is the pastor's salary, the maintenance of the building, light and heat, the wages of a janitor, contributions to various church objects, and the like, to which must be usually added the interest on some debt. The sum thus required varies in Philadelphia from $200 to $5000. A small part of this is raised by a direct tax on each member. Besides this, voluntary contributions by members roughly gauged according to ability, are expected, and a strong public opinion usually compels payment. Another large source of revenue is the collection after the sermons on Sunday, when, amid the reading of notices and a subdued hum of social intercourse, a stream of givers walk to the pulpit and place in the hands of the trustee or steward in charge a contribution, varying from a cent to a dollar or more. To this must be added the steady revenue from entertainments, suppers, socials, fairs, and the like. In this way the Negro churches of Philadelphia raise nearly $100,000 a year. They hold in real estate $900,000 worth of property, and are thus no insignificant element in the economics of the city.

2. Extraordinary methods are used and efforts made to maintain and increase the membership of the various churches. To be a popular church with large membership means ample revenues, large social influence and a leadership among the colored people unequaled in power and effectiveness. Consequently people are attracted to the church by sermons, by music and by entertainments; finally, every year a revival is held, at which considerable numbers of young people are converted. All this is done in perfect sincerity and without much thought of merely increasing membership, and yet every small church strives to be large by

these means and every large church to maintain itself or grow larger. The churches thus vary from a dozen to a thousand members.

3. Without wholly conscious effort the Negro church has become a centre of social intercourse to a degree unknown in white churches even in the country. The various churches, too, represent social classes. At St. Thomas' one looks for the well-to-do Philadelphians, largely descendants of favorite mulatto house-servants, and consequently well-bred and educated, but rather cold and reserved to strangers or newcomers; at Central Presbyterian one sees the older, simpler set of respectable Philadelphians with distinctly Quaker characteristics—pleasant but conservative; at Bethel may be seen the best of the great laboring class—steady, honest people, well dressed and well fed, with church and family traditions; at Wesley will be found the new arrivals, the sight-seers and the strangers to the city—hearty and easy-going people, who welcome all comers and ask few questions; at Union Baptist one may look for the Virginia servant girls and their young men; and so on throughout the city. Each church forms its own social circle, and not many stray beyond its bounds. Introductions into that circle come through the church, and thus the stranger becomes known. All sorts of entertainments and amusements are furnished by the churches: concerts, suppers, socials, fairs, literary exercises and debates, cantatas, plays, excursions, picnics, surprise parties, celebrations. Every holiday is the occasion of some special entertainment by some club, society or committee of the church; Thursday afternoons and evenings, when the servant girls are free, are always sure to have some sort of entertainment. Sometimes these exercises are free, sometimes an admission fee is charged, sometimes refreshments or articles are on sale. The favorite entertainment is a concert with solo singing, instrumental music, reciting, and the like. Many performers make a living by appearing at these entertainments in various cities, and often they are persons of training and ability, although not always. So frequent are these and other church exercises that there are few Negro churches which are not open four to seven nights in a week and sometimes one or two afternoons in addition.

Perhaps the pleasantest and most interesting social intercourse takes place on Sunday; the weary week's work is done, the people have slept late and had a good breakfast, and sally forth to church well dressed and complacent. The usual hour of the morning service is eleven, but people stream in until after twelve. The sermon is usually short and stirring, but in the larger churches elicits little response other than an "Amen" or two. After the sermon the social features begin; notices on the various meetings of the week are read, people talk with each other in subdued tones, take their contributions to the altar, and linger in the aisles and corridors long after dismission to laugh and chat until one or two o'clock. Then they go home to good dinners. Sometimes there is some special three o'clock service, but usually nothing save Sunday-school, until night. Then comes the chief meeting of the day; probably ten thousand Negroes gather every Sunday night in their churches. There is much music, much preaching, some short addresses; many strangers are there to be looked at; many beaus bring out their belles, and those who do not gather in crowds at the church door and escort the young women home. The crowds are usually well behaved and respectable, though rather more jolly than comports with a puritan idea of church services.

In this way the social life of the Negro centres in his church—baptism, wedding and burial, gossip and courtship, friendship and intrigue—all lie in these walls. What wonder that this central club house tends to become more and more luxuriously furnished, costly in appointment and easy of access!

4. It must not be inferred from all this that the Negro is hypocritical or irreligious. His church is, to be sure, a social institution first, and religious afterwards, but nevertheless, its religious activity is wide and sincere. In direct moral teaching and in setting moral standards for the people, however, the church is timid, and naturally so, for its constitution is democracy tempered by custom. Negro preachers are often condemned for poor leadership and empty sermons, and it is said that men with so much power and influence could make striking moral reforms. This is but partially true. The congregation does not follow the moral precepts of the preacher, but rather the preacher follows the standard of his flock, and only exceptional men dare seek to change this. And here it must be remembered that the Negro preacher is primarily an executive officer, rather than a spiritual guide. If one goes into any great Negro church and hears the sermon and views the audience, one would say: either the sermon is far below the calibre of the audience, or the people are less sensible than they look; the former explanation is usually true. The preacher is sure to be a man of executive ability, a leader of men, a shrewd and affable president of a large and intricate corporation. In addition to this he may be, and usually is, a striking elocutionist; he may also be a man of integrity, learning, and deep spiritual earnestness; but these last three are sometimes all lacking, and the last two in many cases. Some signs of advance are here manifest: no minister of notoriously immoral life, or even of bad reputation, could hold a large church in Philadelphia without eventual revolt. Most of the present pastors are decent, respectable men; there are perhaps one or two exceptions to this, but the exceptions are doubtful, rather than notorious. On the whole then, the average Negro preacher in this city is a shrewd manager, a respectable man, a good talker, a pleasant companion, but neither learned nor spiritual, nor a reformer.

The moral standards are therefore set by the congregations, and vary from church to church in some degree. There has been a slow working toward a literal obeying of the puritan and ascetic standard of morals which Methodism imposed on the freedmen; but condition and temperament have modified these. The grosser forms of immorality, together with theatre-going and dancing, are specifically denounced; nevertheless, the precepts against specific amusements are often violated by church members. The cleft between denominations is still wide, especially between Methodists and Baptists. The sermons are usually kept within the safe ground of a mild Calvinism, with much insistence on Salvation, Grace, Fallen Humanity and the like.

The chief function of these churches in morals is to conserve old standards and create about them a public opinion which shall deter the offender. And in this the Negro churches are peculiarly successful, although naturally the standards conserved are not as high as they should be.

5. The Negro churches were the birthplaces of Negro schools and of all agencies which seek to promote the intelligence of the masses; and even to-day no agency serves to disseminate news or information so quickly and effectively among Negroes as the church. The lyceum and lecture here still maintain a feeble but persistent existence, and church newspapers and books are circulated widely. Night schools and kindergartens are still held in connection with churches, and all Negro celebrities, from a bishop to a poet like Dunbar, are introduced to Negro audiences from the pulpits.

6. Consequently all movements for social betterment are apt to centre in the churches. Beneficial societies in endless number are formed here; secret societies keep in touch; co-operative and building associations have lately sprung up; the minister often acts as an employment agent; considerable charitable and relief work is done and special meetings held to aid special projects. The race problem in all its phases is continually being discussed, and, indeed, from this forum many a youth goes forth inspired to work.

Such are some of the functions of the Negro church, and a study of them indicates how largely this organization has come to be an expression of the organized life of Negroes in a great city.

The Present Condition of the Churches—The 2,441 families of the Seventh Ward were distributed among the various denominations, in 1896, as follows:

	Families
Methodists	842
Baptists	577
Episcopalians	156
Presbyterians	74
Catholic	69
Shakers	2
Unconnected and unknown	721
	2,441

Probably half of the "unconnected and unknown" habitually attend church.

In the city at large the Methodists have a decided majority, followed by the Baptists, and further behind, the Episcopalians. Starting with the Methodists, we find three bodies: the African Methodist Episcopal, founded by Allen, the A. M. E. Zion, which sprung from a secession of Negroes from white churches in New York in the eighteenth century; and the A. M. E. Church, consisting of colored churches belonging to the white Methodist Church, like Zoar.

The A. M. E. Church is the largest body and had, in 1897, fourteen churches and missions in the city, with a total membership of 3,210, and thirteen church edifices, seating 6,117 persons. These churches collected during the year, $27,074.13. Their property is valued at $202,229 on which there is a mortgage indebtedness of $30,000 to $50,000. . . .

These churches are pretty well organized, and are conducted with vim and enthusiasm. This arises largely from their system. Their bishops have been in some instances men of piety and ability like the late Daniel A. Payne. In other cases they have fallen far below this standard; but they have always been men of great influence, and had a genius for leadership—else they would not have been bishops. They have large powers of appointment and removal in the case of pastors, and thus each pastor working under the eye of an inspiring chief, strains every nerve to make his church a successful organization. The bishop is aided by several presiding elders, who are traveling inspectors and preachers, and give advice as to appointments. This system results in great unity and power; the purely spiritual aims of the church, to be sure, suffer somewhat, but after all this peculiar organism is more than a church, it is a government of men.

The headquarters of the A. M. E. Church are in Philadelphia. Their publishing house, at Seventh and Pine, publishes a weekly paper, and a quarterly review, besides some books, such as hymnals, church disciplines, short treatises, leaflets and the like. The receipts of this establishment in 1897 were $16,058.26, and its expenditures $14,119.15. Its total outfit and property is valued at $45,513.64, with an indebtedness of $14,513.64.

An episcopal residence for the bishop of the district has recently been purchased on Belmont avenue. The Philadelphia Conference disbursed from the general church funds in 1897, $985 to superannuated ministers, and $375 to widows of ministers. Two or three women missionaries visited the sick during the year and some committees of the Ladies' Mission Society worked to secure orphans' homes. Thus throughout the work of this church there is much evidence of enthusiasm and persistent progress.

There are three churches in the city representing the A. M. E. Zion connection. They are:

Wesley	Fifteenth and Lombard Sts.
Mount Zion	Fifty-fifth above Market St.
Union	Ninth St. and Girard Ave.

No detailed statistics of these churches are available; the last two are small, the first is one of the largest and most popular in the city; the pastor receives $1,500 a year and the total income of the church is between $4,000 and $5,000. It does considerable charitable work among its aged members, and supports a large sick and death benefit society. Its property is worth at least $25,000.

Two other Methodist churches of different denominations are: Grace U. A. M. E., Lombard street, above Fifteenth; St. Matthew Methodist Protestant, Fifty-eighth and Vine streets. Both these churches are small, although the first has a valuable piece of property.

The Methodist Episcopal Church has six organizations in the city among the Negroes; they own church property valued at $53,700, have a total membership of 1202, and an income of $16,394 in 1897. Of this total income, $1,235, or 7 1/2 percent, was given for benevolent enterprises. These churches are quiet and well conducted, and although not among the most popular churches, have nevertheless a membership of old and respected citizens.

Colored M. E. Churches in Philadelphia, 1897.

Church	Members	Salary, etc., of Pastor	Contributions to Presiding Elders and Bishops	Value of Church	Value of Parsonage	Building and Improvements during Year	Paid on Indebtedness	Present Indebtedness	Current Expenses	Benevolent Collections
Bainbridge Street	354	$1312	$151	$20,000	...	$190	$601	$4,433	$1274	$326
Frankford	72	720	35	1,500	...	15	146	130	155	87
Germantown	165	828	72	4,000	...	...	400	1,000	270	177
Haven	72	440	39	3,400	...	24	...	3,836	277	25
Waterloo Street	31	221	27	800	...	450	50	90	22	37
Zoar	508	1270	220	20,000	$4,000	3522	2171	5,800	257	583
Total	1202	$4791	544	$49,700	$4,000	$4201	$3368	$15,289	$2255	$1235

There were in 1896 seventeen Baptist churches in Philadelphia, holding property valued at more than $300,000, having six thousand members, and an annual income of, probably, $30,000 to $35,000. One of the largest churches has in the last five years raised between $17,000 and $18,000.

Colored Baptist Churches of Philadelphia, 1896.

Church	Membership	Value of Property	Expended in Missions, Local and Foreign	Annual Income
Monumental	435	$30,000	$7.00	...
Cherry Street	800	50,000	...	...
Union	1,020	50,000	58.10	...
St. Paul	422	25,000	1.00	...
Ebenezer	189	12,000	3.36	...
Macedonia	76	1,000	3.00	...
Bethsaida	78	...	...	...
Haddington	50	...	...	...
Germantown	305	24,800	...	...
Grace	57	2,000	5.50	...
Shiloh	1,000	50,000	...	$3,600
Holy Trinity	287	10,000	3.00	...
Second, Nicetown	164	2,000	9.73	...
Zion	700	40,000	...	...
Providence	...	...	...	...
Cherry Street Mission	...	...	...	...
Tabernacle	...	...	...	...
Total	5,583	$296,800		

The Baptists are strong in Philadelphia, and own many large and attractive churches, such as, for instance, the Union Baptist Church, on Twelfth street; Zion Baptist, in the northern part of the city; Monumental, in West Philadelphia, and the staid and respectable Cherry Street Church. These churches as a rule have large membership. They are, however, quite different in spirit and methods from the Methodists; they lack organization, and are not so well managed as business institutions. Consequently statistics of their work are very hard to obtain, and indeed in many cases do not even exist for individual churches. On the other hand, the Baptists are peculiarly clannish and loyal to their organization, keep their pastors a long time, and thus each church gains an individuality not noticed in Methodist churches. If the pastor is a strong, upright character, his influence for good is marked. At the same time, the Baptists have in their ranks a larger percentage of illiteracy than probably any other church, and it is often possible for an inferior man to hold a large church for years and allow it to stagnate and retrograde. The Baptist policy is extreme democracy applied to church affairs, and no wonder that this often results in a pernicious dictatorship. While many of the Baptist pastors of Philadelphia are men of ability and education, the general average is below that of the other churches—a fact due principally to the ease with which one can enter the Baptist ministry. These churches support a small publishing house in the city, which issues a weekly paper. They do some charitable work, but not much.

There are three Presbyterian churches in the city:

Name	Members	Value of Property	Annual Income	
Berean	98	$75,000	$1,135	Parsonage
Central	430	50,000	1,800	Parsonage
First African	105	25,000	1,538	

Central Church is the oldest of these churches and has an interesting history. It represents a withdrawal from the First African Presbyterian Church in 1844. The congregation first worshiped at Eighth and Carpenter streets, and in 1845 purchased a lot at Ninth and Lombard, where they still meet in a quiet and respectable house of worship. Their 430 members include some of the oldest and most respectable Negro families of the city. Probably if the white Presbyterians had given more encouragement to Negroes, this denomination would have absorbed the best elements of the colored population; they seem, however, to have shown some desire to be rid of the blacks, or at least not to increase their Negro membership in Philadelphia to any great extent. Central Church is more nearly a simple religious organization than most churches; it listens to able sermons, but does little outside its own doors.

Berean Church is the work of one man and is an institutional church. It was formerly a mission of Central Church and now owns a fine piece of property bought by donations contributed by whites and Negroes, but chiefly by the former. The conception of the work and its carrying out, however, is due to Negroes. This church conducts a successful Building and Loan Association, a kindergarten, a medical dispensary and a seaside home, beside the numerous church societies. Probably no church in the city, except the Episcopal Church of the Crucifixion, is doing so much for the social betterment of the Negro. The First African is the oldest colored church of this denomination in the city.

The Episcopal Church has, for Negro congregations, two independent churches, two churches dependent on white parishes, and four missions and Sunday-schools. . . .

The Episcopal churches receive more outside help than others and also do more general mission and rescue work. They hold $150,000 worth of property, have 900–1,000 members and an annual income of $7,000 to $8,000. They represent all grades of the colored population. The oldest of the churches is St. Thomas. Next comes the Church of the Crucifixion, over fifty years old and perhaps the most effective church organization in the city for benevolent and rescue work. It has been built up virtually by one Negro, a man of sincerity and culture, and of peculiar energy. This church carries on regular church work at Bainbridge and Eighth and at two branch missions; it helps in the Fresh Air Fund, has an ice mission, a vacation school of thirty-five children, and a parish visitor. It makes an especial feature of good music with its vested choir. One or two courses of University Extension lectures are held here each year, and there is a large beneficial and insurance society in active operation, and a Home for the Homeless on Lombard street. This church especially reaches after a class of neglected poor whom the other colored churches shun or forget and for whom there is little fellowship in white churches. The rector says of this work:

"As I look back over nearly twenty years of labor in one parish, I see a great deal to be devoutly thankful for. Here are people struggling from the beginning of one year to another, without ever having what can be called the necessaries of life. God alone knows what a real struggle life is to them. Many of them must always be 'moving on,' because they cannot pay the rent or meet other obligations.

"I have just visited a family of four, mother and three children. The mother is too sick to work. The eldest girl will work when she can find something to do. But the rent is due, and there is not a cent in the house. This is but a sample. How can such people support a church of their own? To many such, religion often becomes doubly comforting. They seize eagerly on the promises of a life where these earthly distresses will be forever absent.

"If the other half only knew how this half is living—how hard and dreary, and often hopeless, life is—the members of the more favored half would gladly help to do all they could to have the gospel freely preached to those whose lives are so devoid of earthly comforts.

"Twenty or thirty thousand dollars (and that is not much), safely invested, would enable the parish to do a work that ought to be done and yet is not being done at present. The poor could then have the gospel preached to them in a way that it is not now being preached."

The Catholic church has in the last decade made great progress in its work among Negroes and is determined to do much in the future. Its chief hold upon the colored people is its comparative lack of discrimination. There is one Catholic church in the city designed especially for Negro work—St. Peter Clavers at Twelfth and Lombard—formerly a Presbyterian church; recently a parish house has been added. The priest in charge estimates that 400 or 500 Negroes regularly attend Catholic churches in various parts of the city. The Mary

Drexel Home for Colored Orphans is a Catholic institution near the city which is doing much work. The Catholic church can do more than any other agency in humanizing the intense prejudice of many of the working-class against the Negro, and signs of this influence are manifest in some quarters.

We have thus somewhat in detail reviewed the work of the chief churches. There are beside these continually springing up and dying a host of little noisy missions which represent the older and more demonstrative worship. A description of one applies to nearly all; take for instance one in the slums of the Fifth Ward:

"The tablet in the gable of this little church bears the date 1837. For sixty years it has stood and done its work in the narrow lane. What its history has been all this time it is difficult to find out, for no records are on hand, and no one is here to tell the tale.

"The few last months of the old order was something like this: It was in the hands of a Negro congregation. Several visits were paid to the church, and generally a dozen people were found there. After a discourse by a very illiterate preacher, hymns were sung, having many repetitions of senseless sentiment and exciting cadences. It took about an hour to work up the congregation to a fervor aimed at. When this was reached a remarkable scene presented itself. The whole congregation pressed forward to an open space before the pulpit, and formed a ring. The most excitable of their number entered the ring, and with clapping of hands and contortions led the devotions. Those forming the ring joined in the clapping of hands and wild and loud singing, frequently springing into the air, and shouting loudly. As the devotions proceeded, most of the worshipers took off their coats and vests and hung them on pegs on the wall. This continued for hours, until all were completely exhausted, and some had fainted and been stowed away on benches or the pulpit platform. This was the order of things at the close of sixty years' history. * * * When this congregation vacated the church, they did so stealthily, under cover of darkness, removed furniture not their own, including the pulpit, and left bills unpaid."

There are dozens of such little missions in various parts of Philadelphia, led by wandering preachers. They are survivals of the methods of worship in Africa and the West Indies. In some of the larger churches noise and excitement attend the services, especially at the time of revival or in prayer meetings. For the most part, however, these customs are dying away. . . .

CHAPTER THREE

Credo

Du Bois wrote the following poem in 1900 at the age of twenty-three. It was sub-sequently published in *Darkwater* (1920), and it is his single most reprinted piece of work. While it is a gentle expression of religious sentiment, its motif of racial pride and its condemnation of injustice and inequality are also quite pronounced and were extremely radical in their day.

I believe in God, who made of one blood all nations that on earth do dwell. I believe that all men, black and brown and white, are brothers, varying through time and opportunity, in form and gift and feature, but differing in no essential particular, and alike in soul and the possibility of infinite development.

Especially do I believe in the Negro Race: in the beauty of its genius, the sweetness of its soul, and its strength in that meekness which shall yet inherit this turbulent earth.

I believe in Pride of race and lineage and self: in pride of self so deep as to scorn injustice to other selves; in pride of lineage so great as to despise no man's father; in pride of race so chivalrous as neither to offer bastardy to the weak nor beg wedlock of the strong, knowing that men may be brothers in Christ, even though they be not brothers in law.

I believe in Service—humble, reverent service, from the blackening of boots to the whitening of souls; for Work is Heaven, Idleness Hell, and Wage is the "Well done!" of the Master, who summoned all them that labor and are heavy laden, making no distinction between the black, sweating cotton hands of Georgia and the first families of Virginia, since all distinction not based on deed is devilish and not divine.

I believe in the Devil and his angels, who wantonly work to narrow the opportunity of struggling human beings, especially if they be black; who spit in the faces of the fallen, strike them that cannot strike again, believe the worst and work to prove it, hating the image which their Maker stamped on a brother's soul.

I believe in the Prince of Peace. I believe that War is Murder. I believe that armies and navies are at bottom the tinsel and braggadocio of oppression and wrong, and I believe that the wicked conquest of weaker and darker nations by nations whiter and stronger but foreshadows the death of that strength.

I believe in Liberty for all men: the space to stretch their arms and their souls, the right to breathe and the right to vote, the freedom to choose their friends, enjoy the sunshine, and ride on the railroads, uncursed by color; thinking, dreaming, working as they will in a kingdom of beauty and love.

I believe in the Training of Children, black even as white; the leading out of little souls into the green pastures and beside the still waters, not for self nor peace, but for life lit by some large vision of beauty and goodness and truth; lest we forget, and the sons of the fathers, like Esau, for mere meat barter their birthright in a mighty nation.

Finally, I believe in Patience—patience with the weakness of the Weak and the strength of the Strong, the prejudice of the Ignorant and the ignorance of the Blind; patience with the tardy triumph of Joy and the mad chastening of Sorrow; patience with God!

CHAPTER FOUR

The Negro Church [Essay]

Du Bois was one of the most vociferous critics of the Black Church. In this piece, published in *The Crisis* in 1912, Du Bois charges that "all is not well with the colored church" and subsequently suggests paths toward improvement.

It happens that during this month, in the North, West, and South, there are meeting the ruling Methodist ecclesiastical bodies representing a membership of 1,175,000 colored Americans. Later, in midsummer, the Baptist conventions, which represented 2,300,000 members, will meet. These three and a half millions of people represent the great middle class of colored Americans. The lowest class of outcasts have never been reached; the highest class of the educated and thoughtful are being gradually lost. The great middle class remains, and in 35,000 churches holding $57,000,000 worth of property they form a peculiar organized government of men. Under some 50 powerful leaders and 30,000 salaried local preachers they raise and expend over 7,000,000 dollars a year.

Before such an organization one must bow with respect. It has accomplished much. It has instilled and conserved morals, it has helped family life, it has taught and developed ability and given the colored man his best business training. It has planted in every city and town of the Union with few exceptions, meeting places for colored folk which vary from shelter to luxurious and beautiful edifices.

Not withstanding this, all is not well with the colored church. First, its fifty leaders are in too many cases not the men they should be. This is not peculiar to the Negro church, but it is true to a larger degree than is healthful. We can point to pure-minded, efficient, unselfish prelates like the last Bishop Paine, the present Bishop Lee and J.W. White. We have men of scholarship and standing like

45

Bishop J. Albert Johnson, and we have efficient men of affairs like John F. Hurst, and M.C.B. Mason and R.H. Boyd.

The trouble is, however, this: there are too few such men. The paths and the higher places are choked with pretentious, ill-trained men and in far too many cases with men dishonest and otherwise immoral. Such men make the walk of upright and business like candidates for power extremely difficult. They put an undue premium upon finesse and personal influence.

Having thus a partially tainted leadership, small wonder that the 30,000 colored ministers fall as a mass far below expectations. There are among them hustling businessmen, eloquent talkers, suave companions and hale fellows, but only here and there does one meet men like Henry L. Phillips of Philadelphia—burning spiritual guides of a troubled, panting people, utterly self-forgetful, utterly devoted to a great ideal of righteousness.

Yet this is precisely the type for which the church—the white church as well as the black church—is crying. This is the only type which will hold thoughtful, reasonable men, to membership with this organization. Today the tendencies are not this way. Today the church is still inveighing against dancing and theatergoing, still blaming educated people for objecting to silly and empty sermons, boasting and noise, still building churches when people need homes and schools, and persisting in crucifying critics rather than realizing the handwriting on the wall.

Let us trust that these great churches in conference, remembering the leaders of the past, and conscious of all that the church has done well, will set their faces to these deeds:

1. Electing as Bishops and leaders only men of honesty, probity, and efficiency and rejecting the noisy and unclean leaders of the thoughtless mob.
2. Weeding out the ministry so as to increase the clean apostles of service and sacrifice.
3. Initiating positive programs of education and social uplift and discouraging extravagant building and mere ostentation.
4. Bending every effort to make the Negro church a place where colored men and women of education and energy can work for the best things regardless of their belief or disbelief in unimportant dogmas and ancient and outworn creeds.

CHAPTER FIVE

Of the Faith of the Fathers

The following chapter comes from Du Bois's most famous book, *The Souls of Black Folk,* published in 1903. Du Bois describes the Black Church as the "social centre" of the black community and its "central club-house," thereby developing his ongoing analysis of the social/communal aspects of early twentieth-century black religious life. But he also illustrates the deeply spiritual components of black religiosity, as well as exploring such matters as the uniqueness of the Negro revival, the transition from African religion to Christianity, and the racist color line that separates white and black even, and perhaps most incredibly, in the realm of religion.

It was out in the country, far from home, far from my foster home, on a dark Sunday night. The road wandered from our rambling log-house up the stony bed of a creek, past wheat and corn, until we could hear dimly across the fields a rhythmic cadence of song,—soft, thrilling, powerful, that swelled and died sorrowfully in our ears. I was a country schoolteacher then, fresh from the East, and had never seen a Southern Negro revival. To be sure, we in Berkshire were not perhaps as stiff and formal as they in Suffolk of olden time; yet we were very quiet and subdued, and I know not what would have happened those clear Sabbath mornings had some one punctuated the sermon with a wild scream, or interrupted the long prayer with a loud Amen! And so most striking to me, as I approached the village and the little plain church perched aloft, was the air of intense excitement that possessed that mass of black folk. A sort of suppressed terror hung in the air and seemed to seize us,—a pythian madness, a demoniac possession, that lent terrible reality to song and word. The black and massive form of the preacher swayed and quivered as the words crowded to his lips and flew at us in singular eloquence. The people moaned and fluttered, and then the gaunt-cheeked brown woman beside me suddenly leaped straight into the air and shrieked like a lost soul, while round about came wail and groan and outcry, and a scene of human passion such as I had never conceived before.

Those who have not thus witnessed the frenzy of a Negro revival in the untouched backwoods of the South can but dimly realize the religious feeling of the slave; as described, such scenes appear grotesque and funny, but as seen they are awful. Three things characterized this religion of the slave,—the Preacher, the Music, and the Frenzy. The preacher is the most unique personality developed by the Negro on American soil. A leader, a politician, an orator, a "boss," an intriguer, an idealist,—all these he is, and ever, too, the centre of a group of men, now twenty, now a thousand in number. The combination of a certain adroitness with deep-seated earnestness, of tact with consummate ability, gave him his preëminence, and helps him maintain it. The type, of course, varies according to time and place, from the West Indies in the sixteenth century to New England in the nineteenth, and from the Mississippi bottoms to cities like New Orleans or New York.

The Music of Negro religion is that plaintive rhythmic melody, with its touching minor cadences, which, despite caricature and defilement, still remains the most original and beautiful expression of human life and longing yet born on American soil. Sprung from the African forests, where its counterpart can still be heard, it was adapted, changed, and intensified by the tragic soul-life of the slave, until, under the stress of law and whip, it became the one true expression of a people's sorrow, despair, and hope.

Finally the Frenzy of "Shouting," when the Spirit of the Lord passed by, and, seizing the devotee, made him mad with supernatural joy, was the last essential of Negro religion and the one more devoutly believed in than all the rest. It varied in expression from the silent rapt countenance or the low murmur and moan to the mad abandon of physical fervor,—the stamping, shrieking, and shouting, the rushing to and fro and wild waving of arms, the weeping and laughing, the vision and the trance. All this is nothing new in the world, but old as religion, as Delphi and Endor. And so firm a hold did it have on the Negro, that many generations firmly believed that without this visible manifestation of the God there could be no true communion with the Invisible.

These were the characteristics of Negro religious life as developed up to the time of Emancipation. Since under the peculiar circumstances of the black man's environment they were the one expression of his higher life, they are of deep interest to the student of his development, both socially and psychologically. Numerous are the attractive lines of inquiry that here group themselves. What did slavery mean to the African savage? What was his attitude toward the World and Life? What seemed to him good and evil,—God and Devil? Whither went his longings and strivings, and wherefore were his heart-burnings and disappointments? Answers to such questions can come only from a study of Negro religion as a development, through its gradual changes from the heathenism of the Gold Coast to the institutional Negro church of Chicago.

Moreover, the religious growth of millions of men, even though they be slaves, cannot be without potent influence upon their contemporaries. The Methodists and Baptists of America owe much of their condition to the silent but potent influence of their millions of Negro converts. Especially is this noticeable in the South, where theology and religious philosophy are on this account a long way behind the North, and where the religion of the poor whites is a plain copy of Negro thought and methods. The mass of "gospel" hymns which has swept through American churches and well-nigh ruined our sense of song consists largely of debased imitations of Negro melodies made by ears that caught the jingle but not the music, the body but not the soul, of the Jubilee songs. It is thus clear that the study of Negro religion is not only a vital part of the history of the Negro in America, but no uninteresting part of American history.

The Negro church of to-day is the social centre of Negro life in the United States, and the most characteristic expression of African character. Take a typical church in a small Virginia town: it is the "First Baptist"—a roomy brick edifice seating five hundred or more persons, tastefully finished in Georgia pine, with a carpet, a small organ, and stained-glass windows. Underneath is a large assembly room with benches. This building is the central club-house of a community of a thousand or more Negroes. Various organizations meet here,—the church proper, the Sunday-school, two or three insurance societies, women's societies, secret societies, and mass meetings of various kinds. Entertainments, suppers, and lectures are held beside the five or six regular weekly religious services. Considerable sums of money are collected and expended here, employment is found for the idle, strangers are introduced, news is disseminated and charity distributed. At the same time this social, intellectual, and economic centre is a religious centre of great power. Depravity, Sin, Redemption, Heaven, Hell, and Damnation are preached twice a Sunday after the crops are laid by; and few indeed of the community have the hardihood to withstand conversion. Back of this more formal religion, the Church often stands as a real conserver of morals, a strengthener of family life, and the final authority on what is Good and Right.

Thus one can see in the Negro church to-day, reproduced in microcosm, all the great world from which the Negro is cut off by color-prejudice and social condition. In the great city churches the same tendency is noticeable and in many respects emphasized. A great church like the Bethel of Philadelphia has over eleven hundred members, an edifice seating fifteen hundred persons and valued at one hundred thousand dollars, an annual budget of five thousand dollars, and a government consisting of a pastor with several assisting local preachers, an executive and legislative board, financial boards and tax collectors; general church meetings for making laws; sub-divided groups led by class leaders, a company of militia, and twenty-four auxiliary societies. The activity of a church like this is immense and far-reaching, and the bishops who preside over these organizations throughout the land are among the most powerful Negro rulers in the world.

Such churches are really governments of men, and consequently a little investigation reveals the curious fact that, in the South, at least, practically every American Negro is a church member. Some, to be sure, are not regularly enrolled, and a few do not habitually attend services; but, practically, a proscribed people must have a social centre and that centre for this people is the Negro church. The census of 1890 showed nearly twenty-four thousand Negro churches in the country, with a total enrolled membership of over two and a half millions, or ten actual church members to every twenty eight persons, and in some Southern states one in every two persons. Besides these there is the large number who, while not enrolled as members, attend and take part in many of the activities of the church. There is an organized Negro church for every sixty black families in the nation, and in some States for every forty families, owning, on an average, a thousand dollars' worth of property each, or nearly twenty-six million dollars in all.

Such, then, is the large development of the Negro church since Emancipation. The question now is, What have been the successive steps of this social history and what are the present tendencies? First, we must realize that no such institution as the Negro church could rear itself without definite historical foundations. These foundations we can find if we remember that the social history of the Negro did not start in America. He was from a definite social environment—the polygamous clan life under the headship of the chief and the potent influence of the priest. His religion was nature-worship, with profound belief in invisible surrounding influences, good and bad, and his worship was through incantation and sacrifice. The first rude change in this life was the slave ship and the West Indian sugar-fields. The plantation organization replaced the clan and tribe, and the white master replaced the chief with far greater and more despotic powers. Forced and long-continued toil became the rule of life, the old ties of blood relationship and kinship disappeared, and instead of the family appeared a new polygamy and polyandry, which, in some cases, almost reached promiscuity. It was a terrific social revolution, and yet some traces were retained of the former group life, and the chief remaining institution was the Priest or Medicine-man. He early appeared on the plantation and found his function as the healer of the sick, the interpreter of the Unknown, the comforter of the sorrowing, the super-natural avenger of wrong, and the one who rudely but picturesquely expressed the longing, disappointment, and resentment of a stolen and oppressed people. Thus, as bard, physician, judge, and priest, within the narrow limits allowed by the slave system, rose the Negro preacher, and under him the first church was not at first by any means Christian nor definitely organized; rather it was an adapta-tion and mingling of heathen rites among the members of each plantation, and roughly designated as Voodooism. Association with the masters, missionary effort and motives of expediency gave these rites an early veneer of Christianity, and after the lapse of many generations the Negro church became Christian.

Two characteristic things must be noticed in regard to the church. First, it became almost entirely Baptist and Methodist in faith; secondly, as a social insti-tution it antedated by many decades the monogamic Negro home. From the very circumstances of its beginning, the church was confined to the plantation, and consisted primarily of a series of disconnected units; although, later on, some freedom of movement was allowed, still this geographical limitation was always important and was one cause of the spread of the decentralized and democratic Baptist faith among the slaves. At the same time, the visible rite of baptism appealed strongly to their mystic temperament. To-day the Baptist Church is still largest in membership among Negroes, and has a million and a half communi-cants. Next in popularity came the churches organized in connection with the white neighboring churches, chiefly Baptist and Methodist, with a few Episco-palian and others. The Methodists still form the second greatest denomination, with nearly a million members. The faith of these two leading denominations was more suited to the slave church from the prominence they gave to religious feeling and fervor. The Negro membership in other denominations has always been small and relatively unimportant, although the Episcopalians and Presby-terians are gaining among the more intelligent classes to-day, and the Catholic Church is making headway in certain sections. After Emancipation, and still ear-lier in the North, the Negro churches largely severed such affiliations as they had had with the white churches, either by choice or by compulsion. The Baptist churches became independent, but the Methodists were compelled early to unite for purposes of episcopal government. This gave rise to the great African Methodist Church, the greatest Negro organization in the world, to the Zion Church and the Colored Methodist, and to the black conferences and churches in this and other denominations.

The second fact noted, namely, that the Negro church antedates the Negro home, leads to an explanation of much that is paradoxical in this communistic institution and in the morals of its members. But especially it leads us to regard this institution as peculiarly the expression of the inner ethical life of a people in a sense seldom true elsewhere. Let us turn, then, from the outer physical development of the church to the more important inner ethical life of the people who compose it. The Negro has already been pointed out many times as a religious animal—a being of that deep emotional nature which turns instinctively toward the supernatural. Endowed with a rich tropical imagination and a keen, delicate appreciation of Nature, the transplanted African lived in a world animate with gods and devils, elves and witches; full of strange influences,—of Good to be implored, of Evil to be propitiated. Slavery, then, was to him the dark triumph of Evil over him. All the hateful powers of the Under-world were striving against him, and a spirit of revolt and revenge filled his heart. He called up all the resources of heathenism to aid,—exorcism and witch-craft, the mysterious Obi worship with its barbarious rites, spells, and blood-sacrifice even, now and then, of human victims. Weird midnight orgies and mystic conjurations were invoked, the witch-woman and the voodoo-priest became the centre of Negro group life, and that vein of vague superstition which characterizes the unlettered Negro even to-day was deepened and strengthened.

In spite, however, of such success as that of the fierce Maroons, the Danish blacks, and others, the spirit of revolt gradually died away under the untiring energy and superior strength of the slave masters. By the middle of the eighteenth century the black slave had sunk, with hushed murmurs, to his place at the bottom of a new economic system, and was unconsciously ripe for a new philosophy of life. Nothing suited his condition then better than the doctrines of passive submission embodied in the new newly learned Christianity. Slave masters early realized this, and cheerfully aided religious propaganda within certain bounds. The long system of repression and degradation of the Negro tended to emphasize the elements of his character which made him a valuable chattel: courtesy became humility, moral strength degenerated into submission, and the exquisite native appreciation of the beautiful became an infinite capacity for dumb suffering. The Negro, losing the joy of this world, eagerly seized upon the offered conceptions of the next; the avenging Spirit of the Lord enjoining patience in this world, under sorrow and tribulation until the Great Day when He should lead His dark children home,—this became his comforting dream. His preacher repeated the prophecy, and his bards sang,—

> "Children, we all shall be free
> When the Lord shall appear!"

This deep religious fatalism, painted so beautifully in "Uncle Tom," came soon to breed, as all fatalistic faiths will, the sensualist side by side with the martyr. Under the lax moral life of the plantation, where marriage was a farce, laziness a virtue, and property a theft, a religion of resignation and submission degenerated easily, in less strenuous minds, into a philosophy of indulgence and crime. Many of the worst characteristics of the Negro masses of to-day had their seed in this period of the slave's ethical growth. Here it was that the Home was ruined under the very shadow of the Church, white and black; here habits of shiftlessness took root, and sullen hopelessness replaced hopeful strife.

With the beginning of the abolition movement and the gradual growth of a class of free Negroes came a change. We often neglect the influence of the freedman before the war, because of the paucity of his numbers and the small weight he had in the history of the nation. But we must not forget that his chief influence was internal,—was exerted on the black world; and that there he was the ethical and social leader. Huddled as he was in a few centres like Philadelphia, New York, and New Orleans, the masses of the freedmen sank into poverty and listlessness; but not all of them. The free Negro leader early arose and his chief characteristic was intense earnestness and deep feeling on the slavery question. Freedom became to him a real thing and not a dream. His religion became darker and more intense, and into his ethics crept a note of revenge, into his songs a day of reckoning close at hand. The "Coming of the Lord" swept this side of Death, and came to be a thing to be hoped for in this day. Through fugitive slaves and irrepressible discussion this desire for freedom seized the black millions still in bondage, and became their one ideal of life. The black bards caught new notes, and sometimes even dared to sing,—

> "O Freedom, O Freedom, O Freedom over me!
> Before I'll be a slave
> I'll be buried in my grave,
> And go home to my Lord
> And be free."

For fifty years Negro religion thus transformed itself and identified itself with the dream of Abolition, until that which was a radical fad in the white North and an anarchistic plot in the white South had become a religion to the black world.

Thus, when Emancipation finally came, it seemed to the freedman a literal Coming of the Lord. His fervid imagination was stirred as never before, by the tramp of armies, the blood and dust of battle, and the wail and whirl of social upheaval. He stood dumb and motionless before the whirlwind: what had he to do with it? Was it not the Lord's doing, and marvellous in his eyes? Joyed and bewildered with what came, he stood awaiting new wonders till the inevitable Age of Reaction swept over the nation and brought the crisis of to-day.

It is difficult to explain clearly the present critical stage of Negro religion. First, we must remember that living as the blacks do in close contact with a great modern nation, and sharing, although imperfectly, the soul-life of that nation, they must necessarily be affected more or less directly by all the religious and ethical forces that are to-day moving the United States. These questions and movements are, however, overshadowed and dwarfed by the (to them) all-important question of their civil, political, and economic status. They must perpetually discuss the "Negro Problem,"—must live, move, and have their being in it, and interpret all else in its light or darkness. With this come, too, peculiar problems of their inner life,—of the status of women, the maintenance of Home, the training of children, the accumulation of wealth, and the prevention of crime. All this must mean a time of intense ethical ferment, of religious heart-searching and intellectual unrest. From the double life every American Negro must live, as a Negro and as an American, as swept on by the current of the nineteenth while yet struggling in the eddies of the fifteenth century,—from this must arise a painful self-consciousness, an almost morbid sense of personality and a moral hesitancy which is fatal to self-confidence. The worlds within and without the Veil of Color are changing, and changing rapidly, but not at the same rate, not in the same way; and this must produce a peculiar wrenching of the soul, a peculiar sense of doubt and bewilderment. Such a double life, with double thoughts, double duties, and double social classes, must give rise to double words and double ideals, and tempt the mind to pretence or revolt, to hypocrisy or radicalism.

In some such doubtful words and phrases can one perhaps most clearly picture the peculiar ethical paradox that faces the Negro of to-day and is tingeing and changing his religious life. Feeling that his rights and his dearest ideals are being trampled upon, that the public conscience is ever more deaf to his righteous appeal, and that all the reactionary forces of prejudice, greed, and revenge are daily gaining new strength and fresh allies, the Negro faces no enviable dilemma. Conscious of his impotence, and pessimistic, he often becomes bitter and vindictive; and his religion, instead of a worship, is a complaint and a curse, a wail rather than a hope, a sneer rather than a faith. On the other hand, another type of mind, shrewder and keener and more tortuous too, sees in the very strength of the anti-Negro movement its patent weaknesses, and with Jesuitic casuistry is deterred by no ethical considerations in the endeavor to turn this weakness to the black man's strength. Thus we have two great and hardly reconcilable streams of thought and ethical strivings; the danger of the one lies in anarchy, that of the other in hypocrisy. The one type of Negro stands almost ready to curse God and die, and the other is too often found a traitor to right and a coward before force; the one is wedded to ideals remote, whimsical, perhaps impossible of realization; the other forgets that life is more than meat and the body more than raiment. But, after all, is not this simply the writhing of the age translated into black, the triumph of the Lie which today, with its false culture, faces the hideousness of the anarchist assassin?

To-day the two groups of Negroes, the one in the North, the other in the South, represent these divergent ethical tendencies, the first tending toward radicalism, the other toward hypocritical compromise. It is no idle regret with which the white South mourns the loss of the old-time Negro,—the frank, honest, simple old servant who stood for the earlier religious age of submission and humility. With all his laziness and lack of many elements of true manhood, he was at least open-hearted, faithful, and sincere. To-day he is gone, but who is to blame for his going? Is it not those very persons who mourn for him? Is it not the tendency, born of Reconstruction and Reaction, to found a society on lawlessness and deception, to tamper with the moral fibre of a naturally honest and straightforward people until the whites threaten to become ungovernable tyrants and the blacks criminals and hypocrites? Deception is the natural defence of the weak against the strong, and the South used it for many years against its conquerors; to-day it must be prepared to see its black proletariat turn that same two-edged weapon against itself. And how natural this is! The death of Denmark Vesey and Nat Turner proved long since to the Negro the present hopelessness of physical defence. Political defence is becoming less and less available, and economic defence is still only partially effective. But there is a patent defence at hand,—the defence of deception and flattery, of cajoling and lying. It is the same defence which peasants of the Middle Age used and which left its stamp on their character for centuries. To-day the young Negro of the South who would succeed cannot be frank and outspoken, honest and self-assertive, but rather he is daily tempted to be silent and wary, politic and sly; he must flatter and be pleasant, endure petty insults with a smile, shut his eyes to wrong; in too many cases he sees positive personal advantage in deception and lying. His real thoughts, his real aspirations, must be guarded in whispers; he must not criticise, he must not complain. Patience, humility, and adroitness must, in these growing black youth, replace impulse, manliness, and courage. With this sacrifice there is an economic opening, and perhaps peace and some prosperity. Without this there is riot, migration, or crime. Nor is this situation peculiar to the Southern United States, is it not rather the only method by which undeveloped races have gained the right to share modern culture? The price of culture is a Lie.

On the other hand, in the North the tendency is to emphasize the radicalism of the Negro. Driven from his birthright in the South by a situation at which every fibre of his more outspoken and assertive nature revolts, he finds himself in a land where he can scarcely earn a decent living amid the harsh competition and the color discrimination. At the same time, through schools and periodicals, discussions and lectures, he is intellectually quickened and awakened. The soul, long pent up and dwarfed, suddenly expands in new-found freedom. What wonder that every tendency is to excess, radical complaint, radical remedies, bitter denunciation or angry silence. Some sink, some rise. The criminal and the sensualist leave the church for the gambling-hell and the brothel, and fill the slums of Chicago and Baltimore; the better classes segregate themselves from the group-life of both white and black, and form an aristocracy, cultured but pessimistic, whose bitter criticism stings while it points out no way of escape. They despise the submission and subserviency of the Southern Negroes, but offer no other means by which a poor and oppressed minority can exist side by side with its masters. Feeling deeply and keenly the tendencies and opportunities of the age in which they live, their souls are bitter at the fate which drops the Veil between; and the very fact that this bitterness is natural and justifiable only serves to intensify it and make it more maddening.

Between the two extreme types of ethical attitude which I have thus sought to make clear wavers the mass of the millions of Negroes, North and South; and their religious life and activity partake of this social conflict within their ranks. Their churches are differentiating,—now into groups of cold, fashionable devotees, in no way distinguishable from similar white groups save in color of skin; now into large social and business institutions catering to the desire for information and amusement of their members, warily avoiding unpleasant questions both within and without the black world, and preaching in effect if not in word: *Dum vivimus, vivamus.*

But back of this still broods silently the deep religious feeling of the real Negro heart, the stirring, unguided might of powerful human souls who have lost the guiding star of the past and seek in the great night a new religious ideal. Some day the Awakening will come, when the pent-up vigor of ten million souls shall sweep irresistibly toward the Goal, out of the Valley of the Shadow of Death, where all that makes life worth living—Liberty, Justice, and Right—is marked "For White People Only."

CHAPTER SIX

Of Alexander Crummell

This chapter, also from *The Souls of Black Folk* (1903), offers a powerful illustration of what it was like to be a black Christian leader in the United States at the turn of the century. We glimpse the story of a strong young man who braved the white racism of his day in pursuit of his spiritual ambition. In exploring the intersection of race and religion, Du Bois reminds us that religious life is never a realm unto itself, but is always and everywhere interwoven with the given social and cultural forces with which it finds itself inevitably enmeshed.

This is the story of a human heart,—the tale of a black boy who many long years ago began to struggle with life that he might know the world and know himself. Three temptations he met on those dark dunes that lay gray and dismal before the wonder-eyes of the child: the temptation of Hate that stood out against the red dawn; the temptation of Despair, that darkened noonday; and the temptation of Doubt, that ever steals along with twilight. Above all you must hear of the vales he crossed,—the Valley of Humiliation and the Valley of the Shadow of Death.

I saw Alexander Crummell first at a Wilberforce commencement season, amid its bustle and crush. Tall, frail, and black he stood, with simple dignity and an unmistakable air of good breeding. I talked with him apart, where the storming of the lusty young orators could not harm us. I spoke to him politely, then curiously, then eagerly, as I began to feel the fineness of his character,—his calm courtesy, the sweetness of his strength, and his fair blending of the hope and truth of life. Instinctively I bowed before this man, as one bows before the prophets of the world. Some seer he seemed, that came not from the crimson Past or the gray To-come, but from the pulsing Now,—that mocking world which

57

seemed to me at once so light and dark, so splendid and sordid. Fourscore years had he wandered in this same world of mine, within the Veil.

He was born with the Missouri Compromise and lay a-dying amid the echoes of Manila and El Caney: stirring times for living, times dark to look back upon, darker to look forward to. The black-faced lad that paused over his mud and marbles seventy years ago saw puzzling vistas as he looked down the world. The slave-ship still groaned across the Atlantic, faint cries burdened the Southern breeze, and the great black father whispered mad tales of cruelty into those young ears. From the low doorway the mother silently watched her boy at play, and at nightfall sought him eagerly lest the shadows bear him away to the land of slaves.

So his young mind worked and winced and shaped curiously a vision of Life; and in the midst of that vision ever stood one dark figure alone,—ever with the hard, thick countenance of that bitter father, and a form that fell in vast and shapeless folds. Thus the temptation of Hate grew and shadowed the growing child,—gliding stealthily into his laughter, fading into his play, and seizing his dreams by day and night with rough, rude turbulence. So the black boy asked of sky and sun and flower the never-answered Why? and loved, as he grew, neither the world nor the world's rough ways.

Strange temptation for a child, you may think; and yet in this wide land to-day a thousand thousand dark children brood before this same temptation, and feel its cold and shuddering arms. For them, perhaps, some one will some day lift the Veil,—will come tenderly and cheerily into those sad little lives and brush the brooding hate away, just as Beriah Green strode in upon the life of Alexander Crummell. And before the bluff, kind-hearted man the shadow seemed less dark. Beriah Green had a school in Oneida County, New York, with a score of mischievous boys. "I'm going to bring a black boy here to educate," said Beriah Green, as only a crank and an abolitionist would have dared to say. "Oho!" laughed the boys. "Ye-es," said his wife; and Alexander came. Once before, the black boy had sought a school, had travelled, cold and hungry, four hundred miles up into free New Hampshire, to Canaan. But the godly farmers hitched ninety yoke of oxen to the abolition schoolhouse and dragged it into the middle of the swamp. The black boy trudged away.

The nineteenth was the first century of human sympathy,—the age when half wonderingly we began to descry in others that transfigured spark of divinity which we call Myself; when clodhoppers and peasants, and tramps and thieves, and millionaires and—sometimes—Negroes, became throbbing souls whose warm pulsing life touched us so nearly that we half gasped with surprise, crying, "Thou too! Hast Thou seen Sorrow and the dull waters of Hopelessness? Hast Thou known Life?" And then all helplessly we peered into those Other-worlds, and wailed "O World of Worlds, how shall man make you one?"

So in that little Oneida school there came to those school-boys a revelation of thought and longing beneath one black skin, of which they had not dreamed before. And to the lonely boy came a new dawn of sympathy and inspiration. The shadowy, formless thing—the temptation of Hate, that hovered between him and the world—grew fainter and less sinister. It did not wholly fade away, but diffused itself and lingered thick at the edges. Through it the child now first saw the blue and gold of life,— the sun-swept road that ran 'twixt heaven and earth until in one far-off wan wavering line they met and kissed. A vision of life came to the growing boy,—mystic, wonderful. He raised his head, stretched himself, breathed deep of the fresh new air. Yonder, behind the forests, he heard strange sounds; then glinting through the trees he saw, far, far away, the bronzed hosts of a nation calling, calling faintly, calling loudly. He heard the hateful clank of their chains; he felt them cringe and grovel, and there rose within him a protest and a prophecy. And he girded himself to walk down the world.

A voice and vision called him to be a priest,—a seer to lead the uncalled out of the house of bondage. He saw the headless host turn toward him like the whirling of mad waters,—he stretched forth his hands eagerly, and then, even as he stretched them, suddenly there swept across the vision the temptation of Despair.

They were not wicked men,—the problem of life is not the problem of the wicked,—they were calm, good men, Bishops of the Apostolic Church of God, and strove toward righteousness. They said slowly, "It is all very natural—it is even commendable; but the General Theological Seminary of the Episcopal Church cannot admit a Negro." And when that thin, half-grotesque figure still haunted their doors, they put their hands kindly, half sorrowfully, on his shoulders, and said, "Now, of course, we—we know how *you* feel about it; but you see it is impossible,—that is—well—it is premature. Sometime, we trust—sincerely trust—all such distinctions will fade away; but now the world is as it is."

This was the temptation of Despair; and the young man fought it doggedly. Like some grave shadow he flitted by those halls, pleading, arguing, half angrily demanding admittance, until there came the final *No:* until men hustled the disturber away, marked him as foolish, unreasonable, and injudicious, a vain rebel against God's law. And then from that Vision Splendid all the glory faded slowly away, and left an earth gray and stern rolling on beneath a dark despair. Even the kind hands that stretched themselves toward him from out the depths of that dull morning seemed but parts of the purple shadows. He saw them coldly, and asked, "Why should I strive by special grace when the way of the world is closed to me?" All gently yet, the hands urged him on,—the hands of young John Jay, that daring father's daring son; the hands of the good folk of Boston, that free city. And yet, with a way to the priesthood of the Church open at last before him, the cloud lingered there; and even when in old St. Paul's the venerable Bishop raised his white arms above the Negro deacon—even then the burden had not lifted from that heart, for there had passed a glory from the earth.

And yet the fire through which Alexander Crummell went did not burn in vain. Slowly and more soberly he took up again his plan of life. More critically he studied the situation. Deep down below the slavery and servitude of the Negro people he saw their fatal weaknesses, which long years of mistreatment had emphasized. The death of strong moral character, of unbending righteousness, he felt, was their great shortcoming, and here he would begin. He would gather the best of his people into some little Episcopal chapel and there lead, teach, and inspire them, till the leaven spread, till the children grew, till the world hearkened, till—till—and then across his dream gleamed some faint after-glow of that first fair vision of youth—only an after-glow, for there had passed a glory from the earth.

One day—it was in 1842, and the springtide was struggling merrily with the May winds of New England—he stood at last in his own chapel in Providence, a priest of the Church. The days sped by, and the dark young clergyman labored; he wrote his sermons carefully; he intoned his prayers with a soft, earnest voice; he haunted the streets and accosted the wayfarers; he visited the sick, and knelt beside the dying. He worked and toiled, week by week, day by day, month by month. And yet month by month the congregation dwindled, week by week the hollow walls echoed more sharply, day by day the calls came fewer and fewer, and day by day the third temptation sat clearer and still more clearly within the Veil; a temptation, as it were, bland and smiling, with just a shade of mockery in its smooth tones. First it came casually, in the cadence of a voice: "Oh, colored folks? Yes." Or perhaps more definitely: "What do you *expect?*" In voice and gesture lay the doubt—the temptation of Doubt. How he hated it, and stormed at it furiously! "Of course they are capable," he cried; "of course they can learn and strive and achieve—" and "Of course," added the temptation softly, "they do nothing of the sort." Of all the three temptations, this one struck the deepest. Hate? He had outgrown so childish a thing. Despair? He had steeled his right arm against it, and fought it with the vigor of determination. But to doubt the worth of his life-work,—to doubt the destiny and capability of the race his soul loved because it was his; to find listless squalor instead of eager endeavor; to hear his own lips whispering, "They do not care; they cannot know; they are dumb driven cattle,—why cast your pearls before swine?"—this, this seemed more than man could bear; and he closed the door, and sank upon the steps of the chancel, and cast his robe upon the floor and writhed.

The evening sunbeams had set the dust to dancing in the gloomy chapel when he arose. He folded his vestments, put away the hymn-books, and closed the great Bible. He stepped out into the twilight, looked back upon the narrow little pulpit with a weary smile, and locked the door. Then he walked briskly to the Bishop, and told the Bishop what the Bishop already knew. "I have failed," he said simply. And gaining courage by the confession, he added: "What I need is a larger constituency. There are comparatively few Negroes here, and perhaps they are not of the best. I must go where the field is wider, and try again." So the Bishop sent him to Philadelphia, with a letter to Bishop Onderdonk.

Bishop Onderdonk lived at the head of six white steps,—corpulent, red-faced, and the author of several thrilling tracts on Apostolic Succession. It was after dinner, and the Bishop had settled himself for a pleasant season of contemplation, when the bell must needs ring, and there must burst in upon the Bishop a letter and a thin, ungainly Negro. Bishop Onderdonk read the letter hastily and frowned. Fortunately, his mind was already clear on this point; and he cleared his brow and looked at Crummell. Then he said, slowly and impressively: "I will receive you into this diocese on one condition: no Negro priest can sit in my church convention, and no Negro church must ask for representation there."

I sometimes fancy I can see that tableau: the frail black figure, nervously twitching his hat before the massive abdomen of Bishop Onderdonk; his threadbare coat thrown against the dark woodwork of the bookcases, where Fox's "Lives of the Martyrs" nestled happily beside "The Whole Duty of Man." I seem to see the wide eyes of the Negro wander past the Bishop's broadcloth to where the swinging glass doors of the cabinet glow in the sunlight. A little blue fly is trying to cross the yawning keyhole. He marches briskly up to it, peers into the chasm in a surprised sort of way, and rubs his feelers reflectively; then he essays its depths, and, finding it bottom-less, draws back again. The dark-faced priest finds himself wondering if the fly too has faced its Valley of Humiliation, and if it will plunge into it,—when lo! it spreads its tiny wings and buzzes merrily across, leaving the watcher wingless and alone.

Then the full weight of his burden fell upon him. The rich walls wheeled away, and before him lay the cold rough moor winding on through life, cut in twain by one thick granite ridge,—here, the Valley of Humiliation; yonder, the Valley of the Shadow of Death. And I know not which be darker,—no, not I. But this I know: in yonder Vale of the Humble stand to-day a million swarthy men, who willingly would

> ". . . bear the whips and scorns of time,
> The oppressor's wrong, the proud man's contumely,
> The pangs of despised love, the law's delay,
> The insolence of office, and the spurns
> That patient merit of the unworthy takes,"—

All this and more would they bear did they but know that this were sacrifice and not a meaner thing. So surged the thought within that lone black breast. The Bishop cleared his throat suggestively; then, recollecting that there was really nothing to say, considerately said nothing, only sat tapping his foot impatiently. But Alexander Crummell said, slowly and heavily: "I will never enter your diocese on such terms." And saying this, he turned and passed into the Valley of the Shadow of Death. You might have noted only the physical dying, the shattered frame and hacking cough; but in that soul lay deeper death than that. He found a chapel in New York,—the church of his father; he labored for it in poverty and starvation, scorned by his fellow priests. Half in despair, he wandered across the sea, a beggar with outstretched hands. Englishmen clasped them,—Wilberforce and Stanley, Thirwell and Ingles, and even Froude and Macaulay; Sir Benjamin Brodie bade him rest awhile at Queen's College in Cambridge, and there he lingered, struggling for health of body and mind, until he took his degree in '53. Restless still, and unsatisfied, he turned toward Africa, and for long years, amid the spawn of the slave-smugglers, sought a new heaven and a new earth.

So the man groped for light; all this was not Life,—it was the world-wandering of a soul in search of itself, the striving of one who vainly sought his place in the world, ever haunted by the shadow of a death that is more than death,—the passing of a soul that has missed its duty. Twenty years he wandered,—twenty years and more; and yet the hard rasping question kept gnawing within him, "What, in God's name, am I on earth for?" In the narrow New York parish his soul seemed cramped and smothered. In the fine old air of the English University he heard the millions wailing over the sea. In the wild fever-cursed swamps of West Africa he stood helpless and alone.

You will not wonder at his weird pilgrimage,—you who in the swift whirl of living, amid its cold paradox and marvellous vision, have fronted life and asked its riddle face to face. And if you find that riddle hard to read, remember that yonder black boy finds it just a little harder; if it is difficult for you to find and face your duty, it is a shade more difficult for him; if your heart sickens in the blood and dust of battle, remember that to him the dust is thicker and the battle fiercer. No wonder the wanderers fall! No wonder we point to thief and murderer, and haunting prostitute, and the never-ending throng of unhearsed dead! The Valley of the Shadow of Death gives few of its pilgrims back to the world.

But Alexander Crummell it gave back. Out of the temptation of Hate, and burned by the fire of Despair, triumphant over Doubt, and steeled by Sacrifice against Humiliation, he turned at last home across the waters, humble and strong, gentle and determined. He bent to all the gibes and prejudices, to all hatred and discrimination, with that rare courtesy which is the armor of pure souls. He fought among his own, the low, the grasping, and the wicked, with that unbending righteousness which is the sword of the just. He never faltered, he seldom complained; he simply worked, inspiring the young, rebuking the old, helping the weak, guiding the strong.

So he grew, and brought within his wide influence all that was best of those who walk within the Veil. They who live without knew not nor dreamed of that full power within, that mighty inspiration which the dull gauze of caste decreed that most men should not know. And now that he is gone, I sweep the Veil away and cry, Lo! the soul to whose dear memory I bring this little tribute. I can see his face still, dark and heavy-lined beneath his snowy hair; lighting and shading, now with inspiration for the future, now in innocent pain at some human wickedness, now with sorrow at some hard memory from the past. The more I met Alexander Crummell, the more I felt how much that world was losing which knew so little of him. In another age he might have sat among the elders of the land in purple-bordered toga; in another country mothers might have sung him to the cradles.

He did his work,—he did it nobly and well, and yet I sorrow that here he worked alone, with so little human sympathy. His name to-day, in this broad land, means little, and comes to fifty million ears laden with no incense of memory or emulation. And herein lies the tragedy of the age: not that men are poor,—all men know something of poverty; not that men are wicked,—who is good? not that men are ignorant,—what is Truth? Nay, but that men know so little of men.

He sat one morning gazing toward the sea. He smiled and said, "The gate is rusty on the hinges." That night at star-rise a wind came moaning out of the west to blow the gate ajar, and then the soul I loved fled like a flame across the Seas, and in its seat sat Death.

I wonder where he is to-day? I wonder if in that dim world beyond, as he came gliding in, there rose on some wan throne a King,—a dark and pierced Jew, who knows the writhings of the earthly damned, saying, as he laid those heart-wrung talents down, "Well done!" while round about the morning stars sat singing.

CHAPTER SEVEN

A Litany at Atlanta

This poem was written in 1906 and subsequently published in *Darkwater* (1920). It was composed in the wake of a gruesome race riot that took place in Atlanta. White mobs killed and assaulted the blacks there, as well as destroying their homes and property. Du Bois was away in Alabama at the time but rushed home to his wife and baby, who were unhurt. He wrote this piece while he was on the train heading home. It is one of the finest examples of "God wrestling" in American literature.

O Silent God, Thou whose voice afar in mist and mystery hath left our ears anhungered in these fearful days—

Hear us, good Lord!

Listen to us, Thy children: our faces dark with doubt are made a mockery in Thy Sanctuary. With uplifted hands we front Thy Heaven, O God, crying:

We beseech Thee to hear us, good Lord!

We are not better than our fellows. Lord; we are but weak and human men. When our devils do deviltry, curse Thou the doer and the deed—curse them as we curse them, do to them all and more than ever they have done to innocence and weakness, to womanhood and home.

Have mercy upon us, miserable sinners!

And yet, whose is the deeper guilt? Who made these devils? Who nursed them in crime and fed them on injustice? Who ravished and debauched their mothers and their grandmothers? Who bought and sold their crime and waxed fat and rich on public iniquity?

Thou knowest, good God!

Is this Thy Justice, O Father, that guile be easier than innocence and the innocent be crucified for the guilt of the untouched guilty?

Justice, O Judge of men!

Wherefore do we pray? Is not the God of the Fathers dead? Have not seers seen in Heaven's halls Thine hearsed and lifeless form stark amidst the black and rolling smoke of sin, where all along bow bitter forms of endless dead?

Awake, Thou that sleepest!

Thou art not dead, but flown afar, up hills of endless light, through blazing corridors of suns, where worlds do swing of good and gentlemen, of women strong and free—far from the cozenage, black hypocrisy, and chaste prostitution of this shameful speck of dust!

Turn again, O Lord; leave us not to perish in our sin!

From lust of body and lust of blood—

Great God, deliver us!

From lust of power and lust of gold—

Great God, deliver us!

From the leagued lying of despot and of brute—

Great God, deliver us!

A city lay in travail, God our Lord, and from her loins sprang twin Murder and black Hate. Red was the midnight; clang, crack, and cry of death and fury filled the air and trembled underneath the stars where church spires pointed silently to Thee. And all this was to sate the greed of greedy men who hide behind the veil of vengeance!

Bend us Thine ear, O Lord!

In the pale, still morning we looked upon the deed. We stopped our ears and held our leaping hands, but they—did they not wag their heads and leer and cry with bloody jaws: *Cease from Crime!* The word was mockery, for thus they train a hundred crimes while we do cure one.

Turn again our captivity, O Lord!

Behold this maimed and broken thing, dear God; it was an humble black man, who toiled and sweated to save a bit from the pittance paid him. They told him: *Work and Rise!* He worked. Did this man sin? Nay, but someone told how someone said another did—one whom he had never seen nor known. Yet for that man's crime this man lieth maimed and murdered, his wife naked to shame, his children to poverty and evil.

Hear us, O heavenly Father!

Doth not this justice of hell stink in Thy nostrils, O God? How long shall the mounting flood of innocent blood roar in Thine ears and pound in our hearts for vengeance? Pile the pale frenzy of blood-crazed brutes, who do such deeds, high on Thine Altar, Jehovah Jireh, and burn it in hell forever and forever!

Forgive us, good Lord; we know not what we say!

Bewildered we are and passion-tossed, mad with the madness of a mobbed and mocked and murdered people; straining at the armposts of Thy throne, we raise our shackled hands and charge Thee, God, by the bones of our stolen fathers, by the tears of our dead mothers, by the very blood of Thy crucified Christ: What meaneth this? Tell us the plan; give us the sign!

Keep not Thou silent, O God!

Sit not longer blind, Lord God, deaf to our prayer and dumb to our dumb suffering. Surely Thou, too, art not white, O Lord, a pale, bloodless, heartless thing!

Ah! Christ of all the Pities!

Forgive the thought! Forgive these wild, blasphemous words! Thou art still the God of our black fathers and in Thy Soul's Soul sit some soft darkenings of the evening, some shadowings of the velvet night.

But whisper—speak—call, great God, for Thy silence is white terror to our hearts! The way, O God, show us the way and point us the path!

Whither? North is greed and South is blood; within, the coward, and without, the liar. Whither? To death?

Amen! Welcome, dark sleep!

Whither? To life? But not this life, dear God, not this. Let the cup pass from us, tempt us not beyond our strength, for there is that clamoring and that clawing within, to whose voice we would not listen, yet shudder lest we must—and it is red. Ah! dear God! It is a red and awful shape.

Selah!

In yonder East trembles a star.

Vengeance is Mine; I will repay, saith the Lord!

Thy Will, O Lord, be done!

Kyrie Eleison!

Lord, we have done these pleading, wavering words.

We beseech Thee to bear us, good Lord!

We bow our heads and hearken soft to the sobbing of women and little children.

We beseech Thee to hear us, good Lord!

Our voices sink in silence and in night.

Hear us, good Lord!

In night, O God of a godless land!

Amen!

In silence, O Silent God.

Selah!

CHAPTER EIGHT

Religion in the South

This chapter comes from *The Negro in the South*, published in 1907. It is a rare volume and is of considerable interest; two of its four chapters were written by Du Bois and the other two by Booker T. Washington, the prominent African-American leader with whom Du Bois would subsequently have a difficult and often antagonistic relationship. In this chapter, Du Bois discusses questions concerning the conversion of enslaved Africans to Christianity, the careers of several prominent black religious leaders, and the glaring hypocrisy of white Christianity alongside white racism.

It is often a nice question as to which is of greater importance among a people—the way in which they earn their living, or their attitude toward life. As a matter of fact these two things are but two sides of the same problem, for nothing so reveals the attitude of a people toward life as the manner in which they earn their living; and on the other hand the earning of a living depends in the last analysis upon one's estimate of what life really is. So that these two questions that I am discussing with regard to the South are intimately bound up with each other.

If we have studied the economic development of the South carefully, then we have already seen something of its attitude toward life; the history of religion in the South means a study of these same facts over which we have gone, from a different point of view. Moreover, as the economic history of the South is in effect the economics of slavery and the Negro problem, so the essence of a study of religion in the South is a study of the ethics of slavery and emancipation.

It is very difficult of course for one who has not seen the practical difficulties that surround a people at any particular time in their battle with the hard facts of this world, to interpret with sympathy their ideals of life; and this is especially difficult when the economic life of a nation has been expressed by such a discredited word as slavery. If, then, we are to study the history of religion in the South, we must first of all divest ourselves of prejudice, pro and con; we must try to put ourselves in the place of those who are seeking to read the riddle of life and grant to them about the same general charity and the same general desire to do right that we find in the average human being. On the other hand, we must not, in striving to be charitable, be false to truth and right. Slavery in the United States was an economic mistake and a moral crime. This we cannot forget. Yet it had its excuses and mitigations. These we must remember.

When in the seventeenth century there grew up in the New World a system of human slavery, it was not by any means a new thing. There were slaves and slavery in Europe, not, to be sure, to a great extent, but none the less real. The Christian religion, however, had come to regard it as wrong and unjust that those who partook of the privileges and hopes and aspirations of that religion should oppress each other to the extent of actual enslavement. The idea of human brotherhood in the seventeenth century was of a brotherhood of co-religionists. When it came to the dealing of Christian with heathen, however, the century saw nothing wrong in slavery; rather, theoretically, they saw a chance for a great act of humanity and religion. The slaves were to be brought from heathenism to Christianity, and through slavery the benighted Indian and African were to find their passport into the kingdom of God. This theory of human slavery was held by Spaniards, French, and English. It was New England in the early days that put the echo of it in her codes . . . and recognition of it can be seen in most of the colonies.

But no sooner had people adopted this theory than there came the insistent and perplexing question as to what the status of the heathen slave was to be after he was Christianized and baptized; and even more pressing, what was to be the status of his children?

It took a great deal of bitter heart searching for the conscientious early slaveholders to settle this question. The obvious state of things was that the new convert awoke immediately to the freedom of Christ and became a freeman. But while this was the theoretical, religious answer, and indeed the answer which was given in several instances, the practice soon came into direct and perplexing conflict with the grim facts of economic life.

Here was a man who had invested his money and his labor in slaves; he had done it with dependence on the institution of property. Could he be deprived of his property simply because his slaves were baptized afterward into a Christian church? Very soon such economic reasoning swept away the theological dogma and it was expressly declared in colony after colony that baptism did not free the slaves. . . . This, of course, put an end to the old doctrine of the heathen slave and it was necessary for the church to arrange for itself a new theory by which it could ameliorate, if not excuse, the position of the slave. The next question was naturally that of the children of slaves born in Christianity and the church for a time hedged unworthily on the subject by consigning to perpetual slavery the children of heathen but not those born of Christian parents; this was satisfactory for the first generation but it fell short of the logic of slavery later, and a new adjustment was demanded.

Here again this was not found difficult. In Virginia there had been built up the beginnings of a feudal aristocracy. Men saw nothing wrong or unthinkable in the situation as it began to develop, but rather something familiar. At the head of the feudal manor was the lord, or master, beneath him the under-lord or overseers and then the artisans, retainers, the free working men and lastly the serfs, slaves or servants as they were called. The servant was not free and yet he was not theoretically exactly a slave, and the laws of Virginia were rather careful to speak very little of slaves.

Serfdom in America as in Europe was to be a matter of status or position and not of race or blood, and the law of the South in the seventeenth and early eighteenth centuries made little or no distinction between black and white bondservants save in the time of their service. The idea, felt rather than expressed, was that here in America we were to have a new feudalism suited to the new country. At the top was the governor of the colony representing the majesty of the English king, at the bottom the serfs or slaves, some white, most of them black.

Slavery therefore was gradually transformed in the seventeenth and eighteenth centuries into a social status out of which a man, even a black man, could escape and did escape; and, no matter what his color was, when he became free, he became free in the same sense that other people were. Thus it was that there were free black voters in the southern colonies (Virginia and the Carolinas) in the early days concerning whose right to vote there was less question than there is concerning my right to vote now in Georgia. . . .

The church recognized the situation and the Episcopal church especially gave itself easily to this new conception. This church recognized the social gradation of men; all souls were equal in the sight of God, but there were differences in worldly consideration and respect, and consequently it was perfectly natural that there should be an aristocracy at the top and a group of serfs at the bottom.

Meantime, however, America began to be stirred by a new democratic ideal; there came the reign of that ruler of men, Andrew Jackson; there came the spread of the democratic churches, Methodist and Baptist, and the democratization of other churches. Now when America became to be looked upon more and more as the dwelling place of free and equal men and when the Methodist and, particularly, the Baptist churches went down into the fields and proselyted among the slaves, a thing which the more aristocratic Episcopal church had never done . . . , there came new questions and new heart-searchings among those who wanted to explain the difficulties and to think and speak clearly in the midst of their religious convictions.

As such people began to look round them the condition of the slaves appalled them. The Presbyterian Synod of South Carolina and Georgia declared in 1833: "There are over two millions of human beings in the condition of heathen and some of them in a worse condition. They may be justly considered the heathen of this country, and will bear a comparison with heathen in any country in the world. The Negroes are destitute of the gospel, and ever will be under the present state of things. In the vast field extending from an entire state beyond the Potomac [i.e., Maryland] to the Sabine River [at the time our southwestern boundary] and from the Atlantic to the Ohio, there are, to the best of our knowledge, not twelve men exclusively devoted to the religious instruction of the Negroes. In the present state of feeling in the South, a ministry of their own color could neither be obtained nor tolerated.

"But do not the Negroes have access to the gospel through the stated ministry of the whites? We answer, no. The Negroes have no regular and efficient ministry; as a matter of course, no churches; neither is there sufficient room in the white churches for their accommodation. We know of but five churches in the slave-holding states built expressly for their use. These are all in the state of Georgia. We may now inquire whether they enjoy the privileges of the gospel in their own houses, and on our plantations? Again we return a negative answer. They have no Bibles to read by their own firesides. They have no family altars; and when in affliction, sickness, or death, they have no minister to address to them the consolations of the gospel, nor to bury them with appropriate services."

The same synod said in 1834: "The gospel as things now are, can never be preached to the two classes (whites and blacks) successfully in conjunction. The galleries or back seats on the lower floor of white churches are generally appropriated to the Negroes, when it can be done without inconvenience to the whites. When it cannot be done conveniently, the Negroes must catch the gospel as it escapes through the doors and windows. If the master is pious, the house servants alone attend family worship, and frequently few of them, while the field hands have no attention at all. So far as masters are engaged in the work [of religious instruction of slaves], an almost unbroken silence reigns on this vast field."

The Rev. C. C. Jones, a Georgian and ardent defender of slavery . . . says of the period 1790–1820: "It is not too much to say that the religious and physical condition of the Negroes were both improved during this period. Their increase was natural and regular, ranging every ten years between thirty-four and thirty-six percent. As the old stock from Africa died out of the country, the grosser customs, ignorance, and paganism of Africa died with them. Their descendants, the country-born, were better looking, more intelligent, more civilized, more susceptible of religious impressions.

"On the whole, however, but a minority of the Negroes, and that a small one, attended regularly the house of God, and taking them as a class, their religious instruction was extensively and most seriously neglected."

And of the decade 1830–40, he insists: "We cannot cry out against the Papists for withholding the Scriptures from the common people and keeping them in ignorance of the way of life, for we withhold the Bible from our servants, and keep them in ignorance of it, while we will not use the means to have it read and explained to them."

Such condition stirred the more radical-minded toward abolition sentiments and the more conservative toward renewed effort to evangelize and better the condition of the slaves. This condition was deplorable as Jones pictures it. "Persons live and die in the midst of Negroes and know comparatively little of their real character. They have not the immediate management of them. They have to do with them in the ordinary discharge of their duty as servants, further than this they institute no inquiries; they give themselves no trouble.

"The Negroes are a distinct class in the community, and keep themselves very much to themselves. They are one thing before the whites and another before their own color. Deception before the former is characteristic of them, whether bond or free, throughout the whole United States. It is habit, a long established custom, which descends from generation to generation. There is an upper and an under current. Some are contented with the appearance on the surface; others dive beneath. Hence the diversity of impressions and representations of the moral and religious condition of the Negroes. Hence the disposition of some to deny the darker pictures of their more searching and knowing friends."

He then enumerates the vice of the slaves: "The divine institution of marriage depends for its perpetuity, sacredness, and value, largely upon the protection given it by the law of the land. Negro marriages are neither recognized nor protected by law. The Negroes receive no instruction on the nature, sacredness, and perpetuity of the institution; at any rate they are far from being duly impressed with these things. They are not required to be married in any particular form, nor by any particular persons."

He continues: "Hence, as may well be imagined, the marriage relation loses much of the sacredness and perpetuity of its character. It is a contract of convenience, profit, or pleasure, that may be entered into and dissolved at the will of the parties, and that without heinous sin, or the injury of the property or interests of any one. That which they possess in common is speedily divided, and the support of the wife and children falls not upon the husband, but upon the master. Protracted sickness, want of industrial habits, of congeniality of disposition, or disparity of age, are sufficient grounds for a separation."

Under such circumstances, "polygamy is practiced both secretly and openly." Uncleanness, infanticide, theft, lying, quarreling, and fighting are noted, and the words of Charles Cotesworth Pinckney in 1829 are recalled: "There needs no stronger illustration of the doctrine of human depravity than the state of morals on plantations in general. Besides the mischievous tendency of bad example in parents and elders, the little Negro is often taught by these natural instructors that he may commit any vice that he can conceal from his superiors, and thus falsehood and deception are among the earliest lessons they imbibe. Their advance in years is but a progression to the higher grades of iniquity. The violation of the Seventh Commandment is viewed in a more venial light than in fashionable European circles. Their depredations of rice have been estimated to amount to twenty-five per cent of the gross average of crops."

John Randolph of Roanoke once visited a lady and "found her surrounded with her seamstresses, making up a quantity of clothing. 'What work have you in hand?' 'O Sir, I am preparing this clothing to send to the poor Greeks.' On taking leave at the steps of her mansion, he saw some of her servants in need of the very clothing which their tender-hearted mistress was sending abroad. He exclaimed, 'Madam, madam, the Greeks are at your door!'"

One natural solution of this difficulty was to train teachers and preachers for the slaves from among their own number. The old Voodoo priests were passing away and already here and there new spiritual leaders of the Negroes began to arise. Accounts of several of these, taken from "The Negro Church," will be given.

Among the earliest was Harry Hosier who traveled with the Methodist Bishop Asbury and often filled appointments for him. George Leile and Andrew Bryan were preachers whose life history is of intense interest. . . .

Lott Carey a free Virginia Negro "was evidently a man of superior intellect and force of character, as is evidenced from the fact that his reading took a wide range—from political economy, in Adam Smith's 'Wealth of Nations,' to the voyage of Captain Cook. That he was a worker as well as a preacher is true, for when he decided to go to Africa his employers offered to raise his salary from $800 to $1,000 a year. Remember that this was over eighty years ago. Carey was not seduced by such a flattering offer, for he was determined.

"His last sermon in the old First Church in Richmond must have been exceedingly powerful, for it was compared by an eyewitness, a resident of another state, to the burning, eloquent appeals of George Whitfield. Fancy him as he stands there in that historic building ringing the changes on the word 'freely,' depicting the willingness with which he was ready to give up his life for service in Africa.

"He, as you may already know, was the leader of the pioneer colony to Liberia, where he arrived even before the agent of the Colonization Society. In his new home his abilities were recognized, for he was made vice governor, and became governor in fact while Governor Ashmun was absent from the colony in this country. Carey did not allow his position to betray the cause of his people, for he did not hesitate to expose the duplicity of the Colonization Society and even to defy their authority, it would seem, in the interests of the people.

"While casting cartridges to defend the colonists against the natives in 1828, the accidental upsetting of a candle caused an explosion that resulted in his death.

"Carey is described as a typical Negro, six feet in height, of massive and erect frame, with the sinews of a Titan. He had a square face, keen eyes, and a grave countenance. His movements were measured; in short, he had all the bearing and dignity of a prince of the blood."

John Chavis was a full-blooded Negro, born in Granville County, N.C., near Oxford, in 1763. He was born free and was sent to Princeton, studying privately under Dr. Witherspoon, where he did well. He went to Virginia to preach to Negroes. In 1802, in the county court, his freedom and character were certified to and it was declared that he had passed "through a regular course of academic studies" at what is now Washington and Lee University. In 1805 he returned to North Carolina, where in 1809 he was made a licentiate in the Presbyterian Church and allowed to preach. His English was remarkably pure, his manner impressive, his explanations clear and concise.

For a long time he taught school and had the best whites as pupils—a United States senator, the sons of a chief justice of North Carolina, a governor of the state and many others. Some of his pupils boarded in the family, and his school was regarded as the best in the State. " All accounts agree that John Chavis was a gentleman," and he was received socially among the best whites and asked to table. In 1830 he was stopped from preaching by the law. Afterward he taught a school for free Negroes in Raleigh.

Henry Evans was a full-blooded Virginia free Negro, and was the pioneer of Methodism in Fayetteville, N.C. He found the Negroes there, about 1800, without any religious instruction. He began preaching and the town council ordered him away; he continued and whites came to hear him. Finally the white auditors outnumbered the blacks and sheds were erected for Negroes at the side of the church. The gathering became a regular Methodist Church, with a white and Negro membership, but Evans continued to preach. He exhibited "rare self-control before the most wretched of castes! Henry Evans did much good, but he would have done more good had his spirit been untrammeled by this sense of inferiority."

His dying words uttered as he stood, aged and bent beside his pulpit, are of singular pathos: "I have come to say my last word to you. It is this: None but Christ. Three times have I had my life in jeopardy for preaching the gospel to you. Three times I have broken ice on the edge of the water and swam across the Cape Fear to preach the gospel to you; and, if in my last hour I could trust to that, or anything but Christ crucified, for my salvation, all should be lost and my soul perish forever."

Early in the nineteenth century Ralph Freeman was a slave in Anson County, N.C. He was a full-blooded Negro, and was ordained and became an able Baptist preacher. He baptized and administered communion, and was greatly respected. When the Baptists split on the question of missions he sided with the anti-mission side. Finally the law forbade him to preach.

Lunsford Lane was a Negro who bought his freedom in Raleigh, N.C., by the manufacture of smoking tobacco. He later became a minister of the gospel, and had the confidence of many of the best people.

The story of Jack of Virginia is best told in the words of a Southern writer:

"Probably the most interesting case in the whole South is that of an African preacher of Nottoway County, popularly known as 'Uncle Jack,' whose services to white and black were so valuable that a distinguished minister of the Southern Presbyterian Church felt called upon to memorialize his work in a biography.

"Kidnapped from his idolatrous parents in Africa, he was brought over in one of the last cargoes of slaves admitted to Virginia and sold to a remote and obscure planter in Nottoway County, a region at that time in the backwoods and destitute particularly as to religious life and instruction. He was converted under the occasional preaching of Rev. Dr. John Blair Smith, president of Hampden-Sidney College, and of Dr. William Hill and Dr. Archibald Alexander of Princeton, then young theologues, and by hearing the Scriptures read.

"Taught by his master's children to read, he became so full of the spirit and knowledge of the Bible that he was recognized among the whites as a powerful expounder of Christian doctrine, was licensed to preach by the Baptist Church, and preached from plantation to plantation within a radius of thirty miles, as he was invited by overseers or masters. His freedom was purchased by a subscription of whites, and he was given a home and tract of land for his support. He organized a large and orderly Negro church, and exercised such a wonderful controlling influence over the private morals of his flock that masters, instead of punishing their slaves, often referred them to the discipline of their pastor, which they dreaded far more.

"He stopped a heresy among the Negroes of Southern Virginia, defeating in open argument a famous fanatical Negro preacher named Campbell, who advocated noise and 'the spirit' against the Bible, and winning over Campbell's adherents in a body. For over forty years, and until he was nearly a hundred years of age, he labored successfully in public and private among black and whites, voluntarily giving up his preaching in obedience to the law of 1832, the result of 'Old Nat's war.'

"The most refined and aristocratic people paid tribute to him, and he was instrumental in the conversion of many whites. Says his biographer, Rev. Dr. William S. White: 'He was invited into their houses, sat with their families, took part in their social worship, sometimes leading the prayer at the family altar. Many of the most intelligent people attended upon his ministry and listened to his sermons with great delight. Indeed, previous to the year 1825, he was considered by the best judges to be the best preacher in that county. His opinions were respected, his advice followed, and yet he never betrayed the least symptoms of arrogance or self-conceit.

"'His dwelling was a rude log cabin, his apparel of the plainest and coarsest materials.' This was because he wanted to be fully identified with his class. He refused gifts of better clothing, saying 'These clothes are a great deal better than are generally worn by people of my color, and besides if I wear finer ones I find I shall be obliged to think about them even at meeting.'"

Thus slowly, surely, the slave, in the persons of such exceptional men, appearing here and there at rare intervals, was persistently stretching upward. The Negroes bade fair in time to have their leaders. The new democratic evangelism began to encourage this, and then came the difficulty—the inevitable ethical paradox.

The good men of the South recognized the needs of the slaves. Here and there Negro ministers were arising. What now should be the policy? On the part of the best thinkers it seemed as if men might strive here, in spite of slavery, after brotherhood; that the slaves should be proselyted, taught religion, admitted to the churches, and, notwithstanding their civil station, looked upon as the spiritual brothers of the white communicants. Much was done to make this true. The conditions improved in a great many respects, but no sooner was there a systematic effort to teach the slaves, even though that teaching was confined to elementary religion, than the various things followed that must follow all intellectual awakenings.

We have had the same thing in our day. A few Negroes of the South have been taught, they consequently have begun to think, they have begun to assert themselves, and suddenly men are face to face with the fact that either one of two things must happen—either they must stop teaching or these people are going to be men, not serfs or slaves. Not only that, but to seek to put an awakening people back to sleep means revolt. It meant revolt in the eighteenth century, when a series of insurrections and disturbances frightened the South tremendously, not so much by their actual extent as by the possibilities they suggested. It was noticeable that many of these revolts were led by preachers.

The revolution in Hayti greatly stirred the South and induced South Carolina to declare in 1800:

"It shall not be lawful for any number of slaves, free Negroes, mulattoes, or mestizoes, even in company with white persons, to meet together and assemble for the purpose of mental instruction or religious worship either before the rising of the sun or after the going down of the same. And all magistrates, sheriffs, militia officers, etc., etc., are hereby vested with power, etc., for dispersing such assemblies."

On petition of the white churches the rigor of this law was slightly abated in 1803 by a modification which forbade any person, before nine o'clock in the evening, "to break into a place of meeting wherein shall be assembled the members of any religious society in this State, provided a majority of them shall be white persons, or otherwise to disturb their devotions unless such persons, etc., so entering said place (of worship) shall first have obtained from some magistrate, etc., a warrant, etc., in case a magistrate shall be then actually within a distance of three miles from such place of meeting; otherwise the provisions, etc. (of the Act of 1800) to remain in full force."

So, too, in Virginia the Haytian revolt and the attempted insurrection under Gabriel in 1800 led to the Act of 1804, which forbade all evening meetings of slaves. This was modified in 1805 so as to allow a slave, in company with a white person, to listen to a white minister in the evening. A master was "allowed" to employ a religious teacher for his slaves. Mississippi passed similar restrictions.

By 1822 the rigor of the South Carolina laws in regard to Negro meetings had abated, especially in a city like Charleston, and one of the results was the Vesey plot.

"The sundry religious classes or congregations, with Negro leaders or local preachers, into which were formed the Negro members of the various churches of Charleston, furnished Vesey with the first rudiments of an organization, and at the same time with a singularly safe medium for conducting his underground agitation. It was customary, at that time, for these Negro congregations to meet for purposes of worship entirely free from the presence of whites. Such meetings were afterward forbidden to be held except in the presence of at least one representative of the dominant race, but during the three or four years prior to the year 1822 they certainly offered Denmark Vesey regular, easy, and safe opportunity for preaching his gospel of liberty and hate. And we are left in no doubt whatever in regard to the uses to which he put those gatherings of blacks.

"Like many of his race, he possessed the gift of gab, as the silver in the tongue and the gold in the full or thick-lipped mouth are oftentimes contemptuously characterized. And, like many of his race, he was a devoted student of the Bible, to whose interpretation he brought, like many other Bible students not confined to the Negro race, a good deal of imagination and not a little of superstition, which, with some natures, is perhaps but another name for the desires of the heart.

"Thus equipped, it is no wonder that Vesey, as he pored over the Old Testament scriptures, found many points of similitude in the history of the Jews and that of the slaves in the United States. They were both peculiar peoples. They were both Jehovah's peculiar peoples, one in the past, the other in the present. And it seemed to him that as Jehovah bent His ear, and bared His arm once in behalf of the one, so would He do the same for the other. It was all vividly real to his thought, I believe, for to his mind thus had said the Lord.

"He ransacked the Bible for apposite and terrible texts whose commands in the olden times, to the olden people, were no less imperative upon the new times and the new people. This new people were also commanded to arise and destroy their enemies and the city in which they dwelt, 'both man and woman, young and old, with the edge of the sword.' Believing superstitiously as he did in the stern and Nemesis-like God of the Old Testament he looked confidently for a day of vengeance and retribution for the blacks. He felt, I doubt not, something peculiarly applicable to his enterprise and intensely personal to himself in the stern and exultant prophecy of Zachariah, fierce and sanguinary words, which were constantly in his mouth: 'Then shall the Lord go forth and fight against those nations as when He fought in the day of battle.' According to Vesey's lurid exegesis 'those nations' in the text meant beyond peradventure the cruel masters, and Jehovah was to go forth to fight them for the poor slaves and on whichever side fought that day the Almighty God on that side would assuredly rest victory and deliverance.

"It will not be denied that Vesey's plan contemplated the total annihilation of the white population of Charleston. Nursing for many dark years the bitter wrongs of himself and race had filled him without doubt with a mad spirit of revenge and had given to him a decided predilection for shedding the blood of his oppressors. But if he intended to kill them to satisfy a desire for vengeance he intended to do so also on broader ground. The conspirators, he argued, had no choice in the matter, but were compelled to adopt a policy of extermination by the necessity of their position. The liberty of the blacks was in the balance of fate against the lives of the whites. He could strike that balance in favor of the blacks only by the total destruction of the whites. Therefore the whites, men, women, and children, were doomed to death."[1]

Vesey's plot was well laid, but the conspirators were betrayed.

Less than ten years after this plot was discovered and Vesey and his associates hanged, there broke out the Nat Turner insurrection in Virginia. Turner was himself a preacher.

"He was a Christian and a man. He was conscious that he was a Man and not a 'thing'; therefore, driven by religious fanaticism, he undertook a difficult and bloody task. Nathaniel Turner was born in Southampton County, Virginia, October 2, 1800. His master was one Benjamin Turner, a very wealthy and aristocratic man. He owned many slaves, and was a cruel and exacting master. Young 'Nat' was born of slave parents, and carried to his grave many of the superstitions and traits of his father and mother. The former was a preacher, the latter a 'mother in Israel.' Both were unlettered but, nevertheless, very pious people.

"The mother began when Nat was quite young to teach him that he was born, like Moses, to be the deliverer of his race. She would sing to him snatches of wild, rapturous songs and repeat portions of prophecy she had learned from the preachers of those times. Nat listened with reverence and awe, and believed everything his mother said. He imbibed the deep religious character of his parents, and soon manifested a desire to preach. He was solemnly set apart to 'the gospel ministry' by his father, the church, and visiting preachers. He was quite low in stature, dark, and had the genuine African features. His eyes were small but sharp, and gleamed like fire when he was talking about his 'mission' or preaching from some prophetic passage of scripture. It is said that he never laughed. He was a dreamy sort of a man, and avoided the crowd.

"Like Moses he lived in the solitudes of the mountains and brooded over the condition of his people. There was something grand to him in the rugged scenery that nature had surrounded him with. He believed that he was a prophet, a leader raised up by God to burst the bolts of the prison-house and set the oppressed free. The thunder, the hail, the storm-cloud, the air, the earth, the stars, at which he would sit and gaze half the night all spake the language of the God of the oppressed. He was seldom seen in a large company, and never drank a drop of ardent spirits. Like John the Baptist, when he had delivered his message, he would retire to the fastness of the mountain or seek the desert, where he could meditate upon his great work."

In the impression of the Richmond *Enquirer* of the 30th of August, 1831, the first editorial or leader is under the caption of "The Banditte." The editor says:

"They remind one of a parcel of blood-thirsty wolves rushing down from the Alps; or, rather, like a former incursion of the Indians upon the white settlements. Nothing is spared; neither age nor sex respected—the helplessness of women and children pleads in vain for mercy. . . . The case of Nat Turner warns us. No black man ought to be permitted to turn preacher through the country. The law must be enforced, or the tragedy of Southampton appeals to us in vain."

Mr. Gray, the man to whom Turner made his confession before dying, said:

"It has been said that he was ignorant and cowardly and that his object was to murder and rob for the purpose of obtaining money to make his escape. It is notorious that he was never known to have a dollar in his life, to swear an oath, or drink a drop of spirits. As to his ignorance, he certainly never had the advantages of an education, but he can read and write, and for natural intelligence and quickness of apprehension is surpassed by few men I have ever seen. As to his being a coward, his reason as given for not resisting Mr. Phipps, shows the decision of his character. When he saw Mr. Phipps present his gun, he said he knew it was impossible for him to escape as the woods were full of men. He, therefore, thought it was better for him to surrender and trust to fortune for his escape.

"He is a complete fanatic or plays his part most admirably. On other subjects he possesses an uncommon share of intelligence, with a mind capable of attaining anything, but warped and perverted by the influence of early impressions. He is below the ordinary stature, though strong and active, having the true Negro face, every feature of which is strongly marked.

"I shall not attempt to describe the effect of his narrative, as told and commented on by himself, in the condemned hole of the prison; the calm deliberate composure with which he spoke of his late deeds and intentions; the expression of his fiend-like face when excited by enthusiasm, still bearing the stains of the blood of the helpless innocence about him, clothed with rags and covered with chains, yet daring to raise his manacled hand to Heaven, with a spirit soaring above the attributes of man. I looked on him and the blood curdled in my veins."[2]

The Turner insurrection is so connected with the economic revolution which enthroned cotton that it marks an epoch in the history of the slave. A wave of legislation passed over the South prohibiting the slaves from learning to read and write, forbidding Negroes to preach, and interfering with Negro religious meetings.

Virginia declared, in 1831, that neither slaves nor free Negroes might preach, nor could they attend religious service at night without permission. In North Carolina slaves and free Negroes were forbidden to preach, exhort or teach "in any prayer-meeting or other association for worship where slaves of different families are collected together" on penalty of not more than thirty-nine lashes. Maryland and Georgia had similar laws. The Mississippi law of 1831 said: It is "unlawful for any slave, free Negro, or mulatto to preach the gospel" upon pain of receiving thirty-nine lashes upon the naked back of the presumptuous preacher. If a Negro received written permission from his master he might preach to the Negroes in his immediate neighborhood, providing six respectable white men, owners of slaves, were present. In Alabama the law of 1832 prohibited the assembling of more than five male slaves at any place off the plantation to which they belonged, but nothing in the act was to be considered as forbidding attendance at places of public worship held by white persons. No slave or free person of color was permitted to "preach, exhort, or harangue any slave or slaves, or free persons of color, except in the presence of five respectable slaveholders, or unless the person preaching was licensed by some regular body of professing Christians in the neighborhood, to whose society or church the Negroes addressed properly belonged."

In the District of Columbia the free Negroes began to leave white churches in 1831 and to assemble in their own.

Thus it was that through the fear of insurrection, the economic press of the new slavery that was arising, and the new significance of slavery in the economics of the South, the strife for spiritual brotherhood was given up. Slavery became distinctly a matter of race and not of status. Long years before, the white servants had been freed and only black servants were left; now social condition came to be not simply a matter of slavery but a matter of belonging to the black race, so that even the free Negroes began to be disfranchised and put into the caste system. . . .

A new adjustment of ethics and religion had to be made to meet this new situation, and in the adjustment no matter what might be said or thought, the Negro and slavery had to be the central thing.

In the adjustment of religion and ethics that was made for the new slavery, under the cotton kingdom, there was in the first place a distinct denial of human brotherhood. These black men were not men in the sense that white men were men. They were different—different in kind, different in origin; they had different diseases . . . they had different feelings; they were not to be treated the same; they were not looked upon as the same; they were altogether apart and, while perhaps they had certain low sensibilities and aspirations, yet so far as this world is concerned, there could be with them neither human nor spiritual brotherhood.

The only status that they could possibly occupy was the status of slaves. They could not get along as freemen; they could not work as freemen; it was utterly unthinkable that people should live with them free. This was the philosophy that was worked out gradually, with exceptions here and there, and that was thought through, written on, preached from the pulpits and taught in the homes, until people in the South believed it as they believed the rising and the setting of the sun.

As this became more and more the orthodox ethical opinion, heretics appeared in the land as they always do. But intolerance and anathema met them. In community after community there was a demand for orthodoxy on this one burning question of the economic and religious South, and the heretics were driven out. The Quakers left North Carolina, the abolitionists either left Virginia or ceased to talk, and throughout the South those people who dared to think otherwise were left silent or dead. . . .

So long as slavery was an economic success this orthodoxy was all powerful; when signs of economic distress appeared it became intolerant and aggressive. A great moral battle was impending in the South, but political turmoil and a development of northern thought so rapid as to be unintelligible in the South stopped this development forcibly. War came and the hatred and moral bluntness incident to war, and men crystallized in their old thought.

The matter now could no longer be argued and thought out, it became a matter of tradition, of faith, of family and personal honor. There grew up therefore after the war a new predicament; a new-old paradox. Upon the whites hung the curse of the past; because they had not settled their labor problem then, they must settle the problem now in the face of upheaval and handicapped by the natural advance of the world.

So after the war and even to this day, the religious and ethical life of the South bows beneath this burden. Shrinking from facing the burning ethical questions that front it unrelentingly, the Southern Church clings all the more closely to the letter of a worn out orthodoxy, while its inner truer soul crouches before and fears to answer the problem of eight million black neighbors. It therefore assiduously "preaches Christ crucified," in prayer meeting *patois*, and crucifies "Niggers" in unrelenting daily life.

While the Church in the North, all too slowly but surely is struggling up from the ashes of a childish faith in myth and miracle, and beginning to preach a living gospel of civic virtue, peace and good will and a crusade against lying, stealing and snobbery, the Southern church for the most part is still murmuring of modes of "baptism," "infant damnation" and the "divine plan of creation."

Thus the post-bellum ethical paradox of the South is far more puzzling than the economic paradox. To be sure there is leaven in the lump. There are brave voices here and there, but they are easily drowned by social tyranny in the South and by indifference and sensationalism in the North. . . .

First of all the result of the war was the complete expulsion of Negroes from white churches. Little has been said of this, but perhaps it was in itself the most singular and tremendous result of slavery. The Methodist Church South simply set its Negro members bodily out of doors. They did it with some consideration for their feelings, with as much kindliness as crass unkindliness can show, but they virtually said to all their black members—to the black mammies whom they have almost fulsomely praised and whom they remember in such astonishing numbers today, to the polite and deferential old servant, to whose character they build monuments—they said to them: "You cannot worship God with us." There grew up, therefore, the Colored Methodist Episcopal Church.

Flagrantly unchristian as this course was, it was still in some ways better than the absolute withdrawal of church fellowship on the part of the Baptists, or the policy of Episcopalians, which was simply that of studied neglect and discouragement which froze, harried, and well nigh invited the black communicants to withdraw.

From the North now came those Negro church bodies born of color discrimination in Philadelphia and New York in the eighteenth century, and thus a Christianity absolutely divided along the color line arose. There may be in the South a black man belonging to a white church today but if so, he must be very old and very feeble. This anomaly—this utter denial of the very first principles of the ethics of Jesus Christ—is today so deep seated and unquestionable a principle of Southern Christianity that its essential heathenism is scarcely thought of, and every revival of religion in this section banks its spiritual riches solidly and unmovedly against the color line, without conscious question.

Among the Negroes the results are equally unhappy. They needed ethical leadership, spiritual guidance, and religious instruction. If the Negroes of the South are to any degree immoral, sexually unchaste, criminally inclined, and religiously ignorant, what right has the Christian South even to whisper reproach or accusation? How often have they raised a finger to assume spiritual or religious guardianship over those victims of their past system of economic and social life?

Left thus unguided the Negroes, with some help from such Northern white churches as dared, began their own religious upbuilding. . . . They faced tremendous difficulties—lack of ministers, money, and experience. Their churches could not be simply centres of religious life—because in the poverty of their organized efforts all united striving tended to centre in this one social organ. The Negro Church consequently became a great social institution with some ethical ideas but with those ethical ideas warped and changed and perverted by the whole history of the past; with memories, traditions, and rites of heathen worship, of intense emotionalism, trance, and weird singing.

And above all, there brooded over and in the church the sense of all their grievances. Whatsoever their own short-comings might be, at least they knew that they were not guilty of hypocrisy; they did not cry "Whosoever will" and then brazenly ostracize half the world. They knew that they opened their doors and hearts wide to all people that really wanted to come in and they looked upon the white churches not as examples but with a sort of silent contempt and a real inner questioning of the genuineness of their Christianity.

On the other hand, so far as the white post-bellum Christian church is concerned, I can conceive no more pitiable paradox than that of the young white

Christian in the South today who really believes in the ethics of Jesus Christ. What can he think when he hangs upon his church doors the sign that I have often seen, "All are welcome." He knows that half the population of his city would not dare to go inside that church. Or if there was any fellowship between Christians, white and black, it would be after the manner explained by a white Mississippi clergyman in all seriousness: "The whites and Negroes understand each other here perfectly, sir, perfectly; if they come to my church they take a seat in the gallery. If I go to theirs, they invite me to the front pew or the platform."

Once in Atlanta a great revival was going on in a prominent white church. The people were at fever heat, the minister was preaching and calling "Come to Jesus." Up the aisle tottered an old black man—he was an outcast, he had wandered in there aimlessly off the streets, dimly he had comprehended this call and he came tottering and swaying up the aisle. What was the result? It broke up the revival. There was no disturbance; he was gently led out, but that sudden appearance of a black face spoiled the whole spirit of the thing and the revival was at an end.

Who can doubt that if Christ came to Georgia today one of His first deeds would be to sit down and take supper with black men, and who can doubt the outcome if He did?

It is this tremendous paradox of a Christianity that theoretically opens the church to all men and yet closes it forcibly and insultingly in the face of black men and that does this not simply in the visible church but even more harshly in the spiritual fellowship of human souls—it is this that makes the ethical and religious problem in the South today of such tremendous importance, and that gives rise to the one thing which it seems to me is the most difficult in the Southern situation and that is, the tendency to deny the truth, the tendency to lie when the real situation comes up because the truth is too hard to face. This lying about the situation of the South has not been simply a political subterfuge against the dangers of ignorance, but is a sort of gasping inner revolt against acknowledging the real truth of the ethical conviction which every true Southerner must feel, namely: that the South is eternally and fundamentally wrong on the plain straight question of the equality of souls before God—of the inalienable rights of all men.

Here are men—they are aspiring, they are struggling piteously forward, they have frequent instances of ability, there is no doubt as to the tremendous strides which certain classes of Negroes have made—how shall they be treated? That they should be treated as men, of course, the best class of Southerners know and sometimes acknowledge. And yet they believe, and believe with fierce conviction, that it is impossible to treat Negroes as men, and still live with them. Right there is the paradox which they face daily and which is daily stamping hypocrisy upon their religion and upon their land.

Their irresistible impulse in this awful dilemma is to point to and emphasize the Negro's degradation, even though they know that it is not the degraded Negro whom they most fear, ostracize, and fight to keep down, but rather the rising, ambitious Negro.

If my own city of Atlanta had offered it today the choice between 500 Negro college graduates—forceful, busy, ambitious men of property and self-respect, and 500 black cringing vagrants and criminals, the popular vote in favor of the criminals would be simply overwhelming. Why? because they want Negro crime? No, not that they fear Negro crime less, but that they fear Negro ambition and success more. They can deal with crime by chain-gang and lynch law, or at least they think they can, but the South can conceive neither machinery nor place for the educated, self-reliant, self-assertive black man.

Are a people pushed to such moral extremities, the ones whose level-headed, unbiased statements of fact concerning the Negro can be relied upon? Do they really know the Negro? Can the nation expect of them the poise and patience necessary for the settling of a great social problem?

Not only is there then this initial falseness when the South excuses its ethical paradox by pointing to the low condition of the Negro masses, but there is also a strange blindness in failing to see that every pound of evidence to prove the present degradation of black men but adds to the crushing weight of indictment against their past treatment of this race.

A race is not made in a single generation. If they accuse Negro women of lewdness and Negro men of monstrous crime, what are they doing but advertising to the world the shameless lewdness of those Southern men who brought millions of mulattoes into the world, and whose deeds throughout the South and particularly in Virginia, the mother of slavery, have left but few prominent families whose blood does not today course in black veins? Suppose today Negroes do steal; who was it that for centuries made stealing a virtue by stealing their labor? Have not laziness and listlessness always been the followers of slavery? If these ten millions are ignorant by whose past law and mandate and present practice is this true?

The truth then cannot be controverted. The present condition of the Negro in America is better than the history of slavery proves we might reasonably expect. With the help of his friends, North and South, and despite the bitter opposition of his foes, South and North, he has bought twelve million acres of land, swept away two-thirds of his illiteracy, organized his church, and found leadership and articulate voice. Yet despite this the South, Christian and unchristian, with only here and there an exception, still stands like a rock wall and says: Negroes are not men and must not be treated as men.

When now the world faces such an absolute ethical contradiction, the truth is nearer than it seems.

It stands today perfectly clear and plain despite all sophistication and false assumption: If the contention of the South is true—that Negroes cannot by reason of hereditary inferiority take their places in modern civilization beside white men, then the South owes it to the world and to its better self to give the Negro every chance to prove this. To make the assertion dogmatically and then resort to all means which retard and restrict Negro development is not simply to stand convicted of insincerity before the civilized world, but, far worse than that, it is to make a nation of naturally generous, honest people to sit humiliated before their own consciences.

I believe that a straightforward, honorable treatment of black men according to their desert and achievement, will soon settle the Negro problem. If the South is right few will rise to a plane that will make their social reception a matter worth consideration; few will gain the sobriety and industry which will deserve the ballot; and few will achieve such solid moral character as will give them welcome to the fellowship of the church. If, on the other hand, Negroes with the door of opportunity thrown wide do become men of industry and achievement, of moral strength and even genius, then such rise will silence the South with an eternal silence.

The nation that enslaved the Negro owes him this trial; the section that doggedly and unreasonably kept him in slavery owes him at least this chance; and the church which professes to follow Jesus Christ and does not insist on this elemental act of justice merits the denial of the Master—"I never knew you."

This, then, is the history of those mighty moral battles in the South which have given us the Negro problem. And the last great battle is not a battle of South or East, of black or white, but of all of us. The path to racial peace is straight but narrow—its following today means tremendous fight against inertia, prejudice, and intrenched snobbery. But it is the duty of men, it is a duty of the church, to face the problem. Not only is it their duty to face it—they must face it, it is impossible not to, the very attempt to ignore it is assuming an attitude. It is a problem not simply of political expediency, of economic success, but a problem above all of religious and social life; and it carries with it not simply a demand for its own solution, but beneath it lies the whole question of the real intent of our civilization: Is the civilization of the United States Christian?

It is a matter of grave consideration what answer we ought to give to that question. The precepts of Jesus Christ cannot but mean that Christianity consists of an attitude of humility, of a desire for peace, of a disposition to treat our brothers as we would have our brothers treat us, of mercy and charity toward our fellow men, of willingness to suffer persecution for right ideals and in general of love not only toward our friends but even toward our enemies.

Judged by this, it is absurd to call the practical religion of this nation Christian. We are not humble, we are impudently proud; we are not merciful, we are unmerciful toward friend and foe; we are not peaceful nor peacefully inclined as our armies and battle-ships declare; we do not want to be martyrs, we would much rather be thieves and liars so long as we can be rich; we do not seek continuously, and prayerfully inculcate, love and justice for our fellow men, but on the contrary the treatment of the poor, the unfortunate, and the black within our borders is almost a national crime.

The problem that lies before Christians is tremendous. . . . and the answer must begin not by a slurring over of the one problem where these different tests of Christianity are most flagrantly disregarded, but it must begin by a girding of ourselves and a determination to see that justice is done in this country to the humblest and blackest as well as to the greatest and whitest of our citizens.

Now a word especially about the Episcopal church, whose position toward its Negro communicants is peculiar. I appreciate this position and speak of it specifically because I am one of those communicants. For four generations my family has belonged to this church and I belong to it, not by personal choice, not because I feel myself welcome within its portals, but simply because I refuse to be read outside of a church which is mine by inheritance and the service of my fathers. When the Episcopal church comes, as it does come today, to the Parting of the Ways, to the question as to whether its record in the future is going to be, on the Negro problem, as disgraceful as it has been in the past, I feel like appealing to all who are members of that church to remember that after all it is a church of Jesus Christ. Your creed and your duty enjoin upon you one, and only one, course of procedure.

In the real Christian church there is neither black nor white, rich nor poor, barbarian, Scythian, bond nor free, but all stand equal before the face of the Master. If you find that you cannot treat your Negro members as fellow Christians then do not deceive yourselves into thinking that the differences that you make or are going to make in their treatment are made for their good or for the service of the world; do not entice them to ask for a separation which your unchristian conduct forces them to prefer; do not pretend that the distinctions which you make toward them are distinctions which are made for the larger good of men, but simply confess in humility and self-abasement that you are not able to live up to your Christian vows; that you cannot treat these men as brothers and therefore you are going to set them aside and let them go their half-tended way.

I should be sorry, I should be grieved more than I can say, to see that which happened in the Southern Methodist Church and that which is practically happening in the Presbyterian Church, and that which will come in other sects—namely, a segregation of Negro Christians, come to be true among Episcopalians.

It would be a sign of Christian disunity far more distressing than sectarianism. I should therefore deplore it; and yet I am also free to say that unless this church is prepared to treat its Negro members with exactly the same consideration that other members receive, with the same brotherhood and fellowship, the same encouragement to aspiration, the same privileges, similarly trained priests and similar preferment for them, then I should a great deal rather see them set aside than to see a continuation of present injustice. All I ask is that when you do this you do it with an open and honest statement of the real reasons and not with statements veiled by any hypocritical excuses.

I am therefore above all desirous that the younger men and women who are today taking up the leadership of this great group of men, who wish the world better and work toward that end, should begin to see the real significance of this step and of the great problem behind it. It is not a problem simply of the South, not a problem simply of this country, it is a problem of the world.

As I have said elsewhere: "Most men are colored. A belief in humanity is above all a belief in colored men." If you cannot get on with colored men in America you cannot get on with the modern world; and if you cannot work with the humanity of this world how shall your souls ever tune with the myriad sided souls of worlds to come?

It may be that the price of the black man's survival in America and in the modern world, will be a long and shameful night of subjection to caste and segregation. If so, he will pay it, doggedly, silently, unfalteringly, for the sake of human liberty and the souls of his children's children. But as he stoops he will remember the indignation of that Jesus who cried, yonder behind heaving seas and years: "Woe unto you scribes and Pharisees, hypocrites, that strain out a gnat and swallow a camel,"—as if God cared a whit whether His Sons are born of maid, wife or widow so long as His church sits deaf to His own calling:

"Ho! every one that thirsteth, come ye to the waters and he that hath no money; come ye, buy and eat; yea, come, buy wine and milk without money and without price!"

NOTES

1. Grimke: "Right on the Scaffold."
2. "The Negro Church," Atlanta University Publications, No. 8.

CHAPTER NINE

Jesus Christ in Georgia

This piece of short fiction was originally published in *The Crisis* in 1911 and was subsequently published, with slight alterations, under the title "Jesus Christ in Texas" in *Darkwater* (1920). It is a gripping tale of race and religion in which Du Bois uses the figure of Jesus Christ as a device to highlight the essence of true Christian ethics, expose the evil of white racism, and elevate the painful reality of black suffering to the status of the heroic and holy. Jesus is depicted not as a fair-haired Anglo but as a "mulatto, surely," his hair curly and his face "olive, even yellow."

The convict guard laughed.

"I don't know," he said, "I hadn't thought of that—"

He hesitated and looked at the stranger curiously. In the solemn twilight he got an impression of unusual height and soft dark eyes.

"Curious sort of acquaintance for the Colonel," he thought; then he continued aloud: "But that nigger there is bad; a born thief and ought to be sent up for life; is practically; got ten years last time—"

Here the voice of the promoter talking within interrupted; he was bending over his figures, sitting by the Colonel. He was slight, with a sharp nose.

"The convicts," he said, "would cost us $96 a year and board. Well, we can squeeze that so that it won't be over $125 apiece. Now, if these fellows are driven, they can build this line within twelve months. It will be running next April. Freights will fall fifty per cent. Why, man, you will be a millionaire in less than ten years."

The Colonel started. He was a thick, short man, with clean-shaven face, and a certain air of breeding about the lines of his countenance; the word millionaire sounded well in his ears. He thought—he thought a great deal; he almost heard the puff of the fearfully costly automobile that was coming up the road, and he said:

"I suppose we might as well hire them."

"Of course," answered the promoter.

The voice of the tall stranger in the corner broke in here:

"It will be a good thing for them?" he said, half in question.

The Colonel moved. "The guard makes strange friends," he thought to himself. "What's this man doing here, anyway?" He looked at him, or rather, looked at his eyes, and then somehow felt a warming toward him. He said:

"Well, at least it can't harm them—they're beyond that."

"It will do them good, then," said the stranger again. The promoter shrugged his shoulders.

"It will do us good," he said.

But the Colonel shook his head impatiently. He felt a desire to justify himself before those eyes, and he answered:

"Yes, it will do them good; or, at any rate, it won't make them any worse than they are."

Then he started to say something else, but here sure enough the sound of the automobile breathing at the gate stopped him and they all arose.

"It is settled, then," said the promoter.

"Yes," said the Colonel, signing his name and turning toward the stranger again.

"Are you going into town?" he asked with the Southern courtesy of white man to white man in a country town. The stranger said he was. "Then come along in my machine. I want to talk to you about this."

They went out to the car. The stranger as he went turned again to look back at the convict. He was a tall, powerfully built black fellow. His face was sullen, with a low forehead, thick, hanging lips, and bitter eyes. There was revolt written about the mouth, and a hangdog expression. He stood bending over his pile of stones pounding listlessly.

Beside him stood a boy of twelve, yellow, with a hunted, crafty look. The convict raised his eyes, and they met the eyes of the stranger. The hammer fell from his hands.

The stranger turned slowly toward the automobile, and the Colonel introduced him. He could not exactly catch the foreign-sounding name, but he mumbled something as he presented him to his wife and little girl, who were waiting. As they whirled away he started to talk, but the stranger had taken the little girl into his lap, and together they conversed in low tones all the way home.

In some way, they did not exactly know how, they got the impression that the man was a teacher, and of course he must be a foreigner. The long cloak-like coat told this. They rode in the twilight through the half-lighted town, and at last drew up before the Colonel's mansion, with its ghostlike pillars.

The lady in the back seat was thinking of the guests she had invited to dinner, and wondered if she ought not to ask this man to stay. He seemed cultured, and she supposed he was some acquaintance of the Colonel's. It would be rather a distinction to have him there, with the Judge's wife and daughter and the Rector. She spoke almost before she thought:

"You will enter and rest awhile?"

The Colonel and the little girl insisted. For a moment the stranger seemed about to refuse. He said he was on his way North, where he had some business for his father in Pennsylvania. Then, for the child's sake, he consented. Up the steps they went, and into the dark parlor and there they sat and talked a long time. It was a curious conversation. Afterward they did not remember exactly what was said, and yet they all remembered a certain strange satisfaction in that long talk.

Presently the nurse came for the reluctant child, and the hostess bethought herself:

"We will have a cup of tea—you will be dry and tired."

She rang and switched on a blaze of light. With one accord they all looked at the stranger, for they had hardly seen him well in the glooming twilight. The woman started in amazement and the Colonel half rose in anger. Why, the man was a mulatto, surely—even if he did not own the Negro blood, their practiced eyes knew it. He was tall and straight, and the coat looked like a Jewish gabardine. His hair hung in close curls far down the sides of his face, and his face was olive, even yellow.

A peremptory order rose to the Colonel's lips, and froze there as he caught the stranger's eyes. Those eyes, where had he seen those eyes before? He remembered them long years ago—the soft, tear-filled eyes of a brown girl. He remembered many things, and his face grew drawn and white. Those eyes kept burning into him, even when they were turned half away toward the staircase, where the white figure of the child hovered with her nurse, and waved goodnight. The lady sank into her chair and thought: "What will the Judge's wife say? How did the Colonel come to invite this man here? How shall we be rid of him?" She looked at the Colonel in reproachful consternation.

Just then the door opened and the old butler came in. He was an ancient black man with tufted white hair, and he held before him a large silver tray filled with a china tea service. The stranger rose slowly and stretched forth his hands as if to bless the viands. The old man paused in bewilderment, tottered and then, with sudden gladness in his eyes, dropped to his knees as the tray crashed to the floor.

"My Lord!" he whispered, "and My God!" But the woman screamed: "Mother's china!"

The doorbell rang.

"Heavens! Here is the dinner party!" exclaimed the lady.

She turned toward the door, but there in the hall, clad in her night clothes, was the little girl. She had stolen down the stairs to see the stranger again, and the nurse above was calling in vain. The woman felt hysterical and scolded at the nurse, but the stranger had stretched out his arms, and with a glad cry the child nestled in them. "Of such," he whispered, "is the Kingdom of Heaven," as he slowly mounted the stairs with his little burden.

The mother was glad; anything to be rid of the interloper even for a moment. The bell rang again, and she hastened toward the door, which the loitering black maid was just opening. She did not notice the shadow of the stranger as he came slowly down the stairs and paused by the newel post, dark and silent.

The Judge's wife entered. She was an old woman, frilled and powdered into a caricature of youth, and gorgeously gowned. She came forward, smiling with extended hands, but just as she was opposite the stranger, a chill from somewhere seemed to strike her, and she shuddered and cried: "What a draft!" as she drew a silken shawl about her and shook hands cordially; she forgot to ask who the stranger was. The Judge strode in unseeing, thinking of a puzzling case of theft.

"Eh? What? Oh—er—yes—good-evening," he said, "good-evening."

Behind them came a young woman in the glory of youth, daintily silked, with diamonds around her fair neck, beautiful in face and form. She came in lightly, but stopped with a little gasp; then she laughed gaily and said:

"Why, I beg your pardon. Was it not curious? I thought I saw there behind your man"—she hesitated ("but he must be a servant," she argued)—"the shadow of wide white wings. It was but the light on the drapery. What a turn it gave me— so glad to be here." And she smiled again. With her came a tall and haughty naval officer. Hearing this lady refer to the servant, he hardly looked at him, but held his gilded cap and cloak carelessly toward him; the stranger took them and placed them carefully on the rack.

Last came the Rector, a man of forty, and well clothed. He started to pass the stranger, stopped and looked at him inquiringly.

"I beg your pardon," he said, "I beg your pardon, I think I have met you?"

The stranger made no answer, and the hostess nervously hurried the guests on. But the Rector lingered and looked perplexed.

"Surely I know you; I have met you somewhere," he said, putting his hand vaguely to his head. "You—you remember me, do you not?"

The stranger quietly swept his cloak aside, and to the hostess's unspeakable relief moved toward the door.

"I never knew you," he said in low tones, as he went.

The lady murmured some faint excuse about intruders, but the Rector stood with annoyance written on his face.

"I beg a thousand pardons," he said to the hostess absently. "It is a great pleasure to be here—somehow I thought I knew that man. I am sure I knew him, once."

The stranger had passed down the steps, and as he went the nurse-maid, lingering at the top of the staircase, flew down after him, caught his cloak, trembled, hesitated, and then kneeled in the dust. He touched her lightly with his hand and said, "Go, and sin no more."

With a glad cry the maid left the house with its open door and turned north, running, while the stranger turned eastward to the night. As they parted a long low howl rose tremulously and reverberated through the town. The Colonel's wife within shuddered.

"The bloodhounds," she said. The Rector answered carelessly.

"Another one of those convicts escaped, I suppose; really, they need severer measures." Then he stopped. He was trying to remember that stranger's name. The Judge's wife looked about for the draft and arranged her shawl. The girl glanced at the white drapery in the hall, but the young officer was bending over her, and the fires of life burned in her veins.

Howl after howl rose in the night, swelled and died away. The stranger strode rapidly along the highway and out into the deep forest. There he paused and stood waiting, tall and still. A mile up the road behind him a man was running, tall and powerful and black, with crime-stained face, with convict's stripes upon him and shackles on his legs. He ran and jumped in little short steps, and the chains rang. He fell and rose again, while the howl of the hounds rung harder behind him.

Into the forest he leaped and crept and jumped and ran, streaming with sweat; seeing the tall form rise before him, he stopped suddenly, dropped his hands in sullen impotence and sank panting to the earth. A bloodhound shot into the woods behind him, howled, whined and fawned before the stranger's feet. Hound after hound bayed, leapt and lay there; then silent, one by one, with bowed head, they crept backward toward the town.

The stranger made a cup of his hands and gave the man water to drink, bathed his hot head, and gently took the chains and irons from his feet. By and by the convict stood up. Day was dawning above the treetops. He looked into the stranger's face, and for a moment a gladness swept over the stains of his face.

"Why, you'se a nigger, too," he said.

Then the convict seemed anxious to justify himself.

"I never had no chance," he said furtively.

"Thou shalt not steal," said the stranger.

The man bridled.

"But how about them? Can they steal? Didn't they steal a whole year's work and then, when I stole to keep from starving—" he glanced at the stranger. "No, I didn't steal just to keep from starving. I stole to be stealing. I can't help stealing. Seems like when I sees things I just must—but, yes, I'll try!"

The convict looked down at his striped clothes, but the stranger had taken off his long coat—and put it around him, and the stripes disappeared. In the opening morning the black man started toward the low log farmhouse in the distance, and the stranger stood watching him. There was a new glory in the day. The black man's face cleared up and the farmer was glad to get him.

All day he worked as he had never worked before, and the farmer gave him some cold food toward night.

"You can sleep in the barn," he said, and turned away.

"How much do I git a day?" asked the man.

The farmer scowled:

"If you'll sign a contract for the season," he said, "I'll give you ten dollars a month."

"I won't sign no contract to be a slave," said the man doggedly.

"Yes, you will," said the farmer, threateningly, "or I'll call the convict guard." And he grinned.

The convict shrunk and slouched to the barn. As night fell he looked out and saw the farmer leave the place. Slowly he crept out and sneaked toward the house. He looked into the kitchen door. No one was there, but the supper was spread as if the mistress had laid it and gone out. He ate ravenously. Then he looked into the front room and listened. He could hear low voices on the porch. On the table lay a silver watch. He gazed at it, and in a moment was beside it, with his hands on it. Quickly he slipped out of the house and slouched toward the field. He saw his employer coming along the highway. He fled back stealthily and around to the front of the house, when suddenly he stopped. He felt the great dark eyes of the stranger and saw the same dark, cloak-like coat, where he was seated on the doorstep talking with the mistress of the house. Slowly, guiltily, he turned back, entered the kitchen and laid the watch where he had found it; and then he rushed wildly with arms outstretched back toward the stranger.

The woman had laid supper for her husband, and going down from the house had walked out toward a neighbor's. She was gone but a little while, and when she came back she started to see a dark figure on the doorsteps under the tall red oak. She thought it was the new Negro hand until he said in a soft voice:

"Will you give me bread?"

Reassured at the voice of a white man, she answered quickly in her soft Southern tones:

"Why, certainly."

She was a little woman. Once she had been handsome, but now her face was drawn with work and care. She was nervous, and was always thinking, wishing, wanting for something. She went in and got him some cornbread and a glass of cool, rich buttermilk, and then came out and sat down beside him. She began, quite unconsciously, to tell him about herself—the things she had done, and had not done, and the things she had wished. She told him of her husband, and this new farm they were trying to buy. She said it was so hard to get niggers to work. She said they ought all to be in the chain gang and made to work. Even then some ran away. Only yesterday one had escaped.

At last she gossiped of her neighbors; how good they were and how bad.

"And do you like them all?" asked the stranger.

She hesitated.

"Most of them," she said; and then, looking up into his face and putting her hand in his as though he were her father, she said:

"There are none I hate; no, none at all."

He looked away and said dreamily:

"You love your neighbor as yourself?" She hesitated—

"I try—" she began, and then looked the way he was looking; down under the hill, where lay a little, half-ruined cabin.

"They are niggers," she said briefly.

He looked at her. Suddenly a confusion came over her, and she insisted, she knew not why—

"But they are niggers."

With a sudden impulse she rose, and hurriedly lighted the lamp that stood just within the door and held it above her head. She saw his dark face and curly hair. She shrieked in angry terror, and rushed down the path; and just as she rushed down, the black convict came running up with hands outstretched. They met in midpath, and before he could stop he had run against her, and she fell heavily to earth and lay white and still. Her husband came rushing up with cry and oath:

"I knew it," he said; "it is that runaway nigger." He held the black man struggling to the earth, and raised his voice to a yell. Down the highway came the convict guard with hound and mob and gun. They poured across the fields. The farmer motioned to them.

"He—attacked—my wife," he gasped.

The mob snarled and worked silently. Right to the limb of the red oak they hoisted the struggling, writhing black man, while others lifted the dazed woman. Right and left as she tottered to the house she searched for the stranger, with a sick yearning, but the stranger was gone. And she told none of her guest.

"No—no—I want nothing," she insisted, until they left her, as they thought, asleep. For a time she lay still listening to the departure of the mob. Then she rose. She shuddered as she heard the creaking of the limb where the body hung. But resolutely she crawled to the window and peered out into the moon-light; she saw the dead man writhe. He stretched his arms out like a cross, looking upward. She gasped and clung to the window sill. Behind the swaying body, and down where the little, half-ruined cabin lay, a single flame flashed up amid the far-off shout and cry of the mob. A fierce joy sobbed up through the terror in her soul and then sank abashed as she watched the flame rise. Suddenly whirling into one great crimson column it shot to the top of the sky and threw great arms athwart the gloom until above the world and behind the roped and swaying form below hung quivering and burning a great crimson cross.

She hid her dizzy, aching head in an agony of tears, and dared not look, for she knew. Her dry lips moved:

"Despised and rejected of men."

She knew, and the very horror of it lifted her dull and shrinking eyelids. There, heaven-tall, earth-wide, hung the stranger on the crimson cross, riven and bloodstained with thorn-crowned head and pierced hands. She stretched her arms and shrieked.

He did not hear. He did not see. His calm dark eyes all sorrowful were fastened on the writhing, twisting body of the thief, and a voice came out of the winds of the night, saying:

"This day thou shalt be with me in Paradise!"

CHAPTER TEN

The Church and the Negro

This essay was published in *The Crisis* in 1913. It is a harsh, succinct condemnation of American Christianity. As in similar works, Du Bois reminds us of the often problematic and troubling relationship between religion and race relations in American history.

The relation of the church to the Negro is, or should be, a very simple proposition. Leaving aside the supernatural significance of the church organization, we have here groups of people working for human uplift and professing the highest and most unselfish morality as exemplified by the life and teaching of Jesus of Nazareth and the Golden Rule.

By this standard all church members should treat Negroes as they themselves would wish to be treated if they were colored. They should do this and teach this and, if need be, die for this creed.

The plain facts are sadly at variance with this doctrine. The church aided and abetted the Negro slave trade; the church was the bulwark of American slavery; and the church today is the strongest seat of racial and color prejudice. If one hundred of the best and purest colored folk of the United States should seek to apply for membership in any white church in this land tomorrow, 999 out of every 1,000 ministers would lie to keep them out. They would not only do this, but would openly and brazenly defend their action as worthy of followers of Jesus Christ.

Yet Jesus Christ was a laborer and black men are laborers; He was poor and we are poor; He was despised of his fellow men and we are despised; He was persecuted and crucified, and we are mobbed and lynched. If Jesus Christ came to America He would associate with Negroes and Italians and working people; He would eat and pray with them, and He would seldom see the interior of the Cathedral of Saint John the Divine.

Why then are His so-called followers deaf, dumb, and blind on the Negro problem—on the human problem?

Because they think they have discovered bypaths to righteousness which do not lead to brotherhood with the poor, the dirty, the ignorant and the black. "Make them servants," they say; "we need cooks." But can a whole race be doomed to menial service in a civilization where menial service is itself doomed? And when menial service has become Service and lost its social stigma, so that white folk want to enter such service, will they welcome black folk as fellow servants? Certainly not, and the slavery argument of this cry stands revealed.

"But," cry others, "let the Negroes themselves bear their own social responsibilities for poverty, ignorance and disease. Segregate them and pile their sins upon them." Indeed! Are the poor alone responsible for poverty? And the ignorant for ignorance? Can the rich be allowed to escape with this spoil and the learned without obligation for his knowledge? If the black men in America are what they are because of slavery and oppression, how cowardly for white Christians to deny their own guilt. The real hypocrisy comes, however, when the Negro, eager to take responsibility, cries out for power with which to bear it and is denied such power. Denied higher training for his leaders, denied industrial opportunity to make a living, the self-assertion and self-defense of the ballot, denied even hospitals and common schools. Thus the church gaily tosses him stones for bread.

Even the rock of "Science" on which the white church rested with such beautiful faith, hoping to prove the majority of humanity inhuman, so that Fifth Avenue Presbyterianism would not have to dirty its dainty fingers with Fifty-third Street Baptists—and black ones at that—even this Rock of Ages is falling before honest investigation.

There is but the Golden Rule left—the despised and rejected Golden Rule. Can the church follow it? Is there common decency enough in the millions of white American church members to dare to treat Negroes as they would like to be treated if they themselves were colored?

The Negro problem is the test of the church.

CHAPTER ELEVEN

The Burden of Black Women

This poem was published in *The Crisis* in 1914.

Dark doughter of the lotus leaves that watch
    the Southern sea,
Wan spirit of a prisoned soul a-panting to
    be free;
The muttered music of thy streams, the
    whispers of the deep
Have kissed each other in God's name and
    kissed a world to sleep.

The will of the world is a whistling wind
    sweeping a cloud-cast sky,
And not from the east and not from the west
    knelled its soul-searing cry;
But out of the past of the Past's grey past,
    it yelled from the top of the sky;
Crying: Awake, O ancient race! Wailing:
    O woman arise!
And crying and sighing and crying again
    as a voice in the midnight cries;
But the burden of white men bore her back,
    and the white world stifled her sighs.

101

The White World's vermin and filth:
    All the dirt of London,
    All the scum of New York;
    Valiant spoilers of women
    And conquerors of unarmed men;
    Shameless breeders of bastards
    Drunk with the greed of gold,
    Baiting their blood-stained hooks
    With cant for the souls of the simple,
    Bearing the White Man's Burden
    Of Liquor and Lust and Lies!
    Unthankful we wince in the East,
    Unthankful we wail from the westward,
    Unthankfully thankful we sing,
    In the un-won wastes of the wild:
        I hate them, Oh!
        I hate them well,
        I hate them, Christ!
        As I hate Hell,
        If I were God
        I'd sound their knell
        This day!
    Who raised the fools to their glory
    But black men of Egypt and Ind?
    Ethiopia's sons of the evening,
    Chaldeans and Yellow Chinese?
    The Hebrew children of Morning
    And mongrels of Rome and Greece?
        Ah, well!

    And they that raised the boasters
    Shall drag them down again:
    Down with the theft of their thieving
    And murder and mocking of men,
    Down with their barter of women
    And laying and lying of creeds,
    Down with their cheating of childhood,
    And drunken orgies of war—

        down,

            down,

                deep down,

Till the Devil's strength be shorn,
Till some dim, darker David a-hoeing of his corn,
And married maiden, Mother of God,
Bid the Black Christ be born!

Then shall the burden of manhood,
Be it yellow or black or white,
And Poverty, Justice and Sorrow—
The Humble and Simple and Strong,
Shall sing with the Sons of Morning
And Daughters of Evensong:

Black mother of the iron hills that guard the
    blazing sea,
Wild spirit of a storm-swept soul a-struggling
    to be free,
Where 'neath the bloody finger marks, thy
    riven bosom quakes,
Thicken the thunders of God's voice, and lo!
    a world awakes!

CHAPTER TWELVE

Jesus Christ in Baltimore

This piece was published in *The Crisis* in 1911.

It seems that it is not only property that is screaming with fright at the black spectre in Baltimore, but religion also. Two churches founded in the name of Him who "put down the mighty from their seats and exalted them of low degree" are compelled to move. Their palatial edifices filled with marble memorials and Tiffany windows are quite useless for the purposes of their religion since black folk settled next door. Incontinently they have dropped their Bibles and gathered up their priestly robes and fled, after selling their property to colored people for $125,000 in good, cold cash.

Where are they going? Uptown. Up to the wealthy and exclusive and socially select. There they will establish their little gods again, and learned prelates with sonorous voices will ask the echoing pews: "How can the Church reach the working man?"

Why not ask the working man? Why not ask black people, and yellow people, and poor people, and all the people from whom such congregations flee in holy terror? The church that does not run from the lowly find the lowly at its doors, and there are some such churches in the land, but we fear that their number in Baltimore is not as great as it should be.

CHAPTER THIRTEEN

Easter

This piece was published in *The Crisis* in 1912.

The winter of despair has long lain upon our souls. Again and again, out of the awful mists of Nowhere, the cold, white hands of God have crept down and gripped His world until the people shivered and starved and children whimpered in their mothers' arms. So was the day of long night.

Now all is changed.

This is the Resurrection Morning. The world-God stands aloft and smiles with splendor on his brows. The waters trickle, the birds sing, and pulses beat in the eternal hills.

"Awake, awake, put on thy strength, O Zion; put on thy beautiful robes."

There is in this round world neither death nor despair, but ever continually, eternally triumphant over mist and mire, crime and cruelty, springs the unending hope of life, of life that is life, that lives.

This alone is real. These other things that fill and, alas! must fill our pages— murder, meanness, the hurting of little children, the dishonoring of womanhood, the starving of souls—all these are but the unsubstantial smoke and shadow that hide the real things. This reality is ever there, howsoever dark the darkness that blackens and hides it.

Richard Brown is real—the modest, good-faced colored boy, told to paint barns when he can paint the morning as he has done on our cover this month; or that Boston black boy told to earn a living when his soul sees visions in the human face; this whole great black and wonderful race (more wonderful perhaps in countless subtle ways than anything this world has seen), whose spirit nothing can break and whose upward rending nothing can stop. This is the eternal reality of the Easter of the world; this is the resurrection of the hope that burned in the breast of Douglass and Garrison, of Phillips, Langston, and John Brown. This is the hope that never dies.

CHAPTER FOURTEEN

The Negro Church

Published in 1903, *The Negro Church* is not only the first extensive, in-depth sociological study of African-American religion specifically, but it is the first book-
length sociological study of religion in general undertaken in the United States.
Employing an array of historical, interview, survey, and participant-observation
research methods, The Negro Church explores multiple aspects of African-
American religious life in the early years of the twentieth century, from church
finances to public opinion to denominational diversity to belief.

While he was at Atlanta University, Du Bois organized annual conferences in
which scholars and specialists would come together to share their research on a
variety of timely black issues, such as the Negro in business, the Negro American
family, the Negro American artisan, and so on. From 1897 to 1914, in addition to
organizing these conferences, Du Bois supervised, edited, and contributed to the
subsequent publication of sixteen monographs following each conference.

Below are excerpts from the monograph published on the religion of African
Americans. Several authors contributed sections to the monograph, including
Du Bois himself. It is largely the sections written by Du Bois that are included
here. Themes include the effects of the slave trade on African religion, the conversion process to Christianity, the conditions of various black churches
through the country, and so on. Du Bois characterized the Black Church as the
"first distinctly Negro American social institution" and illustrates the degree to
which the religious organizations of African Americans can be considered social
as well as spiritual centers.

The Negro Church is the only social institution of the Negroes which started in the African forest and survived slavery; under the leadership of priest or medicine man, afterward of the Christian pastor, the Church preserved in itself the remnants of African tribal life and became after emancipation, the center of Negro social life. So that today the Negro population of the United States is virtually divided into church congregations which are the real units of race life.

Report of the Third Atlanta Conference, 1898

1. Primitive Negro Religion. The prominent characteristic of primitive Negro religion is Nature worship with the accompanying strong belief in sorcery. . . . The slave trade so mingled and demoralized the west coast of Africa for four hundred years that it is difficult to-day to find there definite remains of any great religious system. Ellis tells us of the spirit belief of the Ewne people; they believe that men and all Nature have the indwelling "Kra," which is immortal. That the man himself after death may exist as a ghost, which is often conceived of as departed from the "Kra," as shadowy continuing of the man. So Bryce, speaking of the Kaffirs of South Africa, a branch of the great Bantu tribe, says:

"To the Kaffirs, as to the most savage races, the world was full of spirits—spirits of the rivers, the mountains, and the woods. Most important were the ghosts of the dead, who had power to injure or help the living, and who were, therefore, propitiated by offerings at stated periods, as well as on occasions, when their aid was especially desired. This kind of worship, the worship once most generally diffused throughout the world, and which held its ground among the Greeks and Italians in the most flourishing period of ancient civilization, as it does in China and Japan to-day, was, and is, virtually the religion of the Kaffirs."

The supreme being of the Bantus is the dimly conceived Molimo, the Unseen, who typifies vaguely the unknown powers of nature or of the sky. Among some tribes the worship of such higher spirits has banished fetichism and belief in witchcraft, but among most of the African tribes the sudden and violent changes in government and social organization have tended to overthrow the larger religious conceptions and leave fetichism and witchcraft supreme. This is particularly true on the west coast among the spawn of the slave traders.

There can be no reasonable doubt, however, but that the scattered remains of religious systems in Africa to-day among the Negro tribes are survivals of the religious ideas upon which the Egyptian religion was based. . . .

The early Christian church had an Exarchate of fifty-two dioceses in Northern Africa, but it probably seldom came in contact with purely Negro tribes on account of the Sahara. The hundred dioceses of the patriarchate of Alexandria, on the other hand, embraced Libya, Pentapolis, Egypt, and Abyssinia, and had a

large number of Negroid members. In Western Africa, after the voyage of Da
Gama, there were several kingdoms of Negroes nominally Catholic, and the
church claimed several hundred thousand communicants. These were on the
slave coast and on the eastern coast.

Mohammedanism entered Africa in the seventh and eighth centuries and had
since that time conquered nearly all Northern Africa, the Sudan, and made
inroads into the populations of the west coast . . . and especially is it preserving
the natives against the desolations of Christian rum.

2. *Effect of Transplanting.* It ought not to be forgotten that each Negro slave
brought to America during the four centuries of the African slave trade was
taken from definite and long-formed habits of social, political, and religious life.
These ideas were not the highest, measured by modern standards, but they were
far from the lowest, measured by the standards of primitive man. The unit of
African tribal organization was the clan or family of families ruled by the patri-
arch or his strongest successor; these clans were united into tribes ruled by hereditary or elected chiefs, and some tribes were more or less loosely federated into
kingdoms. . . .

The power of religion was represented by the priest or medicine man. Aided by
an unfaltering faith, natural sharpness and some rude knowledge of medicine, and
supported by the vague sanctions of a half-seen world peopled by spirits, good and
evil, the African priest wielded a power second only to that of the chief, and often
superior to it. In some tribes the African priesthood was organized and something
like systematic religious institutions emerged. But the central fact of African life,
political, social and religious, is its failure to integrate—to unite and systematize
itself in some conquering whole which should dominate the wayward parts. This
is the central problem of civilization, and while there have arisen from time to
time in Africa conquering kingdoms, and some consolidation of power in religion,
it has been continually overthrown before it was strong enough to maintain itself
independently. What have been the causes of this? They have been threefold: the
physical peculiarities of Africa, the character of external conquest, and the slave-
trade—the "heart disease of Africa." The physical peculiarities of the land shut
out largely the influence of foreign civilization and religion and made human
organization a difficult fight for survival against heat and disease; foreign conquest
took the form of sudden incursions, causing vast migrations and uprooting of institutions and beliefs, or of colonizations of strong, hostile and alien races, and
finally for four centuries the slave-trade fed on Africa, and peaceful evolution in
political organization or religious belief was impossible.

Especially did the slave-trade ruin religious evolution on the west coast; the
ancient kingdoms were overthrown and changed, tribes and nations mixed and
demoralized, and a perfect chaos of ideas left. Here it was that animal worship,
fetishism and belief in sorcery and witchcraft strengthened their sway and gained
wider currency than ever.

The first social innovation that followed the transplanting of the Negro was the substitution of the West Indian plantation for the tribal and clan life of Africa. The real significance of this change will not appear at first glance. The despotic political power of the chief was now vested in the white master; the clan had lost its ties of blood relationship and became simply the aggregation of individuals on a plot of ground, with common rules and customs, common dwellings, and a certain communism in property. The two greatest changes, however, were, first, the enforcement of severe and unremitted toil, and, second, the establishment of a new polygamy—a new family life. These social innovations were introduced with much difficulty and met determined resistance on the part of the slaves, especially when there was community of blood and language. Gradually, however, superior force and organized methods prevailed, and the plantation became the unit of a new development. The enforcement of continual toil was not the most revolutionary change which the plantation introduced. Where this enforced labor did not descend to barbarism and slow murder, it was not bad discipline; the African had the natural indolence of a tropical nature which had never felt the necessity of work; his first great awakening came with hard labor, and a pity it was, not that he worked, but that voluntary labor on his part was not from the first encouraged and rewarded. The vast and overshadowing change that the plantation system introduced was the change in the status of women— the new polygamy. This new polygamy had all the evils and not one of the safeguards of the African prototype. The African system was a complete protection for girls, and a strong protection for wives against everything but the tyranny of the husband; the plantation polygamy left the chastity of Negro women absolutely unprotected in law, and practically little guarded in custom. The number of wives of a native African was limited and limited very effectually by the number of cattle he could command or his prowess in war. The number of wives of a West India slave was limited chiefly by his lust and cunning. The black females, were they wives or growing girls, were the legitimate prey of the men, and on this system there was one, and only one, safeguard, the character of the master of the plantation. Where the master was himself lewd and avaricious the degradation of the women was complete. Where, on the other hand, the plantation system reached its best development, as in Virginia, there was a fair approximation of a monogamic marriage system among the slaves; and yet even here, on the best conducted plantations, the protection of Negro women was but imperfect; the seduction of girls was frequent, and seldom did an illegitimate child bring shame, or an adulterous wife punishment to the Negro quarters.

And this was inevitable, because on the plantation the private home, as a self-protective, independent unit, did not exist. That powerful institution, the polygamous African home, was almost completely destroyed and in its place in America arose sexual promiscuity, a weak community life, with common dwelling, meals and child-nurseries. The internal slave trade tended to further weaken natural ties. A small number of favored house servants and artisans were raised above this— had their private homes, came in contact with the culture of the master class, and assimilated much of American civilization. Nevertheless, broadly speaking, the greatest social effect of American slavery was to substitute for the polygamous Negro home a new polygamy less guarded, less effective, and less civilized.

At first sight it would seem that slavery completely destroyed every vestige of spontaneous social movement among the Negroes; the home had deteriorated; political authority and economic initiative was in the hands of the masters, property, as a social institution, did not exist on the plantation, and, indeed, it is usually assumed by historians and sociologists that every vestige of internal development disappeared, leaving the slaves no means of expression for their common life, thought, and striving. This is not strictly true; the vast power of the priest in the African state has already been noted; his realm alone—the province of religion and medicine—remained largely unaffected by the plantation system in many important particulars. The Negro priest, therefore, early became an important figure on the plantation and found his function as the interpreter of the supernatural, the comforter of the sorrowing, and as the one who expressed, rudely, but picturesquely, the longing and disappointment and resentment of a stolen people. From such beginnings arose and spread with marvelous rapidity the Negro Church, the first distinctively Negro American social institution. It was not at first by any means a Christian Church, but a mere adaptation of those heathen rites which we roughly designate by the term Obe Worship, or "Voodoism." Association and missionary effort soon gave these rites a veneer of Christianity, and gradually, after two centuries, the Church became Christian, with a simple Calvinistic creed, but with many of the old customs still clinging to the services. It is this historic fact that the Negro Church of to-day bases itself upon the sole surviving social institution of the African fatherland, that accounts for its extraordinary growth and vitality. We easily forget that in the United States to-day there is a Church organization for every sixty Negro families. This institution, therefore, naturally assumed many functions which the other harshly suppressed social organs had to surrender; the Church became the center of amusements, of what little spontaneous economic activity remained, of education, and of all social intercourse. . . .

4. *Slavery and Christianity.* The most obvious reason for the spread of witchcraft and persistence of heathen rites among Negro slaves was the fact that at first no effort was made by masters to offer them anything better. The reason for this was the widespread idea that it was contrary to law to hold Christians as slaves. One can realize the weight of this if we remember that the Diet of Worms and

Sir John Hawkins' voyages were but a generation apart. From the time of the Crusades to the Lutheran revolt the feeling of Christian brotherhood had been growing, and it was pretty well established by the end of the sixteenth century that it was illegal and irreligious for Christians to hold each other as slaves for life. This did not mean any widespread abhorrence of forced labor from serfs or apprentices and it was particularly linked with the idea that the enslavement of the heathen was meritorious, since it punished their blasphemy on the one hand and gave them a chance for conversion on the other.

When, therefore, the slave-trade from Africa began it met only feeble opposition here and there. That opposition was in nearly all cases stilled when it was continually stated that the slave-trade was simply a method of converting the heathen to Christianity. The corollary that the conscience of Europe immediately drew was that after conversion the Negro slave was to become in all essential respects like other servants and laborers, that is bound to toil, perhaps, under general regulations, but personally free with recognized rights and duties.

Most colonists believed that this was not only actually right, but according to English law. And while they early began to combat the idea they continually doubted the legality of their action in English courts. . . .

The question arose in different form in Massachusetts when it was enacted that only church members could vote. If Negroes joined the church, would they become free voters of the commonwealth? It seemed hardly possible. . . . Nevertheless, up to 1660 or thereabouts, it seemed accepted in most colonies and in the English West Indies that baptism into a Christian church would free a Negro slave. Massachusetts first apparently attacked this idea by enacting in 1641 that slavery should be confined to captives in just wars "and such strangers as willingly sell themselves or are sold to us," meaning by "strangers" apparently heathen, but saying nothing as to the effect of conversion. Connecticut adopted similar legislation in 1650 and Virginia declared in 1661 that Negroes "are incapable of making satisfaction" for time lost in running away by lengthening their time of service, thus implying that they were slaves for life, and Maryland declared flatly In 1663 that Negro slaves should serve "durante vita." In Barbadoes the Council presented, in 1663, an act to the Assembly recommending the christening of Negro children and the instruction of all adult Negroes to the several ministers of the place. . . .

It was not until 1667 that Virginia finally plucked up courage to attack the issue squarely and declared by law:

"Baptisme doth not alter the condition of the person as to his bondage or freedom, in order that diverse masters freed from this doubt may more carefully endeavor the propagation of Christianity."

Following this Virginia took three further decisive steps In 1670, 1682, and 1705. First she declared that only slaves imported from Christian lands should be free. Next she excepted Negroes and mulattoes from even this restriction unless they were born of Christians and were Christians when taken in slavery. Finally, only personal Christianity in Africa or actual freedom in a Christian country excepted a Virginia Negro slave from life-long slavery. . . .

It is clear from these citations that in the seventeenth century not only was there little missionary effort to convert Negro slaves, but that there was on the contrary positive refusal to let slaves be converted, and that this refusal was one incentive to explicit statements of the doctrine of perpetual slavery for Negroes. The French Code Noir of 1685 made baptism and religious instruction of Negroes obligatory. We find no such legislation in English colonies. On the contrary, the principal Secretary of State is informed in 1670 that in Jamaica the number of tippling houses has greatly increased, and many planters are ruined by drink. . . .

In Massachusetts John Eliot and Cotton Mather both are much concerned that "so little care was taken of their (the Negroes') precious and immortal souls," which were left to "a destroying ignorance merely for fear of thereby losing the benefit of their vassalage."

So throughout the colonies it is reported in 1678 that masters, "out of covetousness," are refusing to allow their slaves to be baptized; and in 1700 there is an earnest plea in Massachusetts for religious instruction of Negroes since it is "notorious" that masters discourage the "poor creatures" from baptism. In 1709 a Carolina clergyman writes to the secretary of the Society for the Propagation of the Gospel in England that only a few of 200 or more Negroes in his community were taught Christianity, but were not allowed to be baptized. Another minister writes, a little later, that he prevailed upon a master after much importuning to allow three Negroes to be baptized. In North Carolina In 1700 a clergyman of the Established Church complains that masters will not allow their slaves to be baptized for fear that a Christian slave is by law free. A few were instructed in religion, but not baptized. The Society for the Propagation of the Gospel combated this notion vigorously. . . .

5. *Early Restrictions.* "In the year 1624, a few years after the arrival of the first slave ship at Jamestown, Va., a Negro child was baptized and called William, and from that time on in almost all, if not all, the oldest churches in the South, the names of Negroes baptized into the church of God can be found upon the registers."

It was easy to make such cases an argument for more slaves. James Habersham, the Georgia companion of the Methodist Whitefield, said about 1730:

"I once thought it was unlawful to keep Negro slaves, but I am now induced to think God may have a higher end in permitting them to be brought to this Christian country, than merely to support their masters. Many of the poor slaves in America have already been made freemen of the heavenly Jerusalem and possibly a time may come when many thousands may embrace the gospel, and thereby be brought into the glorious liberty of the children of God. These, and other considerations, appear to plead strongly for a limited use of Negroes; for, while we can buy provisions in Carolina cheaper than we can here, no one will be induced to plant much."

In other cases there were curious attempts to blend religion and expediency, as for instance, in 1710, when a Massachusetts clergyman evolved a marriage ceremony for Negroes in which the bride solemnly promised to cleave to her husband "so long as God in his Providence" and the slave-trade let them live together!

The gradual increase of these Negro Christians, however, brought peculiar problems. Clergymen, despite the law, were reproached for taking Negroes into the church and still allowing them to be held as slaves. On the other hand it was not easy to know how to deal with the black church member after he was admitted. He must either be made a subordinate member of a white church or a member of a Negro church under the general supervision of whites. As the efforts of missionaries, like Dr. Bray, slowly increased the number of converts, both these systems were adopted. But the black congregations here and there soon aroused the suspicion and fear of the masters. . . .

This made Negro members of white churches a necessity in this colony, and there was the same tendency in other colonies. "Maryland passed a law in 1723 to suppress tumultuous meetings of slaves on Sabbath and other holy days," a measure primarily for good order, but also tending to curb independent religious meetings among Negroes. In 1800 complaints of Negro meetings were heard. Georgia in 1770 forbade slaves "to assemble on pretense of feasting," etc., and "any constable," on direction of a justice, is commanded to disperse any assembly or meeting of slaves "which may disturb the peace or endanger the safety of his Majesty's subjects; and every slave which may be found at such meeting, as aforesaid, shall and may, by order of such justice, immediately be corrected, without trial, by receiving on the bare back twenty-five stripes, with a whip, switch, or cowskin," etc. . . . In 1792 in a Georgia act "to protect religious societies in the exercise of their religious duties," punishment was provided for persons disturbing white congregations, but "no congregation or company of Negroes shall upon pretense of divine worship assemble themselves" contrary to the act of 1770. Whether or not such acts tended to curb the really religious meetings of the slaves or not it is not easy to know. Probably they did, although at the same time there was probably much disorder and turmoil among slaves, which sought to cloak itself under the name of the church. This was natural, for such assemblies were the only surviving African organizations, and they epitomized all there was in slave life outside of forced toil. . . .

In some colonies, like North Carolina, masters continued indifferent throughout the larger part of the eighteenth century. In New Hanover county of that state out of a thousand whites and two thousand slaves, 307 masters were baptized in 1742 but only nine slaves. . . .

6. *The Society for the Propagation of the Gospel.* "The Society for the Propagation of the Gospel in Foreign Parts" was incorporated under William III, on the 16th day of June, 1701, and the first meeting of the society under its charter was the 27th of June of the same year. Thomas Laud, Bishop of Canterbury, Primate and Metropolitan of all England, was appointed by his majesty the first president.

This society was formed with the view, primarily, of supplying the destitution of religious institutions and privileges among the inhabitants of the North American colonies, members the established church of England; and, secondarily, of extending the gospel to the Indians and Negroes. The society entered upon its duties with zeal, being patronized by the king and all the dignitaries of the Church of England.

They instituted inquiries into the religious condition of all the colonies, responded to "by the governors and persons of the best note," (with special reference to Episcopacy), and they perceived that their work "consisted of three great branches: the care and instruction of our people settled in the colonies; the conversion of the Indian savages, and the conversion of the Negroes." Before appointing missionaries they sent out a traveling preacher, the Rev. George Keith (an itinerant missionary), who associated with himself the Rev. John Talbot. Mr. Keith preached between North Carolina and Piscataqua river in New England, a tract above eight hundred miles in length, and completed his mission in two years, and returned and reported his labors to the society.

The annual meetings of this society were regularly held from 1702 to 1819 and 118 sermons preached before it by bishops of the Church of England, a large number of them distinguished for piety, learning, and zeal.

In June, 1702, the Rev. Samuel Thomas, the first missionary, was sent to the colony of South Carolina. The society designed he should attempt the conversion of the Yammosee Indians; but the governor, Sir Nathaniel Johnson, appointed him to the care of the people settled on the three branches of Cooper river, making Goose creek his residence. He reported his labors to the society and said "that he had taken much pains also in instructing the Negroes, and learned twenty of them to read." He died in October, 1706. He was succeeded by a number of missionaries. . . .

The society looked upon the instruction and conversion of the Negroes as a principal branch of its care, esteeming it a great reproach to the Christian name that so many thousands of persons should continue in the same state of pagan darkness under a Christian government and living in Christian families as they lay under formerly in their own heathen countries. The society immediately from its first institution strove to promote their conversion, and inasmuch as its income would not enable it to send numbers of catechists sufficient to instruct the Negroes, yet it resolved to do its utmost, and at least to give this work the mark of its highest approbation. Its officers wrote, therefore, to all their missionaries that they should use their best endeavors at proper times to instruct the Negroes, and should especially take occasion to recommend zealously to the masters to order their slaves, at convenient times, to come to them that they might be instructed.

The history of the society goes on to say: "It is a matter of commendation to the clergy that they have done thus much in so great and difficult a work. But, alas! what is the instruction of a few hundreds in several years with respect to the many thousands uninstructed, unconverted, living, dying, utter pagans. It must be confessed what hath been done is as nothing with regard to what a true Christian would hope to see effected." After stating several difficulties in respect to the religious instruction of the Negroes, it is said: "But the greatest obstruction is the masters themselves do not consider enough the obligation which lies upon them to have their slaves instructed." And in another place, "the society have always been sensible the most effectual way to convert the Negroes was by engaging their masters to countenance and promote their conversion." The bishop of St. Asaph, Dr. Fleetwood, preached a sermon before the society in the year 1711, setting forth the duty of instructing the Negroes in the Christian religion. The society thought this so useful a discourse that they printed and dispersed abroad in the plantations great numbers of that sermon in the same year; and in the year 1725 reprinted the same and dispersed again great numbers. The bishop of London, Dr. Gibson, (to whom the care of plantations abroad, as to religious affairs, was committed,) became a second advocate for the conversion of Negroes, and wrote two letters on the subject. The first in 1727, "addressed to masters and mistresses of families in the English plantations abroad, exhorting them to encourage and promote the instruction of their Negroes in the Christian faith. The second in the same year, addressed to the missionaries there, directing them to distribute the said letter, and exhorting them to give their assistance towards the instruction of the Negroes within their several parishes."

The society were persuaded this was the true method to remove the great obstruction to their conversion, and hoping so particular an application to the masters and mistresses from the See of London would have the strongest influence, they printed ten thousand copies of the letter to the masters and mistresses, which were sent to all the colonies on the continent and to all the British islands in the West Indies, to be distributed among the masters of families, and all other inhabitants. The society received accounts that these letters influenced many masters of families to have their servants instructed. The bishop of London soon after wrote "an address to serious Christians among ourselves, to assist the Society for Propagating the Gospel in carrying on this work."

In the year 1783, and the following, soon after the separation of our colonies from the mother country, the society's operations ceased, leaving in all the colonies forty-three missionaries, two of whom were in the Southern States— one in North and one in South Carolina. The affectionate valediction of the society to them was issued in 1785. "Thus terminated the connection of this noble society with our country, which, from the foregoing notices of its efforts, must have accomplished a great deal for the religious instruction of the Negro population."

7. *The Moravians, Methodists, Baptists, and Presbyterians.* The Moravians or United Brethren were the first who formally attempted the establishment of missions exclusively to the Negroes.

A succinct account of their several efforts, down to the year 1790, is given in the report of the Society for the Propagation of the Gospel among the Heathen, at Salem, N.C., October 5th, 1837, by Rev. J. Renatus Schmidt, and is as follows:

"A hundred years have now elapsed since the Renewed Church of the Brethren first attempted to communicate the gospel to the many thousand Negroes of our land. In 1737 Count Zinzendorf paid a visit to London and formed an acquaintance with General Oglethorpe and the trustees of Georgia, with whom he conferred on the subject of the mission to the Indians, which the brethren had already established in that colony (in 1735). Some of these gentlemen were associates under the will of Dr. Bray, who had left funds to be devoted to the conversion of the Negro slaves in South Carolina; and they solicited the Count to procure them some missionaries for this purpose. On his objecting that the Church of England might hesitate to recognize the ordination of the Brethren's missionaries, they referred the question to the Archbishop of Canterbury, Dr. Potter, who gave it as his opinion 'that the Brethren being members of an Episcopal Church, whose doctrines contained nothing repugnant to the Thirty-nine Articles, ought not to be denied free access to the heathen.' This declaration not only removed all hesitation from the minds of the trustees as to the present application, but opened the way for the labors of the Brethren amongst the slave population of the West Indies, a great and blessed work, which has, by the gracious help of God, gone on increasing even to the present day.

"Various proprietors, however, avowing their determination not to suffer strangers to instruct their Negroes, as they had their own ministers, whom they paid for that purpose, our brethren ceased from their efforts. It appears from the letters of Brother Spangenburg, who spent the greater part of the year 1749 at Philadelphia and preached the gospel to the Negroes in that city, that the labors of the Brethren amongst them were not entirely fruitless. Thus he writes, in 1751: 'On my arrival in Philadelphia, I saw numbers of Negroes still buried in all their native ignorance and darkness, and my soul was grieved for them. Soon after some of them came to me, requesting instruction, at the same time acknowledging their ignorance in the most affecting manner. They begged that a weekly sermon might be delivered expressly for their benefit. I complied with their request and confined myself to the most essential truths of scripture. Upwards of seventy Negroes attended on these occasions, several of whom were powerfully awakened, applied for further instruction, and expressed a desire to be united to Christ and his church by the sacrament of baptism, which was accordingly administered to them.'"

At the request of Mr. Knox, the English Secretary of State, an attempt was made to evangelize the Negroes of Georgia. "In 1774 the Brethren, Lewis Muller, of the Academy at Niesky, and George Wagner, were called to North America and in the year following, having been joined by Brother Andrew Broesing, of North Carolina, they took up their abode at Knoxborough, a plantation so called from its proprietor, the gentleman above mentioned. They were, however, almost constant sufferers from the fevers which prevailed in those parts, and Muller finished his course in October of the same year. He had preached the gospel with acceptance to both whites and blacks, yet without any abiding results. The two remaining Brethren being called upon to bear arms on the breaking out of the war of independence, Broesing repaired to Wachovia, in North Carolina, and Wagner set out in 1779 for England."

In the great Northampton revival, under the preaching of Dr. Edwards In 1735-6, when for the space of five or six weeks together the conversions averaged at least "four a day," Dr. Edwards remarks: "There are several Negroes who, from what was seen in them then and what is discernible in them since, appear to have been truly born again in the late remarkable season."

Direct efforts for the religious instruction of Negroes, continued through a series of years, were made by Presbyterians in Virginia. They commenced with the Rev. Samuel Davies, afterwards president of Nassau Hall, and the Rev. John Todd, of Hanover Presbytery.

In a letter addressed to a friend and member of the "Society in London for promoting Christian knowledge among the poor" in the year 1755, he thus expresses himself: "The poor neglected Negroes, who are so far from having money to purchase books, that they themselves are the property of others, who were originally

African savages, and never heard of the name of Jesus or his gospel until they arrived at the land of their slavery in America, whom their masters generally neglect, and whose souls none care for, as though immortality were not a privilege common to them, as with their masters; these poor, unhappy Africans are objects of my companion, and I think the most proper objects of the society's charity. The inhabitants of Virginia are computed to be about 300,000 men, the one-half of which number are supposed to be Negroes. The number of those who attend my ministry at particular times is uncertain, but generally about 300, who give a stated attendance; and never have I been so struck with the appearance of an assembly as when I have glanced my eye to that part of the meeting-house where they usually sit, adorned (for so it has appeared to me) with so many black countenances, eagerly attentive to every word they hear and frequently bathed in tears. A considerable number of them (about a hundred) have been baptized, after a proper time for instruction, having given credible evidence, not only of their acquaintance with the important doctrines of the Christian religion, but also a deep sense of them in their minds, attested by a life of strict piety and holiness. As they are not sufficiently polished to dissemble with a good grace, they express the sentiments of their souls so much in the language of simple nature and with such genuine indications of sincerity, that it is impossible to suspect their professions, especially when attended with a truly Christian life and exemplary conduct. There are multitudes of them in different places, who are willingly and eagerly desirous to be instructed and embrace every opportunity of acquainting themselves with the doctrines of the gospel; and though they have generally very little help to learn to read, yet to my agreeable surprise, many of them by dint of application in their leisure hours, have made such progress that they can intelligibly read a plain author, and especially their Bibles; and pity it is that any of them should be without them.

"The Negroes, above all the human species that I ever knew, have an ear for music and a kind of ecstatic delight in psalmody, and there are no books they learn so soon or take so much pleasure in as those used in that heavenly part of divine worship."

The year 1747 was marked, in the colony of Georgia, by the authorized introduction of slaves. Twenty-three representatives from the different districts met in Savannah, and after appointing Major Horton president, they entered into sundry resolutions, the substance of which was "that the owners of slaves should educate the young and use every possible means of making religious impressions upon the minds of the aged, and that all acts of inhumanity should be punished by the civil authority."

Methodism was introduced in New York in 1766, and the first missionaries were sent out by Mr. Wesley from New York in 1769. One of these says: "The number of blacks that attend the preaching affects me much." The first regular conference was held in Philadelphia, 1773. From this year to 1776 there was a great revival of religion in Virginia under the preaching of the Methodists in connection with Rev. Mr. Jarratt of the Episcopal Church, which spread through fourteen counties in Virginia and two in North Carolina. One letter states "the chapel was full of white and black;" another, "hundreds of Negroes were among them, with tears streaming down their faces." At Roanoke another remarks: "In general the white people were within the chapel and the black people without."

At the eighth conference in Baltimore in 1780 the following question appeared in the minutes: "Question 25. Ought not the assistant to meet the colored people himself and appoint helpers in his absence, proper white persons, and not suffer them to stay late and meet by themselves? Answer. Yes." Under the preaching of Mr. Garretson in Maryland "hundreds, both white and black, expressed their love for Jesus."

The first return of colored members distinct from white occurs in the minutes of 1786; White 18,791, colored 1,890. "It will be perceived from the above," says Dr. Bangs in his history of the Methodist Episcopal Church, "that a considerable number of colored persons had been received into the church, and were so returned in the minutes of the conference. Hence it appears that at an early period of the Methodist ministry in this country it had turned its attention to this part of the population."

In 1790 it was again asked: "What can be done to instruct poor children, white and black, to read? Answer. Let us labor as the heart and soul of one man to establish Sunday-schools in or near the place of public worship. Let persons be appointed by the bishops, elders, deacons, or preachers, to teach gratis all that will attend and have a capacity to learn." . . .

The first Baptist church in this country was founded in Providence, R. I., by Roger Williams in 1639. Nearly one hundred years after the settlement of America "only seventeen Baptist churches had arisen in it." The Baptist church in Charleston, S.C., was founded In 1690. The denomination advanced slowly through the middle and Southern States, and in 1790 it had churches in them all. Revivals of religion were enjoyed, particularly one in Virginia, which commenced In 1785 and continued until 1791 or 1792. "Thousands were converted and baptized, besides many who joined the Methodists and Presbyterians. A large number of Negroes were admitted to the Baptist Churches during the seasons of revival, as well as on ordinary occasions. They were, however, not gathered into churches distinct from the whites south of Pennsylvania except in Georgia."

"In general the Negroes were followers of the Baptists in Virginia, and after a while, as they permitted many colored men to preach, the great majority of them went to hear preachers of their own color, which was attended with many evils." . . .

George Leile or Lisle, sometimes called George Sharp, was born in Virginia about 1750. His master sometime before the American war removed and settled in Burke county, Georgia. Mr. Sharp was a Baptist and a deacon in a Baptist church, of which Rev. Matthew Moore was pastor. George was converted and baptized under Mr. Moore's ministry. . . .

About nine months after George Leile left Georgia, Andrew, surnamed Bryan, a man of good sense, great zeal, and some natural elocution, began to exhort his black brethren and friends. He and his followers were reprimanded and forbidden to engage further in religious exercises. He would, however, pray, sing, and encourage his fellow-worshippers to seek the Lord. Their persecution was carried to an inhuman extent. Their evening assemblies were broken up and those found present were punished with stripes! Andrew Bryan and Sampson, his brother, converted about a year after him, were twice imprisoned, and they with about fifty others were whipped. When publicly whipped, and bleeding under his wounds, Andrew declared that he rejoiced not only to be whipped, but would freely suffer death for the cause of Jesus Christ, and that while he had life and opportunity he would continue to preach Christ. He was faithful to his vow and, by patient continuance in well-doing, he put to silence and shamed his adversaries, and influential advocates and patrons were raised up for him. Liberty was given Andrew by the civil authority to continue his religious meetings under certain regulations. His master gave him the use of his barn at Brampton, three miles from Savannah, where he preached for two years with little interruption. . . .

The number of Baptists in the United States this year was 73,471, allowing one-fourth to be Negroes the denomination would embrace between 18,000 and 19,000.

The returns of colored members in the Methodist denomination from 1791 to 1795, inclusive, were 12,884, 13,871, 16,227, 13,814, 12,179. . . .

8. *The Sects and Slavery.* The approach of the Revolution brought heart-searching on many subjects, and not the least on slavery. The agitation was noticeable in the legislation of the time, putting an end to slavery in the North and to the slave-trade in all states. Religious bodies particularly were moved. In 1657 George Fox, founder of the Quakers, had impressed upon his followers in America the duty of converting the slaves, and he himself preached to them in the West Indies. The Mennonite Quakers protested against slavery in 1688, and from that time until the Revolution the body slowly but steadily advanced, step by step, to higher ground until they refused all fellowship to slaveholders. Radical Quakers, like Hepburn and Lay, attacked religious sects and Lay called preachers "a sort of devils that preach more to hell than they do to heaven, and

so they will do forever as long as they are suffered to reign in the worst and mother of all sins, slave-keeping."

In Virginia and North Carolina this caused much difficulty owing to laws against manumission early in the nineteenth century, and the result was wholesale migration of the Quakers. . . .

Judge Sewall, among the Massachusetts Congregationalists, had declared, in 1700, that slavery and the slave-trade were wrong, but his protest was unheeded. Later, in 1770 and after, strong Congregational clergymen, like Samuel Hopkins and Ezra Stiles, attacked slavery, but so democratic a church could take no united action. Although Whitefield came to defend the institution, John Wesley, founder of the Methodists, called the slave-trade the "sum of all villanies," and the General Conference in America, 1780, declared slavery "contrary to the laws of God, man, and nature and hurtful to society." From this high stand, however, the church quickly and rather ignominiously retreated. By 1780 it only sought the destruction of slavery "by all wise and prudent means," while preachers were allowed to hold their slaves in slave states. In 1787 the General Conference urged preachers to labor among slaves and receive worthy ones into full membership and "to exercise the whole Methodist discipline among them." Work was begun early among the slaves and they had so many members that their churches in the south were often called Negro churches. The church yielded further ground to the pro-slavery sentiment in 1816, but in 1844 the censure of a bishop who married a slaveholder rent the church in twain on the question.

The Baptists had Negro preachers for Negro members as early as 1773. They were under the supervision of whites and had no voice in general church affairs. The early Baptists held few slaves, and they were regarded as hostile to slavery in Georgia. The Philadelphia Association approved of abolition as early as 1789, and a Virginia Association urged emancipation in the legislature about the same time. In Kentucky and Ohio the Baptist Associations split on the question. The Baptists early interested themselves in the matter of slave marriages and family worship, and especially took spiritual care of the slaves of their own members. They took a stand against the slave-trade in 1818 and 1835. After the division on the subject of missions the Missionary Baptists began active proselyting among the slaves.

The Presbyterian Synod of 1787 recommended efforts looking toward gradual emancipation, and in 1795 the question of excluding slaveholders was discussed, but it ended in an injunction of "brotherly love" for them. In 1815, 1818, and 1835 the question was dismissed and postponed, and finally in 1845 the question was dropped on the ground that Christ and the Apostles did not condemn slavery. At the time of the war the church finally divided. . . .

13. *The Negro Church in 1890*. (From the Eleventh United States Census). There were in the United States in 1890, 23,462 Negro churches. Outside of these there were numbers of Negroes who are members of white churches, but they are not distinguished from others:

We may now consider these organizations by denominations:

REGULAR BAPTISTS (COLORED)

The colored Baptists of the South constitute the most numerous body of Regular Baptists. Not all colored Baptists are embraced in this division; only those who have separate churches, associations, and state conventions. There are many colored Baptists in Northern States, who are mostly counted as members of churches, belonging to white associations. . . .

The first state convention of colored Baptists was organized in North Carolina in 1866, the second in Alabama, and the third in Virginia in 1867, the fourth in Arkansas in 1868, and the fifth in Kentucky in 1869. There are colored conventions in fifteen states and the District of Columbia.

In addition to these organizations the colored Baptists of the United States have others more general in character: The American National Convention, the purpose of which is "to consider the moral, intellectual, and religious growth of the denomination," to deliberate upon questions of general concern, and to devise methods to bring the churches and members of the race closer together; the Consolidated American Missionary Convention, the General Association of the Western States and Territories, the Foreign Mission Convention of the United States, and the New England Missionary Convention. All except one are missionary in their purpose.

The Regular Baptists (colored) are represented in fifteen states, all in the South, or on the border, and the District of Columbia. In Virginia and Georgia they are very numerous, having in the latter 200,516, and in the former 199,871 communicants. . . .

AFRICAN METHODIST EPISCOPAL ZION

A congregation of colored people, organized in New York City, in 1796, was the nucleus of the African Methodist Episcopal Zion Church. This congregation originated in a desire of colored members of the Methodist Episcopal Church to hold separate meetings in which they "might have an opportunity to exercise their spiritual gifts among themselves, and thereby be more useful to one another." They built a church, which was dedicated in 1800, the full name of the denomination subsequently organized being given to it.

The church entered into an agreement in 1801 by which it was to receive certain pastoral supervision from the Methodist Episcopal Church. It had preachers of its own, who supplied its pulpit in part. In 1820 this arrangement terminated, and in the same year a union of colored churches in New York, New Haven, Long Island, and Philadelphia was formed, and rules of government adopted. Thus was the African Methodist Episcopal Zion Church formally organized.

The first annual conference was held in 1821. It was attended by nineteen preachers, representing six churches and 1,426 members. Next year James Varick was chosen superintendent of the denomination, which was extended over the states of the North chiefly, until the close of the civil war, when it entered the South to organize many churches.

In its polity lay representation has long been a prominent feature. Laymen are in its annual conferences as well as in its general conference, and there is no bar to the ordination of women. Until 1880 its superintendents or bishops were elected for a term of four years. In that year the term of the office was made for life or during good behavior. Its system is almost identical with that of the Methodist Episcopal Church, except the presence of laymen in the annual conference, the election of presiding elders on the nomination of the presiding bishop, instead of their appointment by the bishop alone, and other small divergences. Its general conference meets quadrennially. Its territory is divided into seven episcopal districts, to each of which a bishop is assigned by the general conference.

The church is represented in twenty-eight states and the District of Columbia. It is strongest in North Carolina, where it has 111,919 communicants. Alabama comes next, with 79,231 communicants. . . .

COLORED METHODIST EPISCOPAL

The Colored Methodist Episcopal Church was organized in 1870 of colored members and ministers of the Methodist Episcopal Church, South.

Before the late civil war the Methodist Episcopal Church, South, did a large evangelistic work among the Negroes. Bishop McTyeire, of that body, in his "History of Methodism," says:

"As a general rule Negro slaves received the gospel by Methodism from the same preachers and in the same churches with their masters, the galleries or a portion of the body of the house being assigned to them. If a separate building was provided, the Negro congregation was an appendage to the white, the pastor usually preaching once on Sunday for them, holding separate official meetings with their leaders, exhorters, and preachers, and administering discipline, and making return of members for the annual minutes." For the Negroes on plantations, who were not privileged to attend organized churches, special missions were begun as early as 1829. In 1845, the year which marks the beginning of the separate existence of the Methodist Episcopal Church, South, there were in the Southern conferences of Methodism, according to Bishop McTyeire, 124,000 members of the slave population, and in 1860 about 207,000.

In 1866, after the opening of the South to Northern churches had given the Negro members opportunity to join the African Methodist Episcopal, the African Methodist Episcopal Zion, and other Methodist bodies, it was found that of the 207,742 colored members which the church, South, had in 1800 only 78,742 remained. The general conference of 1866 authorized these colored members, with their preachers, to be organized into separate congregations and annual conferences, and the general conference of 1870 appointed two bishops to organize the colored conferences into a separate and independent church. This was done in December, 1870, the new body taking the name "Colored Methodist Episcopal Church." Its rules limited the privilege of membership to Negroes. The Colored Methodist Episcopal Church has the same articles of religion, the same form of government, and the same discipline as its parent body. Its bishops are elected for life. One of them, Bishop L. H. Holsey, says that for some years the body encountered strong opposition from colored people because of its relation to the Methodist Episcopal Church, South, but that this prejudice has now almost entirely disappeared.

CUMBERLAND PRESBYTERIAN (COLORED)

This body was organized in May, 1869, at Murfreesboro, Tenn., under the direction of the General Assembly of the Cumberland Presbyterian Church. It was constituted of colored ministers and members who had been connected with that church. Its first synod, the Tennessee, was organized in 1871. . . .

17. A Southern City. There are in the city of Atlanta, Ga., the following Negro churches:

The Negro population of Atlanta (1900) was 35,727. This means one church to every 662 men, women, and children, or one to every 130 families. Half the total population is enrolled in the church, probably nearly two-thirds of the adult population. The active paying membership is much smaller.

There are 29 Baptist churches, with an active membership of over 5,000, and $60,000 worth of real estate.

Three extracts, from the reports of first-hand young investigators, throw some general light on the general character of these churches:

From an old colored citizen of Atlanta, I learned of the marked advancement he has witnessed in the erection of church edifices and in the character of worship. Just after the war, when the colored people were in their bitter struggle for the necessities of life, he says the race worshipped in box cars frequently, for they could not always obtain houses. As conditions changed the churches were moved to better quarters. The people generally supported the church very well until finally the Negro began to pattern his churches after the white churches, building structures which were far too costly for the Negro's financial status at the time. It seemed very sad to this old man that the "worship of the good, old time" was not what it used to be.

The character of the pastors of the seven Methodist churches in my district seems, in every case, to be good. Such phrases as "you could not find any one to say anything against his character," express the sentiments of the members of these churches. The education of the pastors is fair, although there are exceptions. Among the schools represented by the different pastors, are: Bennet College, Clark University, Turner Theological Seminary (Morris Brown Theological Department), and Gammon Theological Seminary.

The education of the members seems to vary from fair to very poor. In the case of my largest church (membership 740) a large number of the members were graduates of Clark University, and nearly all have a fair education. However, in the smaller churches, having from 16 to 277 members, the education of the congregations was very meagre.

A great majority of the members of the smaller churches are common laborers and are quite poor. The members of the larger churches are in moderate circumstances, and although most of them are laborers, there is a fair percent of artisans and business men among them.

Most of the churches have relief societies to look after the charity and relief work. Some churches did no special relief work. One church, however, has a deaconess, who devotes her time to such work. The money expended in such work varied from nothing to $100 in the different churches. That spent for missions varied from nothing to $200.

The government of all Baptist churches is extremely democratic. Each member has the power of taking part in any of the general meetings and of voting. The financial and business matters of the church are attended to by the deacons' board. The power of the pastor varies somewhat according to the different congregations, and the difference of esteem in which the pastor is held sometimes governs his influence and sway over them.

All Baptists agree that each church is complete in itself and has the power, therefore, to choose its own ministers and to make such rules as it deems to be most in accordance with the advancement of its best interest and the purpose of its existence. The time that a pastor is to serve is not fixed but varies according to the wishes of the people. If the people like the pastor, he is kept as long as he desires to remain, but if they do not, he is put out immediately.

The general condition of the ten Baptist churches in this part of the city shows that on a whole their work is not progressing very fast. Over half of them are very small, with very small memberships, and very ignorant and illiterate pastors. And certainly where there are ignorant leaders of ignorant people not very much progress or good influence can be expected to follow. The places of meeting are not comfortable, being poorly lighted and unclean most of the time, and in some cases the church was situated in an unhealthy place. These, however, represent the worst half; and on the other hand, the larger churches are progressing very fast and their influence is gradually but surely spreading far and wide, and includes all grades of society. Many of the most influential and wealthy Negro churches of the city are Baptist.

The pastors of the Congregational, Episcopal, and Presbyterian churches have excellent characters, and are doing much towards lifting the moral standard and religious life of the people. Not only are they earnest workers, but they are also well equipped for their work. They are well educated, one being a graduate of Fisk and Yale Universities, another is a graduate of St. Augustine College, Raleigh, N.C., and took a post graduate course at Howard University, Washington, D.C., and one is a graduate of Lincoln University, who completed both the college and theological courses. They have excellent reputations, and are held in high esteem by their Alma Maters. The Yale graduate is well known North and South. The character of the members of these churches is good. They are quiet and intelligent, and there is no emotionalism in the churches. Most of the members of these churches are at least high school graduates, and a large per cent is composed of business and professional men and women. . . .

No. 24. Primitive Baptist—Active members thirty.

The pastor can read and write, but is not well educated. His character is good, but he will not do laborious work, which the members think he ought to do outside his church work. Most of the members were slaves, and the church is about twenty-eight years old. It has no influence except among its members and it began where it now stands, and was organized by most of the present members. No collection is taken except on communion day. The building is an old wooden one of rough lumber, raised about five feet from the ground. I looked through one of the cracks to get a view of the interior. Its seating capacity is about seventy-five. The benches are of rough lumber. The lamps (four oil lamps) are hanging from the shabby ceiling. I saw a large Bible upon an altar of dressed lumber. One of the oldest members told me that he gave all the coal and oil used this year. He

said that the church had a meeting once a month, and every three months communion and washing of feet. They believed in having no music, save singing.
They believed in the pastor's working for his living just as the members did, and
because the present pastor would not do this they were going to let him go. I
could not find the pastor nor could they tell me where he or any of the other
members lived.

This is an example of church communion among lowly ignorant and old people—a survival from the past. Such groups tend to change—to absorption into
some larger group or to degenerate through bad leaders and bad members. Two
other specimens of this type follow:

No. 5. Baptist—Fourteen active members.

The old store, which is used for church purposes, is a very shabby building.
A few chairs, two lamps, and a small table and a Bible make up the furniture.
All of the members are old and ignorant. There is no Sunday-school connected
with the church. The church government is a pure democracy, the pastor and
the active members governing the church. The members are ignorant and of
questionable character. The pastor is an old and ignorant man, but is fairly
good. He went away two years ago and left his flock because they did not give
him the proper support. The church did not split but degenerated. Very little
charitable work is done. When one of the members is sick he is given aid if he
asks to be aided. There are several ignorant Negroes living in the vicinity of
the church.

No. 26. Baptist (Missionary)—165 active members.

The education of the pastor is fair, but his character is not good. He has the
reputation of being very immoral. He is, however, a good speaker. There are a few
intelligent members, but the larger portion of the members are very illiterate.
There is connected with the church an organized body of women (Woman's Mission) which looks after the poor, the old, and the sick. The church was organized
in 1878, in the old barracks of this city. It has had eight pastors since its organization, and it is very influential over a large number of people in the vicinity. The
church building is large and was once a beautiful wooden structure, but at present it is very much in need of repairs. It is furnished fairly well on the inside, and
is situated in one of the black belts of Atlanta. There is an official board
appointed by or elected by the church. This official board attends to the affairs
of the church. The pastor presides over the meetings. The pastor now in charge
was once forced to give up his charge and leave the city, so the general report
goes, because of his immorality. There were seven preachers called during his
absence and two church splits, brought about through the pastors who were leading. Then the first pastor was recalled. While many of the members and the pas-

tor bear the reputation of being immoral, they are also said to be very good to the poor. The entire collection of every fifth Sunday goes to the poor. There is a fairly good Sunday-school connected with the church, and the Sunday-school has recently purchased an organ for the church. The church debt is $400.

To reform a perverted group like this is extremely difficult, and yet the work is slowly going on.

No. 30. Colored Methodist Episcopal—Fifty active members.

The church was first begun with one family, at the old barracks, in a one-room cabin. From there it was moved to Peters street, to Shell hall, where it was joined by a second family. Then it was moved to Markham street, where it was joined by others; then to Hunter street, in a white church, where it was burned. It was then re-established at Taylor street, in a store house, from whence it was moved to its present site. It now has a fair brick building, which cost about $3,000, and is fairly well-furnished inside. The present building and parsonage were built largely by the co-operative labor of its own members. The pastors are noisy but of pretty good education.

No. 34. Methodist Episcopal—115 active members.

The pastor has attended Clark University, and is a graduate of Gammon. He is well-liked by his parishioners. The church recruits its members from the railroad hands and their families, who are for the greater part uneducated. Some charitable work is done by different societies in the church. Such, for instance, as aiding paupers. The church is nineteen years old. It is not in debt, and has a large membership. Its influence is wide-spread, being one of the largest churches in this particular section. The church has connected with it a Woman's Home Missionary Society and an Epworth League. Through the missionary society and through the help department of the league, much charitable work is being done in the community. I am told that during this year a poor woman was taken and given a decent burial whereas otherwise the county would have had it to do. There is also a parsonage adjoining the church, which, together with the church, is estimated to be worth $1,500.

The services in churches of this type are calculated to draw the crowd, and are loud and emotional. . . .

No. 42. African Methodist Episcopal—600 active members.

The pastor is of good character and education, a graduate of Howard University Theological School. The members vary from the old, poor, and respectable, to the young and well educated. In 1866 this church was organized by Rev. J. J. Wood; the membership increased steadily until 1868. The church moved into a new building. This old structure itself is yet sufficiently well preserved to show what a nice building it was. . . . The present structure is a handsome one, with a beautiful interior. The building is granite and is finished inside in yellow pine. Beautiful glass windows adorn the church and there are electric light fixtures and theatre chairs in the auditorium, while a $2,500 pipe organ also adds to the beauty. The church is very large, having a seating capacity of 3,000. The total membership is about 1,400, and is composed of some of the most influential and cultured colored people of the city, a considerable number being school teachers and property owners and respected people. The church is valued at $50,000 and a statement of the money paid out during the previous year shows a total of $4,964.86, which includes $984.86 for salary to the pastor and $3,020 for the church debt. This church does a great deal of relief work among the indigent members. Last year the amount expended was $200 for such work and $360 for missions; $500 was given to the general connections.

The growth of such great Negro institutions involves much effort and genius for organization. The greatest danger is that of the "split;" that is, the withdrawal of a dissatisfied minority and the formation of a new church. . . .

No. 54. Christian—Thirty active members.

The leader and pastor is a man of questionable character. The members are mainly the middle working classes of average intelligence. Very little charitable and relief work is done because the church has a hard time to keep on its feet. The church drew out of No. 37 in 1897 and established this church, and since that time the young church has been struggling for existence. The church build-ing is a large barn-like structure, roughly finished on the outside and rather crudely furnished on the inside. It will accommodate about 400 people. . . .

32. Negro Laymen and the Church. Some 200 Negro laymen of average intelli-gence, in all parts of the country, were asked a schedule of questions and answered as follows. The states represented are Georgia, Alabama, Florida, Louisiana, Mississippi, Texas, North Carolina, South Carolina, Virginia, Ken-tucky, Tennessee, Arkansas, Colorado, Illinois and Pennsylvania. The answers of a few ministers are included:

So far as you have observed what is the present condition of our churches in your community?

Very good	23
Good	49
Progressing, improving, prosperous	16
Heavy financial burdens hindering spiritual conditions	9
Fair financially, low spiritually; more intelligent	3
Not so well attended as formerly, but attendants more devoted	2
Good, bad and indifferent	6
Fair, with vast room for improvement	13

Well attended, but mostly in financial straits	12
Poor, bad; not what they should be	12
Here and there a sign of improvement	1
Too much involved with financial efforts	5
Lack of piety and true missionary spirit; need of earnest preachers	2
At a standstill spiritually; not influential enough among the young	2
As far as general improvement is concerned, would say,	
Congregationalists, the Methodists, then Baptists	1
Retrograding spiritually	4
Can't say, don't know; not answered	5

Is their influence, on the whole, toward pure, honest, upright living on the part of the members?

Yes	71
To a very large extent	13
To some extent	17
Room for improvement	5
Not so on account of preacher	1
Belief and doctrine advocated too much to have influence	
for good, upright living	1
Purport simply to bear good influence over the people	1
Not sufficient emphasis laid on Christian living	2
Influence good, but members do not live as they should	2
Cannot say positively yes, though there are exceptions	3
No	17
Generally so; much advancement	6
Not answered	5

Are the ministers usually good men? If not, what are their chief faults? Cite some specific cases, with or without names:

Yes	37
Generally good men	10
Majority good; some exceptions. Faults: Intemperance, dishonesty,	
careless living, selfish ambition, sexual impurity	31
Some good, some bad	9
Some good, majority bad	4
Few good, majority bad	3
Not intelligent	6

Fairly good	3
Chief faults: Selfishness and dogmatism	4
Fault of some: Immorality	8
Fault of some: Deceptiveness	1
Fault of some: Too great love for money	3
Moral status low	1
Faults: Lack of earnestness, sexual impurity, intemperance, love of worldly things	6
Proportion of good ones is increasing	2
Fault of some: Bigamy	1
Only a few whom I have not heard rumors about	1
Appear good, but do not know how to influence the young	1
"No better than they ought to be"	2
Some good, but among others the chief faults are sexual impurity, improper attention to women, and selfishness	4
No, not generally so	6
Miscellaneous	7
Unanswered	5

Of the ministers whom you know, how many are notoriously immoral? What direction does their immorality take: sexual impurity, dishonesty in money matters, drunkenness, or what? Cite some particular instances, with or without names:

None immoral; all good men	28
Very few immoral	2
Some few are not what they should be; do not come up to the true standard	4
One or more are lax in financial matters	8
Some few are sexually impure and dishonest in money matters; majority good	12
Intemperate	8
Some intemperate; some cannot be trusted in money matters	1
Chief faults of some: Sexual impurity and intemperance	8
Chief fault: Sexual impurity	12
Many guilty of all	6
Not answered	17

Some of the answers are:

ALABAMA

I can name a few who are said to be immoral, but cannot say from personal knowledge that they are notoriously immoral.—*Girard*.

I believe we have some ministers who are guilty of every fault named in question four, but I think that one of their worst habits is in their tearing down good church buildings; and in their rebuilding they don't seem to have any care for the strain they place upon their members.—*Mobile*.

I think proselyting and exaggerating minor doctrinal differences a real hindrance. Also the loose methods in vogue of conducting church finances—both in collecting and expending—a serious drawback.—*Mobile*.

Two at present in the city. I know others, but they are not preaching here now. Sexual impurity. They are the only ones in the city with the degree of D.D.—one a Methodist, the other Baptist. They both ruined the good names of two young women.—*Mobile*.

COLORADO

I know some 500 ministers. Of that number probably about 100 are immoral; 10 percent of the 100 are sexually immoral, 20 percent dishonest, 70 percent drink.—*Colorado Springs*.

FLORIDA

I know of no minister who is notoriously immoral. Yet occasionally there comes a little confusion in the churches here because when money is collected for one purpose, through the minister's influence it is used for another. Such actions always do cause church fusses which last for some time.—*Gainesville*.

I know of five around this city who are grossly immoral. Their immorality takes these directions: intemperance, sexual immorality, and dishonesty in money matters. Two cases of gross immorality came to light recently on two preachers. One preacher has recently been dropped for dishonesty in money matters.—*Jacksonville*.

GEORGIA

I cannot say how many; perhaps twenty. Women and unfair dealings in money matters. I have known comparatively few who drink, and still fewer who drink to excess.—*Atlanta.*

About one-tenth of all the ministers in that community (Perry, Ga.) are notoriously immoral, especially in the direction of sexual impurity, dishonesty and drunkenness.—*Atlanta.*

One of the most common and general faults against preachers is their failure to pay promptly financial obligations. I know a few who are said to be guilty of sexual impurity, some others who get drunk.—*Atlanta.*

I know ten and could name more if I would strain my memory who are notoriously immoral. Some of these are sexual impurity, dishonesty in money matters and drunkenness. I have seen this on the streets of Albany. I have not seen any preacher drunk on the streets here in Brunswick.—*Brunswick.*

By common report, yes. Sexual impurity, dishonesty in money matters lead in order given. I know ministers who drink, but they never to my knowledge become intoxicated.—*College.*

I could name as many as ten who drink whiskey and are untruthful. Many are dishonest in money matters. There is a preacher near my home who is a downright drunkard. He first led his members astray by indulging them in this evil habit, so that now it is a corrupt church.—*Jewells.*

What is the greatest need of our churches?

An earnest, consecrated, educated, wide-awake, intelligent ministry	24
An educated, well-trained Christian ministry	25
A good, pure ministry	6
True conversion, practical religion, true Christianity	4
Honest, upright leaders, both preachers and officers	9
Earnest, educated, consecrated Christian workers	5
Consecrated ministers and faithful members	5
More money and better preachers	5
The spirit of Christ and the Holy Ghost	2
Finance	3
Unity and practical Christian living	1
Do not know	1

Some answers are:

I think there is need of improvement in intellect and in a financial way.—*Vincent, Ark.*

A practical knowledge of right and wrong.—*Mobile, Ala.*

Regard for spiritual ideals.—*Mobile, Ala.*

A more perfect knowledge of the requirement of Jesus upon his followers.— *Colorado Springs, Col.*

Downright seriousness and actual missionary spirit and efforts.—*Denver, Col.*

High-toned Christian ministers in the pulpits and teachers of the same kind in Sunday-schools.—*Atlanta, Ga.*

Able and pure men as pastors and a warm oratory to reach and hold the masses.—*Atlanta, Ga.*

I should say more spiritual life. This lack is very general in our churches of today.—*Atlanta, Ga.*

First of all, better men in the ministry. It would follow that the members would be better.—*Augusta, Ga.*

The greatest need is to live up to what we preach. Do away with so much emotion and do practical work. "If ye love me keep my commandments."— *Brunswick, Ga.*

1. Properly trained ministers. 2. Upright, cultured and Christian officers who possess business knowledge. 3. Bibles for congregational reading. 4. Song books for congregational singing.—*Macon, Ga.*

Decidedly, an educated ministry and a higher standard of morality.—*Rome, Ga.*

1. Pure ministry. 2. Less costly edifices. 3. More charitable work. 4. Practical sermons, i.e., how to live, etc.—*Savannah, Ga.*

Thoughtful workers.—*Thomasville, Ga.*

Moral ministers who are able to chastise immorality.—*Princeton, Ky.*

1. The Holy Spirit's power. 2. Clean, heroic, unselfish pastors who love God, righteousness and souls. 3. Deacons who fill the scripture standard. 4. Members who fear God because they are really new creatures in Christ.—*Jackson, Miss.*

The continued emphasizing of intelligent worship, spirituality instead of formality and efforts to keep them from substituting respectability and high social forms for Christian piety.—*Allegheny City, Pa.*

Good preachers, who read, study, and can apply what they read. Thinkers who will make the churches attractive. Church boards composed of those who are not afraid to hold their preacher to a certain standard or get rid of him.— *Darlington, S.C.*

33. Southern Whites and the Negro Church. The difficulty of getting valuable expressions on the Negro churches from Southern white people is that so few of them know anything about these churches. No human beings live further apart than separate social classes, especially when lines of race and color and historic antipathies intervene. Few white people visit Negro churches and those who do go usually for curiosity or "fun," and consequently seek only certain types. The endeavor was made in this case, however, to get the opinion of white people whose business relations or sympathies have brought them into actual contact with these churches. A few of the names in this list are of Northern people, but the great majority are white Southerners. The circular sent out was as follows:

> Your name has been handed to us as that of a person interested in the Negroes of your community and having some knowledge of their churches. We are making a study of Negro churches and would particularly like to have your opinion on the following matters:
> 1. What is the present condition of the Negro churches in your community?
> 2. Is their influence, on the whole, toward pure, honest life?
> 3. Are the Negro ministers in your community good men?
> 4. Are the standards of Negro morality being raised?
> We would esteem it a great favor if you would give us your opinion on these points.

R. B. Smith, County School Commissioner of Greene County, Woodville, Ga.:

1. Not good.
2. No.
3. No.
4. No.

I have given you my candid opinion of such churches and ministers that I know. There are some exceptions to the above. 1. There is a Presbyterian Church in Greensboro that has an intelligent pastor who is a good, true man. 2. I also think that the Methodist Church of same place is also doing pretty good work. A large portion of the ministers are ignorant and in some instances are bad men. I am truly sorry to have to write the above, but it is too true.

W. J. Groom, Princeton, Ky.:

1. Very slow, if any advancement.
2. No.
3. Very few.
4. No.

I regret to say, in my opinion, the Negro race has not advanced religiously, morally or financially. They have some few commendable ministers, but the majority are immoral and dishonest. . . .

A Real Estate Agent, Florence, S.C.:

The Methodist Episcopal Church, North, and the Baptist Church: these churches were well attended, and one reason was that the ministers were their political leaders. Of late years a good many men who have learned to read and write have been going about preaching, some I know of no character. The consequence has been that many new congregations have been started, and although not large, the tendency has been to do more harm than good. These Negro ministers (so-called) are too lazy to work, and make their money in an easy way, principally from the most ignorant Negro women. At present, I think the Negro ministers at the established Methodist Episcopal Church, North, the African Methodist Episcopal Church and Baptist Church are very good men; have not heard anything against their characters. But my opinion is that for real religious training of the Negro the Episcopal Church and Roman Catholic Church would be the best for the Negro, the first named from the example and training, and the latter the confession they would have to make to the priest—the latter more from fear. My opinion, again, is that the Negroes are more immoral, as they read and know what has been done and is being done by the immoral, unreligious white men of the country, and I believe that the example set by the white men of low character has been the greatest cause for the immorality of the Negro. Take for example that crime of rape. I don't know of a section where the whites are refined, nice people and treat the Negroes nicely, but let them know their places, where such an attempt has occurred. How can you expect the Negro women to be virtuous when the white men will continue to have intercourse with them? How can you blame the Negroes for committing murder when the example is set them by the white man?

We must face the truth. If any dirty work is to be done a white man hires a Negro to do it for him. If a member of a church does not wish to be seen going to buy whisky he sends a Negro. If these are facts, what an example to set to an inferior race! And they are facts and a shame on our white race. It seems to me that the Negroes are more immoral here than they used to be and the fault is due mostly to the example set them by the white men. . . .

Wm. Hayne Leavell, Minister, Houston, Tex.:

I am sorry to have to answer you that since coming to Texas I have not been able to know anything of the Negroes or their churches. Out here they seem to be a very different sort from those among whom I was brought up, and in whom I have always been interested, and by whom always been well received. Here they are altogether to themselves, and I do not think I know personally a solitary

Negro minister. It is true I have for ten years been a man busily driven, but the one or two attempts I have made to help the Negroes have not encouraged me to try again. I know only that there are very many church organizations of the various denominations, but of their quality I know nothing. . . .

E. C. Moncure, Judge County Court, Bowling Green, Va.:

First, I have great sympathy with the Negro race and my opinion if anything, I fear, will be a little biased in their favor.

The Negro seems to be naturally a very religious person, full of emotion and human sympathy, mixed up with some superstition and suspicion.

The Negroes are devoted to their churches and will undergo many privations to contribute to church building. They have great pride in their churches, and to be turned out of church is the most humiliating condition in their minds. A Negro convicted of larceny will suffer under the burden of his humiliation from being "turned out of the church" much more than from his disgrace of criminal conviction. Of course that remark does not apply to those who are the leaders of the church. Twenty-five years ago the Negro churches were controlled by much inferior men than to-day. The Negro churches in any community of to-day are quite well organized, with well-attended Sunday-schools, and are progressing. They have an over-zeal in building church houses, and are striving to emulate the white people in having good and neat houses. Their church discipline is rather loose. This, in a measure, comes from the great number of unconverted persons in their churches, for all Negroes must belong to the church; and a great many of their preachers are not educated and not of the highest character, so that they are not particular enough in receiving candidates into their communion. But, in my opinion, the Negroes are gradually improving along many lines. The trouble is with us white people, who, setting a judgment on their progress, expect and demand too much in a small space of time. But the influence toward pure, honest lives, upon the whole, is good; that is, the preponderating influence.

Of the colored registered vote lately voting on local option in my county, the abridged electorate, consisting principally of the educated and owners of property, nearly as a unit voted against whiskey.

Not all of the Negro ministers of my community are good men. In the main, they are, but some are ignorant and superstitious. But with all this, I am clearly of the opinion that the standards of Negro morality are being slowly and gradually raised.

To sum up, I do not think that Negro education and evangelization are failures by any means. In my acquaintance there are some noble examples of progress, faithfulness and devotion to principle.

CHAPTER FIFTEEN

The White Christ

This piece was published in *The Crisis* in 1915.

It seems fair to judge the Christianity of white folk by two present-day developments: the World War and Billy Sunday. As to the widespread and costly murder that is being waged today by the children of the Prince of Peace, comment is quite unnecessary. It simply spells the failure of Christianity. As to Billy Sunday, there is room for opinions. Personally we do not object to him; he is quite natural under the circumstances and a fit expression of his day. He is nearly the same thing as the whirling dervish, the snake-dancer, and devotee of "Mumbo Jumbo." Such methods of appealing to primitive passions and emotions have been usual in the history of the world. Today they are joined, in the case of Mr. Sunday, to picturesque abuse of the English langauge, unusual contortions, and a curious moral obtuseness which allows Mr. Sunday to appropriate a whole speech belonging to Robert Ingersoll and use it as his own. The result has been a large number of converts and widespread demand for Mr. Sunday's services. All this seems necessary. Evidently Mr. Sunday's methods are the only ones that appeal to white Christians. Reason does not appeal. Suffering and poverty does not appeal. The lynching and burning of human beings and torturing of women has no effect. But the contortions of Mr. Sunday bring people down the sawdust trail.
Selah!

But hereafter let no white man sneer at the medicine men of West Africa or the howling of the Negro revival. The Negro church is at least democratic. It welcomes everybody. It draws no color line.

CHAPTER SIXTEEN

The Gospel According to Mary Brown

This short story was published in *The Crisis* in 1919. It is a creative rendition of the Gospel story of Mary and Jesus, set in the early twentieth-century American South and played out by poor southern black people. The construction of Jesus as a black man was a poignant and radical move on the part of Du Bois, who often pointed out that although white Americans claimed Jesus as their savior, it was black Americans who actually lived more Christlike lives.

She was very small and pretty and black and lived in the cabin beyond the Big Road and down the lane by the creek, there where field on field of green cotton was flowering in the spring. And one night as she sat there all alone and wistful, watching the stars, a woman passed by and hailed her. She shrank back in the shadows, but the woman smiled and said full softly:

"Fear not, Mary: for thou hast found favor with God."

And then Mary knew, and she brought out the Old Book and read the lines aloud, following them with her little dark finger:

"My soul doth—magnify the Lord. . . .

"For He hath regarded the low—estate of his handmaiden, for behold from—henceforth all—generations shall call me blessed . . ."

Even as she read the door flew wide, and Pain stood beside her. He thrust and threw her poor little body and wracked and burst her thews in sunder. She moaned, but did not scream—and thus at last, in years of hours, she brought forth her first-born son; and she called his name Joshua.

Day after day she sat and watched his perfect little form. Was he not a beautiful baby? His skin was black velvet; his eyes were star-sown midnights, set in milk; his tiny teeth, white pearls; and his hair all tender tendrils of silk.

Sometimes—some very little times—a pain caught her as she cuddled him close. Would it not be better for him if he were whiter? Brown, or yellow, or dusky cream? Then she would say fiercely: No! No! Is not Love, who is God, his Father? And would his Father send a black baby to this world just to make him suffer?

And so each night after work she took him out beneath the stars, and the glory of the Lord shone round about them, and she heard the angels singing:

"Glory to God in the highest and on earth Peace, good-will toward men."

Thus did Mary, the mother, begin to dream dreams. And the child grew and waxed strong in spirit, filled with wisdom, and the grace of God was upon him.

Now his mother went to town every Christmas to settle for her crops, but it was not until he was twelve years old that he went with her, and saw town for the first. How marvelous and wonderful to him was the revelation.

Mary finished her work and started home, but Joshua tarried behind. When Mary found him not, she turned back seeking him. After three days she found him in a church, sitting in the midst of the deacons, both hearing them and asking them questions:

Why were colored folk poor?

Why were they afraid?

Whose father was God?

Did the deacons know God? Well, he did. God was his own Father.

And all that heard him were astonished at his understanding and answers. But his mother said unto him:

"Son, why did you do me this-a-way?"

And he answered: "Wist ye not, that I must be about my Father's business."

And Mary caught her breast in pain, for how may a father be mentioned when one's father is only God? But she kept all his sayings in her heart.

So Joshua went back to the plantation and worked. He ploughed and picked cotton and hoed and drove mules and, finally, learned to be a carpenter; and always he increased in wisdom and stature and in favor with God and man.

But not, alas! with all white men. Most of them mistrusted him. They could not place him. He was neither sullen nor impudent. But he looked at them with a certain, clear understanding and calm sense of authority; he carried himself like a man, and this they resented.

"Is not this the carpenter, the son of Mary?" they asked. "Didn't we keep him on the plantation and out of school? And yet, he's strutting and talking and preaching; he's putting ideas into niggers' heads." And they slipped down to the old wooden church by the creek and listened to him preach.

The people were scattered on the green under the trees, eating their lunch out of baskets. And Joshua opened his mouth and taught them, saying:

"Blessed are the poor; blessed are they that mourn; blessed are the meek; blessed are the merciful; blessed are they which are persecuted. All men are brothers and God is the Father of all."

Then all the multitude lifted up their voices and sang: "Good news, the Chariot's a comin'."

"What kind of talk is this?" said the White Folk. "Behold, he stirreth up the people."

Whereupon they took council together. They stopped his preaching and doubled his work. They cursed and drove his hearers; they warned and beat them.

Mary watched all this in mounting terror. She saw the hurt in Joshua's eyes and the bitterness in his heart. She knew that he suffered, not simply in himself, but with every other sufferer. That he was wounded by every sin and bruised by every injustice. He was oppressed and he was afflicted, yet he opened not his mouth. She saw him walk daily, despised and rejected of men, a man of sorrows and acquainted with grief. The world hid its face from him and esteemed him not.

Bitter, ever more bitter, grew the White Folk at his silent protest—his humble submission to wrong. They seized him and questioned him.

"What do you mean by this talk about all being brothers—do you mean social equality?"

"What do you mean by 'the meek shall inherit the earth'—do you mean that niggers will own our cotton land?"

"What do you mean by saying God is you-all's father—is God a nigger?"

And Joshua flamed in mighty anger and answered and said: "Woe unto you, Scribes and Pharisees, hypocrites! Fill ye up then the measure of your fathers, Ye serpents, ye generation of vipers, how can ye escape the damnation of hell!"

In wild fury the mob seized him and haled him before a judge.

The Judge—he was from the North—was sorely puzzled. "What shall I do with him?" he asked helplessly.

"Kill the nigger," yelled the mob.

"Why, what evil hath he done?"

But they cried out the more, saying: "Let him be crucified."

Thereupon the Judge washed his hands of the whole matter, saying: "I am innocent of his blood."

And so swiftly he was sentenced for treason and inciting murder and insurrection; quickly they hurried him to the jail-yard, where they stripped him, and spit upon him, and smote him on the head, and mocked, and lynched him. And sitting down, they watched him die.

And Joshua said: "Father, forgive them, for they know not what they do."

Now far down in the cabin beyond the Big Road and down the lane by the creek, there where field on field on bronze-stalked cotton lay bursting in white clouds awaiting the pickers, a mother strove with heaven, on her knees. And she cried!

"God, you ain't fair—You ain't fair, God! You didn't ought to do it—if you didn't want him black, you didn't have to make him black; if you didn't want him unhappy, why did you let him think? And then you let them mock him, and hurt him, and lynch him! Why, why did you do it God?"

And then afar she heard the faint pit-a-pat of running feet; she paused on her knees. Pit-a-pat they came across the field, down the Big Road, along the lane; pit-a-pat-pit-a-pat; and then she heard the hard breathing—ha-ha! Ha-ha!—Pit-a-pat—pit-a-pat, until suddenly a flying sweat-swarthed figure rushed on her, crying:

"Mary—Mary—he is not dead: He is risen!"

He came in the twilight, walking slowly, with head thrust slightly forward, as was his wont, and eyes upon the ground. But the heart of Mary leapt within her. For his hair shone, the lines were gone from his face, and the sorrow slept in his eyes. His clothes were white and whole and clean, and his voice was the voice of God.

And Mary said: "Where was you, Son?"

And he answered and said: "I was crucified, dead, and buried. I descended into Hell. On the third day I rose from the dead. I ascended into Heaven, and sit on the right hand of my Father, from whence I shall come to judge the Quick and the Dead."

And softly Mary laid herself down at His feet, and died.

CHAPTER 17

The Second Coming

This short story, published in *Darkwater* (1920), is yet another play on the Gospels. Du Bois employs religious themes mixed with social commentary in this narrative of the birth of the black Christ.

Three bishops sat in San Francisco, New Orleans, and New York, peering gloomily into three flickering fires, which cast and recast shuddering shadows on book-lined walls. Three letters lay in their laps, which said:

"And thou, Valdosta, in the land of Georgia, art not least among the princes of America, for out of thee shall come a governor who shall rule my people."

The white bishop of New York scowled and impatiently threw the letter into the fire. "Valdosta?" he thought,—"That's where I go to the governor's wedding of little Marguerite, my white flower,—" Then he forgot the writing in his musing, but the paper flared red in the fireplace.

"Valdosta?" said the black bishop of New Orleans, turning uneasily in his chair. "I must go down there. Those colored folk are acting strangely. I don't know where all this unrest and moving will lead to. Then, there's poor Lucy—" And he threw the letter into the fire, but eyed it suspiciously as it flamed green. "Stranger things than that have happened," he said slowly, "and ye shall hear of wars and rumors of wars . . . for nation shall rise against nation and kingdom against kingdom."

In San Francisco the priest of Japan, abroad to study strange lands, sat in his lacquer chair, with face like soft-yellow and wrinkled parchment. Slowly he wrote in a great and golden book: "I have been strangely bidden to the Val d'Osta, where one of those religious cults that swarm here will welcome a prophet. I shall go and report to Kioto."

147

So in the dim waning of the day before Christmas three bishops met in Valdosta and saw its mills and storehouses, its wide-throated and sandy streets, in the mellow glow of a crimson sun. The governor glared anxiously up the street as he helped the bishop of New York into his car and welcomed him graciously.

"I am troubled," said the governor, "about the niggers. They are acting queerly. I'm not certain but Fleming is back of it."

"Fleming?'"

"Yes! He's running against me next term for governor; he's a fire-brand; wants niggers to vote and all that—pardon me a moment, there's a darky I know—" and he hurried to the black bishop, who had just descended from the "Jim-Crow" car, and clasped his hand cordially. They talked in whispers. "Search diligently," said the governor in parting, "and bring me word again." Then returning to his guest, "You will excuse me, won't you?" he asked, "but I am sorely troubled! I never saw niggers act so. They're leaving by the hundreds and those who stay are getting impudent! They seem to be expecting something. What's the crowd, Jim?"

The chauffeur said that there was some sort of Chinese official in town and everybody wanted to glimpse him. He drove around another way.

It all happened very suddenly. The bishop of New York, in full canonicals for the early wedding, stepped out on the rear balcony of his mansion, just as the dying sun lit crimson clouds of glory in the East and burned the West.

"Fire!" yelled a wag in the surging crowd that was gathering to celebrate a southern Christmas eve; all laughed and ran.

The bishop of New York did not understand. He peered around. Was it that dark, little house in the far backyard that flamed? Forgetful of his robes he hurried down,—a brave, white figure in the sunset. He found himself before an old, black, rickety stable. He could hear the mules stamping within.

No. It was not fire. It was the sunset glowing through the cracks. Behind the hut its glory rose toward God like flaming wings of cherubim. He paused until he heard the faint wail of a child. Hastily he entered. A white girl crouched before him, down by the very mules' feet, with a baby in her arms,—a little mite of a baby that wailed weakly. Behind mother and child stood a shadow. The bishop of New York turned to the right, inquiringly, and saw a black man in bishop's robes that faintly re-echoed his own. He turned away to the left and saw a golden Japanese in golden garb. Then he heard the black man mutter behind him: "But He was to come the second time in clouds of glory, with the nations gathered around Him and angels—" at the word a shaft a of glorious light fell full upon the child, while without came the tramping of unnumbered feet and the whirring of wings.

The bishop of New York bent quickly over the baby. *It was black!* He stepped back with a gesture of disgust, hardly listening to and yet hearing the black bishop who spoke almost as if in apology:

"She's not really white; I know Lucy—you see, her mother worked for the governor—" The white bishop turned on his heel and nearly trod on the yellow priest who knelt with bowed head before the pale mother and offered incense and a gift of gold.

Out into the night rushed the bishop of New York. The wings of the cherubim were folded black against the stars. As he hastened down the front staircase the governor came rushing up the street steps.

"We are late!" He cried nervously. "The bride awaits!" He hurried the bishop to the waiting limousine, asking him anxiously: "Did you hear anything? Do you hear that noise? The crowd is growing strangely on the streets and there seems to be a fire over towards the East. I never saw so many people here—I fear violence—a mob—a lynching—I fear—hark!"

What was that which he, too, heard beneath the rhythm of unnumbered feet? Deep in his heart a wonder grew. What was it? Ah, he knew! It was music,—some strong and mighty chord. It rose higher as the brilliantly lighted church split the night and swept radiantly toward them. So high and clear that music flew, it seemed above, around, behind them. The governor, ashen-faced, crouched in the car; but the bishop said softly as the ecstasy pulsed in his heart:

"Such music, such wedding music! What choir is it?"

CHAPTER EIGHTEEN

The Prayers of God

This poem comes from *Darkwater*, published in 1920.

Name of God's Name!
Red murder reigns;
All hell is loose;
On gold autumnal air
Walk grinning devils, barbed and hoofed;
While high on hills of hate,
Black-blossomed, crimson-sky'd,
Though sittest, dumb.

Father Almighty!
This earth is mad!
Palsied, our cunning hands;
Rotten, our gold;
Our argosies reel and stagger
Over empty seas;
All the long aisles
Of Thy Great Temples, God,
Stink with the entrails
Of our souls.
And Thou art dumb.

Above the thunder of Thy Thunders, Lord,
Lightening Thy Lightnings,
Rings and roars

The dark damnation
Of this hell of war.
Red piles the pulp of hearts and heads
And little children's hands.

Allah!
Elohim!
Very God of God!
Death is here!
Dead are the living;
   Deep-dead the dead.
Dying are earth's unborn—
The babes' wide eyes of genius and of joy,
Poems and prayers, sun-glows and earth-songs,
Great-pictured dreams,
Enmarbled phantasies,
High hymning heavens—all
In this dread night
Writhe and shriek and choke and die
This long ghost-night—
While Thou art dumb.

Have mercy!
Have mercy upon us, miserable sinners!
Stand forth, unveil Thy Face,
Pour down the light
That seethes above Thy Throne,
And blaze this devil's dance to darkness!
Hear!
Speak!
In Christ's Great Name—

I hear!
Forgive me, God!
Above the thunder I hearkened;
Beneath the silence, now,—
I hear!

(Wait, God, a little space.
It is so strange to talk with Thee—
Alone!)

This gold?
I took it.

Is it Thine?
Forgive; I did not know.
Blood? Is it wet with blood?
'Tis from my brother's hands.
(I know; his hands are mine.)
It flowed for Thee, O Lord.

War? Not so; not war—
Dominion, Lord, and over black, not white;
Black, brown, and fawn,
And not Thy Chosen Brood, O God,
We murdered.
To build Thy Kingdom,
To drape our wives and little ones,
And set their souls a-glitter—
For this we killed these lesser breeds
And civilized their dead,
Raping red rubber, diamonds, cocoa, gold!

For this, too, once, and in Thy Name,
I lynched a Nigger—

    (He raved and writhed,
    I heard him cry,
    I felt the life-light leap and lie,
    I saw him crackle there, on high,
    I watched him wither!)

Thou?
Thee?
I lynched Thee?

Awake me, God! I sleep!
What was that awful word Thou saidst?
That black and riven thing—was it Thee?
That gasp—was it Thine?
This pain—is it Thine?
Are, then, these bullets piercing Thee?
Have all the wars of all the world,
Down all dim time, drawn blood from Thee?
Have all the lies and thefts and hates—
Is this Thy Crucifixion, God,
And not that funny, little cross,

With vinegar and thorns?
Is this Thy kingdom here, not there,
This stone and stucco drift of dreams?

Help!
I sense that low and awful cry—
Who cries?
Who weeps?
With silent sob that rends and tears—
Can God sob?

Who prays?
I hear strong prayers throng by,
Like mighty winds on dusky moors—
Can God pray?

Prayest Thou, Lord, and to me?
Thou needest me?
Thou *needest* me?
Thou needest *me?*
Poor, wounded soul!
Of this I never dreamed. I thought—

Courage, God
I come!

CHAPTER NINETEEN

A Hymn to the Peoples

This poem comes from *Darkwater,* published in 1920.

O Truce of God!
And primal meeting of the Sons of Man,
Foreshadowing the union of the World!
From all the ends of earth we come!
Old Night, the elder Sister of Day,
Mother of Dawn in the golden East,
Meets in the misty twilight with her brood,
Pale and black, tawny, red and brown,
The mighty human rainbow of the world,
Spanning its wilderness of storm.

Softly in sympathy the sunlight falls,
Rare is the radiance of the moon;
And on the darkest midnight blaze the stars—
The far-flown shadows of whose brilliance
Drop like a dream on the dim shores of Time,
Forecasting Days that are to these
As day to night.

So sit we all as one.
So, gloomed in tall and stone-swathed groves,
The Buddha walks with Christ!
And Al-Koran and Bible both be holy!

Almighty Word!
In this Thine awful sanctuary,
First and flame-haunted City of the Widened World,
Assoil us, Lord of Lands and Seas!

We are but weak and wayward men,
Distraught alike with hatred and vainglory;
Prone to despise the Soul that breathes within—
High visioned hordes that lie and steal and kill,
Sinning the sin each separate heart disclaims,
Clambering upon our riven, writhing selves,
Besieging Heaven by trampling men to Hell!

We be blood-guilty! Lo, our hands be red!
Not one may blame the other in this sin!
But here—here in the white Silence of the Dawn,
Before the Womb of Time,
With bowed hearts all flame and shame,
We face the birth-pangs of a world:
We hear the stifled cry of Nations all but born—
The wail of women ravished of their stunted brood!
We see the nakedness of Toil, the poverty of Wealth,
We know the Anarchy of Empire, and doleful Death
   of Life!
And hearing, seeing, knowing all, we cry:

Save us, World-Spirit, from our lesser selves!
Grant us that war and hatred cease,
Reveal our souls in every race and hue!
Help us, O Human God, in this Thy Truce,
To make Humanity divine!

CHAPTER TWENTY

Pontius Pilate

As in "The Gospel According to Mary Brown" and "The Second Coming," this piece of short fiction, published in *The Crisis* in 1920, employs scenes and images from the Gospels to illustrate and comment upon the lives of African Americans in the early twentieth century.

Pontius Pilate, Federal Governor of Mississippi, sat in the Judgment seat at Jackson. Before him stretched a table of shining gold and the morning sun sang through the eastern windows. It lighted the faces of the Chief Priest and the Elders as they bent eagerly toward him, and twisted itching hands.

He was fingering a pile of silver money which seemed to have been tossed or thrown upon the table before him.

"This-er-Iscariot fellow," he began in a low, inquiring voice, while his eyes sought the haunting shadows of the long, crimson curtains at his back.

A bishop interrupted him: a tall and mighty bishop cassocked, ringed, and jewelled:

"Just a case of uneasy conscience—a worthless fellow—we shall give this to foreign missions, shall we not, and seek Souls for the Kingdom?" And he gathered up and counted out thirty pieces—"and now to the main matter."

"I don't see how I can pardon this Barabbas," said the Governor, speaking with sudden vehemence. "He is a criminal and a drunkard—he has killed men before and—"

"Now, now, Governor!" interrupted the Judge, "Jack Barabbas is not so bad— quarrelsome, to be sure, when in liquor, and quick to defend his honor as every white man should be. Moreover—hark!"

Something floated in by the window. It was a low, but monstrous sound and in it lay anger and blood.

"See, Governor? Hear that? The Saturday crowds are in town and Jack is a prime favorite—you know they're none too well disposed toward you and the Government since this new usurpation of federal power."

"That's just it," answered the Governor angrily, straightening in his chair and flashing challenging glances right and left: "Lawlessness has brought Mississippi to this pass and yet you want me not only to pardon a notorious criminal, but also to condemn an innocent man."

"Innocent?" cried several voices, but the great voice of the Bishop outdrowned them all.

"You do not understand," he said ominously, thrusting forward his great bulk and towering over the nervous frame of the Governor. The Governor stiffened but did not quail. "You are northern born—you live far from our problem—our fearful Problem. Remember, Sir, in Mississippi there is one Crime of Crimes, one beside which all crimes fade to innocence—Murder, Arson, Rape, Theft—all are nothing beside the crime of Race Equality. Sir, this man, whom we have brought before you, not only preaches openly the equality of all men, but (and the Bishop shuddered) *practices it!*"

And then the flying words of all the eager, angry councilors raised and swept across the golden board and up the crimson curtains and down the open, sun-flushed windows:

"Do you know what he wants?"—"He wants equality for Everybody—everybody, mind you"—"Turks, Jews, Niggers, Dagoes, Chinks, Japs"—"everybody"—"talking, sleeping, kissing, marrying"—"the damned scoundrel!"—"and do you know why he wants it?"—"He's nothing but a—"—"He's a Bolshevist—a Red Revolutionist"—"He is going to overthrow all government—"

And then in a shriek—"He claims to be God and King."

Slowly, Pilate arose.

"Bring him in," he said.

They swung the crimson curtains back and there in the shadows stood the Christ.

Pontius Pilate shuddered. "Art thou King?" he whispered.

And the answer came calm and clear, "Yes!"

The cry of the mob below shivered to a shriek, while the Chief Priest and the Elders stood in a silence that was ominous.

Pilate turned.

"I find no fault in this man," he said doggedly, as his hands trembled.

"He blasphemed against the White Race," hissed the Bishop.

But Pilate continued: "You have brought this man before me as a dangerous agitator. I have examined him before you and have found no fault in him. I will therefore fine him and let him go.

But the council cried in one voice.

"Away with Christ—and pardon Barabbas!"

"I'll pardon Barabbas if you insist—but Christ—"

Again the groan of the mob rose and flooded in at the window, breaking the sunshine.

Pilate stirred uneasily—"I won't punish him," he said testily. "I know no law."

"Sir, we know our unwritten law. The crowd below—"

"I'll have no violence," cried Pilate. "It was just this lynching business that led the federal government to interfere in Mississippi—"

"Your Excellency, consider a moment," interrupted the State's Attorney. "You incur no responsibility. You simply deliver this man into our hands; and by your pardon of Barabbas the crowd will be mollified and—"

"And what?" asked the Governor.

"Well, there will be less likelihood of violence."

Pilate arose agitated. "I'll have nothing to do with it," he said. "I wash my hands of the whole thing."

The councilors bowed and turned to the door. The shout of the mob rose and rent the courtyard and the sunlight died:

—Lynch him! Lynch the damned—!

For a moment Pilate hesitated with clenched hands and riven face. Then slowly he left the chamber.

It was late afternoon and Pilate stood in the clean, cool bathroom, washing his hands. His wife hurried in.

"Pontius," she said hesitatingly, "have nothing to do with that just man—for I have suffered—"

"There, there! It's all right," he said, chucking her under the chin. "Don't meddle in politics." They both started, for they heard the mad music of myriad feet, the laughter, screaming and cursing of men, and the shrill babble of women's voices; and then over the height of the hills rolled the far-off echo of that world-worn cry:

"My God, my God! Why has Thou forsaken me!"

CHAPTER TWENTY-ONE

The Gift of the Spirit

This chapter comes from *The Gift of Black Folk*, published in 1924. Reminiscent of material covered in *The Negro Church* and "Religion in the South," subjects include the conversion of the African slaves and early black American church organizations and leaders.

> How the fine sweet spirit of black folk, despite superstition and passion has breathed the soul of humility and forgiveness into the formalism and cant of American religion.

Above and beyond all that we have mentioned, perhaps least tangible but just as true, is the peculiar spiritual quality which the Negro has injected into American life and civilization. It is hard to define or characterize it—a certain spiritual joyousness; a sensuous, tropical love of life, in vivid contrast to the cool and cautious New England reason; a slow and dreamful conception of the universe, a drawling and slurring of speech, an intense sensitiveness to spiritual values—all these things and others like to them, tell of the imprint of Africa on Europe in America. There is no gainsaying or explaining away this tremendous influence of the contact of the north and south, of black and white, of Anglo Saxon and Negro.

One way this influence has been brought to bear is through the actual mingling of blood. But this is the smaller cause of Negro influence. Heredity is always stronger through the influence of acts and deeds and imitations than through actual blood descent; and the presence of the Negro in the United States quite apart from the mingling of blood has always strongly influenced the land. We

161

have spoken of its influence in politics, literature and art, but we have yet to speak of that potent influence in another sphere of the world's spiritual activities: religion.

America early became a refuge for religion—a place of mighty spaces and glorious physical and mental freedom where silent men might sit and think quietly of God and his world. Hither out of the blood and dust of war-wrecked Europe with its jealousies, blows, persecutions and fear of words and thought, came Puritans, Anabaptists, Catholics, Quakers, Moravians, Methodists—all sorts of men and "isms" and sects searching for God and Truth in the lonely bitter wilderness.

Hither too came the Negro. From the first he was the concrete test of that search for Truth, of the strife toward a God, of that body of belief which is the essence of true religion. His presence rent and tore and tried the souls of men. "Away with the slave!" some cried—but where away and why? Was not his body there for work and his soul—what of his soul? Bring hither the slaves of all Africa and let us convert their souls, this is God's good reason for slavery. But convert them to what? to freedom? to emancipation? to being white men? Impossible. Convert them, yes. But let them still be slaves for their own good and ours. This was quibbling and good men felt it, but at least here was a practical path, follow it.

Thus arose the great mission movements to the blacks. The Catholic Church began it and not only were there Negro proselytes but black priests and an order of black monks in Spanish America early in the 16th century. In the middle of the 17th century a Negro freedman and charcoal burner lived to see his son, Francisco Xavier de Luna Victoria, raised to head the Bishopric of Panama where he reigned eight years as the first native Catholic Bishop in America.

In Spanish America and in French America the history of Negro religion is bound up with the history of the Catholic Church. On the other hand in the present territory of the United States with the exception of Maryland and Louisiana organized religion was practically and almost exclusively Protestant and Catholics indeed were often bracketed with Negroes for persecution. They could not marry Protestants at one time in colonial South Carolina; Catholics and Negroes could not appear in court as witnesses in Virginia by the law of 1705; Negroes and Catholics were held to be the cause of the "Negro plot" in New York in 1741.

The work then of the Catholic Church among Negroes began in the United States well into the 19th century and by Negroes themselves. In Baltimore, for instance, in 1829, colored refugees from the French West Indies established a sisterhood and academy and gave an initial endowment of furniture, real estate and some $50,000 in money. In 1842 in New Orleans, four free Negro women gave their wealth to form the Sisters of the Holy Family and this work expanded and grew especially after 1893 when a mulatto, Thomy Lafon, endowed the work with over three quarters of a million dollars, his life savings.

Later, in 1896, a colored man, Colonel John McKee of Philadelphia, left a million dollars in real estate to the Catholic Church for colored and white orphans.

Outside of these colored sisterhoods and colored philanthropists, the church hesitated long before it began any systematic proselyting among Negroes. This was because of the comparative weakness of the church in early days and later when the Irish migration strengthened it the new Catholics were thrown into violent economic competition with slaves and free Negroes, and their fight to escape slave competition easily resolved itself into a serious anti-Negro hatred which was back of much of the rioting in Cincinnati, Philadelphia and New York. It was not then until the 20th century that the church began active work by establishing a special mission for Negroes and engaging in it nearly two hundred white priests. This new impetus was caused by the benevolence of Katherine Drexel and the Sisters of the Blessed Sacrament. Notwithstanding all this and since the beginning of the 18th century only six Negroes have been ordained to the Catholic priesthood.

The main question of the conversion of the Negro to Christianity in the United States was therefore the task of the Protestant Church and it was, if the truth must be told, a task which it did not at all relish. The whole situation was fraught with perplexing contradictions; Could Christians be slaves? Could slaves be Christians? Was the object of slavery the Christianizing of the black man, and when the black man was Christianized was the mission of slavery done and ended? Was it possible to make modern Christians of these persons whom the new slavery began to paint as brutes? The English Episcopal Church finally began the work in 1701 through the Society for the Propagation of the Gospel. It had notable officials, the Archbishop of Canterbury being its first president; it worked in America 82 years, accomplishing something but after all not very much, on account of the persistent objection of the masters. The Moravians were more eager and sent missionaries to the Negroes, converting large numbers in the West Indies and some in the United States in the 18th century. Into the new Methodist Church which came to America in 1766, large numbers of Negroes poured from the first, and finally the Baptists in the 18th century had at least one fourth of their membership composed of Negroes, so that in 1800 there were 14,000 black Methodists and some 20,000 black Baptists.[1]

It must not be assumed that this missionary work acted on raw material. Rather it reacted and was itself influenced by a very definite and important body of thought and belief on the part of the Negroes. Religion in the United States was not simply brought to the Negro by the missionaries. To treat it in that way is to miss the essence of the Negro action and reaction upon American religion.

We must think of the transplanting of the Negro as transplanting to the United States a certain spiritual entity, and an unbreakable set of world-old beliefs, manners, morals, superstitions and religious observances. The religion of Africa is the universal animism or fetishism of primitive peoples, rising to polytheism and approaching monotheism chiefly, but not wholly, as a result of Christian and Islamic missions. Of fetishism there is much misapprehension. It is not mere senseless degradation. It is a philosophy of life. Among primitive Negroes there can be, as Miss Kingsley reminds us, no such divorce of religion from practical life as is common in civilized lands. Religion is life, and fetish an expression of the practical recognition of dominant forces in which the Negro lives. To him all the world is spirit. . . .

At first sight it would seem that slavery completely destroyed every vestige of spontaneous social movement among the Negroes; the home had deteriorated; political authority and economic initiative was in the hands of the masters; property, as a social institution, did not exist on the plantation; and, indeed, it is usually assumed by historians and sociologists that every vestige of internal development disappeared, leaving the slaves no means of expression for their common life, thought, and striving. This is not strictly true; the vast power of the priest in the African state still survived; his realm alone—the province of religion and medicine—remained largely unaffected by the plantation system in many important particulars. The Negro priest, therefore, early became an important figure on the plantation and found his function as the interpreter of the supernatural, the comforter of the sorrowing, and as the one who expressed, rudely, but picturesquely, the longing and disappointment and resentment of a stolen people. From such beginnings arose and spread with marvellous rapidity the Negro church, the first distinctively Negro American social institution. It was not at first by any means a Christian Church, but a mere adaptation of those heathen rites which we roughly designate by the term Obe Worship or "Voodooism." Association and missionary effort soon gave these rites a veneer of Christianity, and gradually, after two centuries, the Church became Christian, with a simple Calvinistic creed, but with many of the old customs still clinging to the services. It is this historic fact that the Negro Church today bases itself upon the sole surviving social institution of the African fatherland, that accounts for its extraordinary growth and vitality. We easily forget that in the United States today there is a Church organization for every sixty Negro families. This institution, therefore, naturally assumed many functions which the other harshly suppressed social organs had to surrender; the Church became the center of amusements, of what little spontaneous economic activity remained, of education, and of all social intercourse, of music and art.

For these reasons the tendency of the Negro worshippers from the very first was to integrate into their own organizations. As early as 1775 distinct Negro congregations with Negro ministers began to appear here and there in the United States. They multiplied, were swept away, effort was made to absorb them in the white church, but they kept on growing until they established national bodies with Episcopal control or democratic federation and these organizations today form the strongest, most inclusive and most vital of the Negro organizations. They count in the United States four million members and their churches seat these four million and six million other guests. They are houses in 40,000 centers, worth $60,000,000 and have some 200,000 leaders.

On the part of the white church this tendency among the Negroes met with alternate encouragement and objection: encouragement because they did not want Negroes in their churches even when they occupied the back seats or in the gallery; objection when the church became, as it so often did, a center of intelligent Negro life and even of plotting against slavery. There arose out of the church the first leaders of the Negro group; and in the first rank among these stands Richard Allen. . . .

It will be seen that the development of the Negro church was not separate from the white. Black preachers led white congregations, white preachers addressed blacks. In many other ways Negroes influenced white religion continuously and tremendously. There was the "Shout," combining the trance and demoniac possession as old as the world, and revivified and made wide-spread by the Negro religious devotees in America. Methodist and Baptist ways of worship, songs and religious dances absorbed much from the Negroes and whatever there is in American religion today of stirring and wild enthusiasm, of loud conversions and every day belief in an anthropomorphic God owes its origin in a no small measure to the black man.

Of course most of the influence of the Negro preachers was thrown into their own churches and to their own people and it was from the Negro church as an organization that Negro religious influence spread most widely to white people. Many would say that this influence had little that was uplifting and was a detriment rather than an advantage in that it held back and holds back the South particularly in its religious development. There is no doubt that influences of a primitive sort and customs that belong to the unlettered childhood of the race rather than to the thinking adult life of civilization crept in with the religious influence of the slave. Much of superstition, even going so far as witchcraft, conjury and blood sacrifice for a long time marked Negro religion here and there in the swamps and islands. But on the other hand it is just as true that the cold formalism of upper class England and New England needed the wilder spiritual emotionalism of the black man to weld out of both a rational human religion based on kindliness and social uplift; and whether the influence of Negro religion was on the whole good or bad, the fact remains that it was potent in the white South and still is.

Several black leaders of white churches are worth remembering. Lemuel Hayes was born in Connecticut in 1753 of a black father and white mother. He received his Master of Arts from Middlebury College in 1804, was a soldier in the Revolution and pastored various churches in New England. . . .

The story of Jack of Virginia is best told in the words of a Southern writer:

"Probably the most interesting case in the whole South is that of an African preacher of Nottoway county, popularly known as 'Uncle Jack,' whose services to white and black were so valuable that a distinguished minister of the Southern Presbyterian Church felt called upon to memorize his work in a biography.

"Kidnapped from his idolatrous parents in Africa, he was brought over in one of the last cargoes of slaves admitted to Virginia and sold to a remote and obscure planter in Nottoway county, a region at that time in the backwoods and destitute particularly as to religious life and instruction. He was converted under the occasional preaching of Rev. Dr. John Blair Smith, President of Hampden-Sidney College, and of Dr. William Hill and Dr. Archibald Alexander of Princeton, then young theologues, and by hearing the scriptures read. Taught by his master's children to read, he became so full of the spirit and knowledge of the Bible that he was recognized among the whites as a powerful expounder of Christian doctrine, was licensed to preach by the Baptist Church, and preached from plantation to plantation within a radius of thirty miles, as he was invited by overseers or masters. His freedom was purchased by a subscription of whites, and he was given a home and a tract of land for his support. He organized a large and orderly Negro church, and exercised such a wonderful controlling influence over the private morals of his flock that masters, instead of punishing their slaves, often referred them to the discipline of their pastor, which they dreaded far more.

"He stopped a heresy among the Negro Christians of Southern Virginia, defeating in open argument a famous fanatical Negro preacher named Campbell, who advocated noise and 'the spirit' against the Bible, winning over Campbell's adherents in a body. For over forty years and until he was nearly a hundred years of age, he labored successfully in public and private among black and whites, voluntarily giving up his preaching in obedience to the law of 1832, the result of 'Old Nat's war.' . . .

"The most refined and aristocratic people paid tribute to him, and he was instrumental in the conversion of many whites. Says his biographer, Rev. Dr. William S. White: 'He was invited into their houses, sat with their families, took part in their social worship, sometimes leading the prayer at the family altar. Many of the most intelligent people attended upon his ministry and listened to

his sermons with great delight. Indeed, previous to the year 1825, he was considered by the best judges to be the best preacher in that county. His opinions
were respected, his advice followed, and yet he never betrayed the least symptoms of arrogance or self-conceit. His dwelling was a rude log cabin, his apparel
of the plainest and coarsest materials.' This was because he wished to be fully
identified with his class. He refused gifts of better clothing saying 'These clothes
are a great deal better than are generally worn by people of my color, and besides
if I wear them I find shall be obliged to think about them even at meeting.'"

All this has to do with organized religion.

But back of all this and behind the half childish theology of formal religion
there has run in the heart of black folk the greatest of human achievements, love
and sympathy, even for their enemies, for those who despised them and hurt
them and did them nameless ill. They have nursed the sick and closed the star-
ing eyes of the dead. They have given friendship to the friendless, they have
shared the pittance of their poverty with the outcast and nameless; they have
been good and true and pitiful to the bad and false and pitiless and in this lies
the real grandeur of their simple religion, the mightiest gift of black to white
America.

Above all looms the figure of the Black Mammy, one of the most pitiful of the
world's Christs. Whether drab and dirty drudge or dark and gentle lady, she
played her part in the uplift of the South. She was an embodied Sorrow, an
anomaly crucified on the cross of her own neglected children for the sake of the
children of masters who bought and sold her as they bought and sold cattle.
Whatever she had of slovenliness or neatness, of degradation or of education she
surrendered it to those who lived to lynch her sons and ravish her daughters.
From her great full breast walked forth governors and judges, ladies of wealth and
fashions, merchants and scoundrels who lead the South. And the rest gave her
memory the reverence of silence. But a few snobs have lately sought to advertise
her sacrifice and degradation and enhance their own cheap success by building
on the blood of her riven heart a load of stone miscalled a monument.

In religion as in democracy, the Negro has been a peculiar test of white pro-
fession. The American church, both Catholic and Protestant, has been kept
from any temptation to over-righteousness and empty formalism by the fact that
just as Democracy in America was tested by the Negro, so American religion
has always been tested by slavery and color prejudice. It has kept before America's truer souls the spirit of meekness and self abasement, it has compelled
American religion again and again to search its heart and cry "I have sinned;"
and until the day comes when color caste falls before reason and economic
opportunity the black American will stand as the last and terrible test of the
ethics of Jesus Christ.

Beyond this the black man has brought to America a sense of meekness and humility which America never has recognized and perhaps never will. If there is anybody in this land who thoroughly believes that the meek shall inherit the earth they have not often let their presence be known. On the other hand it has become almost characteristic of America to look upon position, selfassertion, determination to go forward at all odds, as typifying the American spirit. This is natural. It is at once the rebound from European oppression and the encouragement which America offers physically, economically and socially to the human spirit. But on the other hand, it is in many of its aspects a dangerous and awful thing. It hardens and hurts our souls, it contradicts our philanthropy and religion; and here it is that the honesty of the black race, its hesitancy and heart searching, its submission to authority and its deep sympathy with the wishes of the other man comes forward as a tremendous, even though despised corrective. It is not always going to remain; even now we see signs of its disappearance before contempt, lawlessness and lynching. But it is still here, it still works and one of the most magnificent anomalies in modern human history is the labor and fighting of a half-million black men and two million whites for the freedom of four million slaves and these same slaves, dumbly but faithfully and not wholly unconsciously, protecting the mothers, wives and children of the very white men who fought to make their slavery perpetual.

This then is the Gift of Black Folk to the new world. Thus in singular and fine sense the slave became master, the bond servant became free and the meek not only inherited the earth but made that heritage a thing of questing for eternal youth, of fruitful labor, of joy and music, of the free spirit and of the ministering hand, of wide and poignant sympathy with men in their struggle to live and love which is, after all, the end of being.

CHAPTER TWENTY-TWO

The Color Line and the Church

This piece was published in *The Crisis* in 1929. Describing American Christianity as "Jim Crowed from top to bottom," Du Bois succinctly discusses the tensions between white and black Americans within the specific context of religious institutions.

When the Reverend Mr. Blackshear of St. Matthew's Protestant Episcopal Church, Brooklyn, invited Negroes out of his parish, there was much tumult and shouting, which has now died away. Matters will now settle back to normal: Negroes will fade out of Mr. Blackshear's church; as the surrounding community becomes more and more "colored," this branch of the Church of Christ will move to a whiter neighborhood and St. Matthew's will be "transferred" or sold to colored folk.

And yet even this usual solution will not settle the matter. Mr. Blackshear and his vestry, in drawing the color line in his church, simply followed the policy of American Christianity. The American Church of Christ is Jim Crowed from top to bottom. No other institution in America is built so thoroughly or more absolutely on the color line. Everybody knows this. Why then abuse Mr. Blackshear? He may be a blunt and tactless fool, but he is doing exactly what his church has done for 250 years, and, in this policy, the Episcopalians have been followed by the Catholic Church of America, and, in later years, by the Methodists, Baptists, and Presbyterians.

The reason for this is clear, if we regard the church as a group of ordinary human beings with human ignorance, prejudice, and cruelty, as well as charity and good will. White Americans prefer not to associate with Negroes, neither in homes, theaters, streetcars, nor churches. This is evidently what the younger churchmen (some of whom are beginning their second fifty years of life) almost tearfully acknowledge when they profess a "general guilt and perplexity."

But these gentlemen cannot escape the dilemma into which this confession forces them. The church does not usually profess to be a group of ordinary human beings. It claims Divine Sanction, It professes to talk with God and to receive directly His Commandments. Its ministers and members do not apparently have to acquire Truth by bitter experience and long intensive study: Truth is miraculously revealed to them.

If, therefore, in the midst and in the face of this divine revelation of truth which is weekly thundered from their pulpits, they then turn around and confess that they are acting just like ordinary human beings, what becomes of all these pretensions of supernatural revelation?

In other words, the church faces today, as in other days, and with American Negro problems as in other social problems, an inexorable dilemma: whether the church must acknowledge itself to be a human organization largely composed of the rich and respectable, desirous of better things and groping for social uplift but restrained by inherited prejudice, economic privilege, and social fear; or the church may continue to insist on its divine origin, supernatural power, and absolute and immediate knowledge of Truth.

In the latter case, when the church meets the Negro problem, it writes itself down as a deliberate hypocrite and systematic liar. It does not say "Come unto me all ye that labor"; it does not "love its neighbor as itself"; it does not welcome "Jew and Gentile, barbarian, Scythian, bond and free"; and yet it openly and blatantly professes all this.

On the other hand, a great human institution for social uplift and wider humanity has no reason to be ashamed in confessing its mistakes so long as it does with energy and determination work to correct them. In the past, the church has opposed every great modern social reform; it opposed the spread of democracy, universal education, trade unionism, the abolition of poverty, the emancipation of women, the spread of science, the freedom of art and literature, and the emancipation of the Negro slave. When the reform was gained, the church righted itself, led usually by some schismatic and heretical part of itself, came over on the Lord's side and usually did not hesitate both to claim a preponderant share of the glory of victory and again to emphasize its supernatural claims.

It is the latter development that disturbs and angers right-thinking men. No one utterly condemns a Blackshear, born and raised in Texas and educated in a theological seminary, for crassly drawing a color line in human relations. What else could be humanly expected? We can only insist on facing facts, investigating consequences, and telling the truth about this miserable tangle in human relationships.

Do we get this? No! We get casuistry, molasses and a little well-bred whining. We get a repetition of the "divine Mission of Christianity"; and then silence and quiet persistence in the exact wrong that raised the controversy.

Examine the reply of Blackshear's "Reverend Father in God," Bishop Stires. It is little short of delicious. He says that when black folk appeared in his parish "he never found it necessary to suggest that he did not desire any more." Of course, he did not. His black parishioners were in the position of that well-known "darky" who once tried repeatedly and persistently to join an Episcopal church. At last he gave up and explained the matter to the rector:

"Naw, Suh, naw Suh, I ain't aimin' to jine yo' church. You see hit's this-a-way: last night as I was prayin' for grace, I done see Jesus. And Jesus done said to me, sezzee, Rastus, son, don't try to get into dat 'Pinsopal Church no mo'. I done been tryin' to git in dar mahself for mighty nigh two thousand years and ah ain't made it yit!"

And so Bishop Stires cannot find a thing that he can do; and the younger churchmen will not find a change that they can agree upon. And the church militant will prescribe a large amount of soothing syrup, while Bishop Manning and his ilk, wrapped in decorous and Episcopal silence, will devote his time and great talents to the Cathedral of St. John the Divine.

CHAPTER TWENTY-THREE

Will the Church
Remove the Color Line?

This piece was published in *The Christian Century* in 1931. Addressing the problem of the "color line" permeating American Christianity, Du Bois condemns the church for its inability to act and its hypocrisy in matters of social and racial justice.

Will the church of tomorrow solve the problem of the color line? The problem of the color line, particularly in America, is well known. It is the question of the treatment and place in society and in the state of the descendants of African slaves who were freed by the Civil War. Not only are these persons, numbering some 12,000,000 or more, more physically distinct from the nation because of color and race, but also otherwise segregated because slavery made them poor, kept them ignorant, and plunged them into such sickness and crime as poverty and ignorance always cause. For these and other reasons they form in the United States an inferior social caste.

This is the problem of the color line as it presents itself in the United States. But, of course, the color line extends beyond our own country. The majority of the people of the world are colored and belong to races more or less distinct from the white people of Europe and North America. Because, however, of imperial aggression and industrial exploitation, most of these colored peoples are under the political or commercial domination of white Europe and America, and their consequent problems of self-government, social status, and work and wages present the greatest difficulties the world over.

SCIENTIFIC POSTULATES

In addition to all this, various scientific questions have become involved. The attitude of science toward colored races has greatly changed in the last four centuries, but there arose in the nineteenth century a question that persists in the minds of large numbers of white people today, as to how far the earth is inhabited by nations and races essentially equal in their gifts and power of accomplishment, or how far the world is a hierarchy headed by the white people, with other groups graduating down by grades of color to smaller and smaller brain power, ability and character.

What now should be the relation of the great racial groups of the world? Shall they live together as brothers? Shall they organize and regard each other as potential or actual enemies? Or shall their relation be that of rulers and ruled, with the races that are now dominated held in subjection, either by physical force or by their own submission to what they come to realize or are forced to admit is the greater power, or greater ability, or greater desert of the white race?

Here, then, is the problem of the color line and it is not only the most pressing social question of the modern world; it is an ethical question that confronts every religion and every conscience.

This paper is a frank attempt to express my belief that the Christian church will do nothing conclusive or effective; that it will not settle these problems; that, on the contrary, it will as long as possible and wherever possible avoid them; that in this, as in nearly every great modern moral controversy, it will be found consistently on the wrong side and that when, by the blood and tears of radicals and fanatics of the despised and rejected largely outside the church, some settlement of these problems is found, the church will be among the first to claim full and original credit for this result.

THE CHURCH AND SLAVERY

The proof of this to me lies chiefly in the history of the Christian church and Negro slavery in America. Unfortunately, the editor of the *Christian Century* has not space for me to go into this matter in detail, and perhaps many of us would rather forget it; and yet we cannot forget that under the aegis and protection of the religion of the Prince of Peace—of a religion which was meant for the lowly and unfortunate—there arose in America one of the most stupendous institutions of human slavery that the world has seen. The Christian church sponsored and defended this institution, despite occasional protest and effort at amelioration here and there. The Catholic Church approved of and defended slavery; the

Episcopal church defended and protected slavery; the Puritans and Congregationalists recognized and upheld slavery; the Methodists and Baptists stood staunchly behind it; the Quakers gave their consent to it. Indeed, there was not a single branch of the Christian church that did not in the end become part of an impregnable bulwark defending the trade in human beings and the holding of them as chattel slaves. There must have been between 1619 and 1863 in the United States alone 10,000,000 sermons preached from the text, "Servants, obey your masters, for this is well pleasing in the sight of the Lord"! Then, finally, when the conscience of mankind began to revolt and abolition became a dream, a propaganda, political scheme, what was the attitude of the church?

GARRISON'S TESTIMONY

The only Christian body that gave the abolitionists aid and countenance was the Quakers, who, toward the end of the eighteenth century and in the beginning of the nineteenth, gradually took a stand against slavery and began to agitate for emancipation.

William Lloyd Garrison, reviewing the attitude of the Christian church as a whole, said in the *Liberator* in 1835: "It is a fact, alike indisputable and shameful, that the Christianity of the nineteenth century in this country, is preached and professed by those who hold their brethren in bondage as brute beasts! And so entirely polluted has the church become, that it has not moral power enough to excommunicate a member who is guilty of man-stealing! Whether it be Unitarian or orthodox, Baptist or Methodist, Universalist or Episcopal, Roman Catholic or Christian, it is full of innocent blood—it is the stronghold of slavery—it recognizes as members those who grind the faces of the poor, and usurp over the helpless the prerogatives of the Almighty! At the South, slaves and slaveholders, the masters and their victims, the spoilers and the spoiled, make up the Christian church! The churches at the North partake of the guilt of oppression, inasmuch as they are in full communion with those at the South."

Frederick Douglass added in 1845: "I can see no reason, but the most deceitful one, for calling the religion of this land Christianity."

AFTER EMANCIPATION

After emancipation and in those pregnant twenty years from 1863 to 1883, years whose history has not yet been completely weighed nor written, the world, moral and economic, accepted the fact of free Negroes in America. What attitude should be taken toward these new freedmen and citizens? The church, which had been busy with nursing and relief of the wounded, became involved in schemes for education of refugees, almost before it knew it. The extension of the New England ideal of universal education to black folk was an easy and momentous step. Nevertheless, only part of the church accepted it. The Catholics and the Episcopalians did practically nothing. The Southern white Methodists and Baptists naturally took no part. The Presbyterians took but a small part.

The New England Congregationalists, followed by the Northern Methodists and Baptists, stepped forward eagerly and inaugurated what has sometimes been called the ninth crusade, the crusade for Negro education. It was a splendid movement, and has had tremendous results, and it was perhaps the one great effort of any considerable part of the Christians in America in behalf of the Negroes.

RISE OF COLOR CASTE

But after an effort extending over about thirty years, reactions set in, even in the Congregational Church. The effort of the South to disfranchise the Negro and to establish a color caste received sympathy in the North for economic reasons and because of the new industrial imperialism which was sweeping the world. Many began to express a fear lest the Negro become "overeducated" and too ambitious, and America began to face frankly the problem as to just what it wanted the American Negro to be. Was he to be trained as a free citizen, economically and socially equal to other Americans, or was he to be trained as a servile caste, the recipient of charity and good will, but not a full-fledged member of American democracy?

Thus, the new color caste idea arose in the country and swept over the churches. The Christian church began openly to join those who decried political equality on the part of Negroes, who discountenanced social intercourse between black and white, and who believed that Negroes should be satisfied with humble service and low wages.

What, finally, has been the attitude of the Christian church toward [the] Negro caste from Reconstruction down until this day? While the church has hesitated and made numbers of explanations and excuses, it is fair to say that the white Christian church has accepted the program of caste for Negroes. The Congregational Church stood by its ideals longest, but gradually the contributions for Negro education fell off and the interest in the Negro dwindled. Catholics were forced to face the problem of proselyting among Negroes by the gift of Catherine Drexel. But the work was handicapped by the fact that in 150 years the Catholic church had ordained but seven Negro priests and most of its schools and semi-naries refuse, even today, to admit Negro students. It began the new proselyting by giving charity to the very poor and ignorant, and as these entered the church, they hastened to segregate in separate congregations under white priests, who usu-ally had not the faintest conception of the problems of the black folk.

AFRICAN MISSIONS

The Methodist Church, South, got rid of Negroes absolutely and formed a new Negro church. The Northern Methodist Church segregated them into separate conferences, and several times they invited all of them to join the Negro Methodists. Today, the Negro membership of the Methodist Episcopal church is almost entirely a separate institution, although it is still represented in the gen-eral conference. The Baptists have no national unity and are separated individ-ually into colored and white churches, which more and more have no common meeting ground, although there is some co-operation in education and mission-ary work. The Episcopal church is divided, with very few exceptions, into col-ored and white congregations, and for its colored congregations it has ordained black bishops.

Thus, gradually the Christian church has lessened its support of Negro educa-tion; has seldom taken any stand against lynching and mob violence; against dis-crimination, or even against laws which in most states of the Union class all Negro women and prostitutes together, so far as legal marriage with whites is concerned.

The Christian church thus acquiesced in a new and strict drawing of the color line, not only in political and civil life, but even in church work. Nothing illus-trates this better than the attitude of white churches today toward Christian mis-sions in Africa. Remember that the whole argument of the church for centuries in support of Negro slavery was that this was God's method of redeeming hea-then Africa. For a long time this was interpreted as meaning that a few slaves were to be converted to Christianity; then, as gradually voluntary emancipation freed more of the slaves, these slaves were to return to Africa and be the efficient and logical means of converting the Africans.

NEGROES AND MISSIONS

Numbers of American Negroes today would be willing to work in Africa. What does the Christian church say to this? Out of 158 African missionaries in 1928, the Protestant Episcopal Church had one American Negro; the Presbyterian two out of eighty-eight; the Northern Baptists one out of twenty; the Methodist Episcopal Church five out of ninety-one; the American board four out of 97. Of 793 other missionaries to Africa sent out by American missionary societies, including the United Presbyterians, the United Missionary Society, the United Brethren, the African Inland Mission, the Friends, the Brethren-in-Christ, the Southern Baptists, the Women's General Mission Society of the United Presbyterian Church, the Lutherans, and the Sudan Interior mission, there is not a single American Negro! What is the reason for this? As a matter of fact, missionary societies of the United States started out, for the most part, with the obvious policy of sending Negroes to convert Africa. Then they found out that this involved social equality between white and black missionaries; the paying of Negro missionaries on the same scale as white missionaries, and their promotion and treatment as civilized beings. With few exceptions, American white Christianity could not stand this, and they consequently changed their policy.

LESS DISCRIMINATION OUTSIDE CHURCH

Here, then, we may well pause and let the matter stand, with this summing up of the situation: The Christian church in this country, on the whole, instead of exhibiting itself as a unifying human force, moving toward the brotherhood of men, regardless of lines of color, condition or caste, has shown less unity than almost any other human institution. In education, we have a great deal of separation by color and race, nevertheless, throughout most of the country, and in the case of the majority of its inhabitants, white and colored children attend the same school, and to some extent, white and colored teachers teach regardless of race, as in New York City. In labor and general economic organization, there is widespread separation by race in the United States. Nevertheless, both white and black labor is employed in the United States side by side in many of the great industries. In literature and art, and to some extent in science, there is a great deal less discrimination by race than there is in Christianity. Even in matters of amusement and public enjoyment, colored people more often attend the same parks, the same theater and the same movie house and enjoy treatment in the same institutions for public entertainment, than [If] they attend the same church.

Thus, the record of the church, so far as the Negro is concerned, has been almost complete acquiescence in caste, until today there is in the United States no organization that is so completely split along the color line as the Christian church —the very organization that according to its tenets and beliefs should be no respecter of persons and should draw no line between white or black, "Jew or Gentile, barbarian, Scythian, bond or free."

TOO MUCH TO HOPE

Looking these facts squarely in the face, what can we say as to the possibility of the church in the future settling the problem of the color-blind leading the world toward treating Negroes and colored people as men and brothers? If we conceive the church as a social organization of well-meaning but average human beings, we can only hope that while they will not lead public opinion toward world brotherhood, yet as they see the light and the trend, they will be willing, slowly but surely, to follow and just as they came to recognize the freedom of the slave, they will in time come to conceive the essential equality of all men. But it is too much to imagine that such an organization will oppose wealth and power and withstand respectable conservatism by choosing the right first and adhering at any social cost to the choice which its principles and conscience dictate.

This conception of the church is violently repudiated by all but the most advanced and radical religionists. The church, as a whole, insists on a divine mission and divine guidance and the indisputable possession of the truth. Is there anything in the record of the church in America in regard to the Negro to prove this? There is not. If the treatment of the Negro by the Christian church is called "divine," this is an attack on the conception of God more blasphemous than any which the church has always been so ready and eager to punish.

WHAT OF THE FUTURE?

Thus, judging from the past, I see no reason to think that the attitude of the Christian church toward problems of race and caste is going to be anything different from its attitude in the past. It is mainly a social organization, pathetically timid and human; it is going to stand on the side of wealth and power; it is going to espouse any cause which is sufficiently popular, with eagerness; it is, on the other hand, often going to transgress its own fine ethical statements and be deaf to its own Christ in unpopular and weak causes. And then when human brotherhood is a fact and the color line is remembered only as a fatal aberration and disease of the twentieth century, the Christian church, if it still survives, is going to take the same attitude which it took after emancipation in 1863: From a thousand pulpits it will thunder the triumph of Christianity and the way in which the Lord has led his people.

CHAPTER TWENTY-FOUR

The Son of God

This short story was published in *The Crisis* in 1933. It is yet another dramatic portrayal of Jesus as a suffering black man amid the racist and oppressive social conditions of the early twentieth century. This story, like "The Gospel According to Mary Brown" and "Jesus Christ in Georgia," makes it easy to understand how and why the Gospel story of Jesus resonated—and continues to resonate—with African Americans.

Joe struck her hard, right in the face. Mary swayed back a little toward the bureau, but said nothing and stood slim and straight. He wanted to hit her again and started to, but he could not. It was extraordinary how she always impressed him. Those black somber pupils set in the ivory white of her eyes; the rich smooth brown skin and above, the nimbus of grey-black hair, lifted like an aureole. She gave an extraordinary impression of innocence, purity and power, in spite of all he knew,—in spite of what she had just told him.

"Why the hell don't you tell me who his father is?" he snarled again, feeling all the while his first revulsion and anger ebbing slowly away. But Mary only repeated slowly what she had said before:

"He is the Son of God!"

So Joe turned and stormed out into the night. He couldn't make it out. What would the fellows say? How had he come to marry this black girl anyway? He hadn't meant to; but somehow she fascinated him; the curving beauty of her perfect form; the delicate softness of her skin; the dark and secret brooding that ever lurked in her eyes. Besides, he had wanted to get married. He wanted to be decent and have a family, and now here was this mess. Here she was already with child and she had told him so after he had married her. Well, he'd get rid of her

181

and damned quick. He would drive her out. Then he thought of the new cottage with a sharp twinge of regret.. Of course it wasn't so much,—only two rooms; but it was new; it was his. He had built it himself with her sitting by, singing low songs. It was in a sense the masterpiece of an untutored but earnest artist.

And now this had to come. He couldn't figure it out. He couldn't see what had gotten into her. She never went with anybody but him. It had been hard at first even to get her to look at him. He clenched his hands, striding through the fields, across the branch and up the hill into the sun-set. If it was some of that damned white trash beyond the hill he would have to kill him, of course; but somehow he knew it wasn't. But who else could it be? None of the colored boys had dared look at her since he had marked her for his own.

Then somehow as the weeks passed the pain and bitterness of it faded away. He couldn't make up his mind what he ought to do. There was that air of still and pure loveliness about her; inexplicable, contradictory, unworldly. Uncanny it was, but there. And so he did nothing but waited in surly pain; and late in December, the boy was born, and Joe was holding him wonderingly in his arms, while she lay strait and terrible still. At first, he groaned for he thought her dead but she opened her calm, dark eyes and fixed them on him. And her eyes spoke,—and he knew that she was saying again:

"He is the Son of God."

As weeks and months passed, that happened which he was sure never could happen. The child became his child; he loved it passionately, and it was only when he was angry or a little drunk that he could remember that it wasn't his. Then he swore at Mary or sulked or demanded angrily again: "Who's his father anyway?" It was marvelous, the fascination of that wee bit of life; the soft per-fection of its body; the light that grew daily in its eyes; the little curling tendrils of its hair. There came the days of its first teeth and its standing alone. Its little low gurgles of delight, its wild griefs, and the outstretching of its arms.

Naturally Joe wanted, and yet he did not want the boy named after him; it ought to be and of a surety it ought not to be. "No," he said one day. "Call it what you damned please. But not Joe—not after me." So she called it Joshua and for months Joe searched his memory and the country round for a Joshua; but he found none.

And always silently to and fro went the slim mother, like a certain dark and silver wisp of summer rain or a shadow upon a sun-lit hill. She talked little and yet she listened and put the answering word in just where it made Joe know that she was listening and understanding. Of his work, of his trouble, the old plow, the lame mule, the vagaries of the second-hand Ford, and the boy. Then slowly, she smiled. It always ended there as so often he did not mean it should. It always ended with the boy. For still and always to her, he was the Son of God.

Joshua grew into a silent, brooding but infinitely sympathetic child, whose smile was benediction. He asked few questions and took no orders, and went his own still way. Joe always remembered with a grim satisfaction about the boy at Quarterly meeting. Joshua was twelve then and had already incurred the bitter dislike of the Methodist preacher, whom he had very calmly but decisively disputed in Sunday School. Joe was tickled. He hated that preacher anyway. Always interfering. Sure, he might be right. Probably was. But he had no business to be so nosey and he took too much of the people's money. And then Joe found Joshua at noon standing up in the midst of the preachers, telling them what was what; not as sharply and blusteringly, as Joe would have liked, and yet with a certain assurance and decision that tickled Joe infinitely. He dragged Joshua home, chuckling as he went, in the midst of stern advice.

"You just let them preachers alone. They know lots more than you do, and you can't be sassy to your elders."

Then he would chuckle again and Joshua always remained silent.

And so years went on, ever more swiftly, until there came a question as to what Joshua was going to do for a living after he finished the elementary schools. Joe insisted that he should become a farmer and help him. His mother suggested rather dreamily that he might be a lawyer. Joshua said he was going to be a carpenter and a carpenter he became. A rather good carpenter but slow, and often called away on business of his own. His father's business, he called it.

"It ain't no business of mine," growled Joe.

Then at last Joe began to complain. "First thing you know that fellow is going to be a gangster. He's hanging around with a lot of Communists and talking on street corners, and saying things about property that white folks ain't going to stand for. The police will get after him one of these days and first thing you know he'll be in jail."

But his mother sewed and washed and swept and grew thinner and taller as her eyes grew larger. Only she muttered, as always:

"He is the Son of God."

Once they heard a strange tale from Bethany, a neighboring town. The mob had beat Laz Simmons, one of Joshua's pals, and left him for dead, lying in the gutter. Martha, his sister, ran ten miles to get Joshua and begged him for help when none others dared touch the body. Joshua wept. He bore him home.

"He was nearly dead," said Joe.

"He was dead," said Mary.

"Don't be a fool. He's alive and well."

Mary answered, "He said: 'Laz, get up.' And he got up."

"Yes," sneered Joe, "and them crackers will get Joshua yet for that."

That night Mary went to prayer meeting and shouted before the Lord, waving like a palm in a storm. And as she swayed, she cried with a great voice:

"He is the Resurrection and the Life. He that believeth in Him, though he were dead, yet shall he live!"

Joe didn't like it, Joshua was always out of a job and never had made much money. He didn't dress up, but went about hatless and in old, run-down shoes. He wouldn't get married and didn't seem interested in any of the nice girls; and yet one day he walked down Main Street with Jackson's Babe, a strumpet. Joe nearly struck her when he met them, but Joshua glared at him and they passed on. Joe couldn't figure it out; but boys will be boys, and he remembered that he himself—

Then Joshua kept running with curious people. Outcasts and tramps. Lately he had found a new religion. He was holding meetings and haranguing on street corners, and there were white women listening.

Once in curiosity, Joe and Mary slipped down town, and standing apart, shadowed by a tree, listened to Joshua talk. Joe was disappointed to find that the "harangue" which he had heard about was more like teaching. Joshua was sitting on an old fence that ran back of the courthouse and talking to a funny looking crowd:

"Heaven is going to be filled with people who are down-hearted and you that are mourning will get a lot of comfort some day. It's meek folk who are lucky, and going to get everything; and you that are hungry, too. Poor people are better than rich people because they work for what they wear and eat. There won't be any rich people in Heaven. You got to be easy on guys when they do wrong. Then they'll be easy on you, when you get in bad. God's sons are those that won't quarrel. You must treat other people just like you want to be treated. Let'm call you names. Listen! They have called some of the biggest folks that ever lived, dirty names. What's the difference? Which ones do we remember? Don't work all the time. Sit down and rest and sing sometimes. Everthing's all right. Give God time. And say, you know how folks use to think they must get even with their enemies? Well, I'll tell you what: you just love your enemies. And if anybody hits you, don't hit 'em back. Just let them go on beating you—"

"Come on," growled Joe. "I ain't never heard so much damned nonsense since I was borned."

At last Joshua went away on a long journey; he did not say good-bye but cried at the gate.

"Hail, Mary!"

And gripping Joe's hand, was gone. The years heavy-footed rolled on. "He will be 25 today," they said; "Today he will be thirty!" They heard rumors of strange things that he did.

"He may come home rich," growled Joe testily.

But Mary mused.

"He is despised and rejected of men,
A man of sorrows and acquainted with grief."

Then at last it came like a flash in the sky, when the young man was in his early thirties, yet seemed to them still a baby. He had been seized by a mob and they had hanged him at sunset. The charge against him wasn't clear: "Worshipping a new God." "Living with white women!" "Getting up a revolution." "Stealing or blasphemy," the neighbors muttered. Joe came home cursing and half drunk.

"Trying to get out of his place; that's it," he yelled. "Criticizing white folk—I told him—I warned him—"

But Mary left her tub; set aside her broom and laid the thimble and scissors carefully in the machine drawer; she put on her black dress and went into the parlor and sat there in the darkness, tall and stern, with an oil lamp in the window that lit the rigid halo of her hair and threw across the yard the black shadow of a noosed and hanging rope. And Mary said;

"His name shall be called Wonderful, Councillor, the Mighty God, the Ever-Lasting Father and the Prince of Peace."

"You crazy fool," shrieked Joe. "You always was dippy about that idiot."

But Mary talked on.

"Behold the Sign of Salvation—a noosed rope."

Joe flung out of the room and fell down the steps and crawled out to the barn and leaned against it; gripping its planks with bleeding hands.

He saw the shadow of the Noose across the world and heard Mary's voice looming in the night:

"He is the Son of God!"

And Joe buried his head in the dirt and sobbed.

CHAPTER TWENTY-FIVE

Jacob and Esau

The following essay was delivered as the commencement address to the graduating class of Talladega College of 1944. In addition to offering a scathing critique of how Jews and Christians have traditionally viewed the characters of Jacob and Esau (lauding the former and condemning the latter), Du Bois exhibits his ability to employ biblical stories and images to address the pressing social problems of his day.

I remember very vividly the Sunday-school room where I spent the Sabbaths of my early years. It had been newly built after a disastrous fire; the room was large and full of sunlight; nice new chairs were grouped around where the classes met. My class was in the center, so that I could look out upon the elms of Main Street and see the passers-by. But I was interested usually in the lessons and in my fellow students and the frail rather nervous teacher, who tried to make the Bible and its ethics clear to us. We were a trial to her, full of mischief, restless and even noisy; but perhaps more especially when we asked questions. And on the story of Jacob and Esau we did ask questions. My judgment then and my judgment now is very unfavorable to Jacob. I thought that he was a cad and a liar and I did not see how possibly he could be made the hero of a Sunday-school lesson.

Many days have passed since then and the world has gone through astonishing changes. But basically, my judgment of Jacob has not greatly changed and I have often promised myself the pleasure of talking about him publicly, and especially to young people. This is the first time that I have had the opportunity.

My subject then is "Jacob and Esau," and I want to examine these two men and the ideas which they represent; and the way in which those ideas have come to our day. Of course, our whole interpretation of this age-old story of Jewish mythology has greatly changed. We look upon these Old Testament stories today not as untrue and yet not as literally true. They are simple, they have their truths, and yet they are not by any means the expression of eternal verity. Here were brought forward for the education of Jewish children and for the interpretation of Jewish life to the world, two men: one small, lithe and quick-witted; the other tall, clumsy and impetuous; a hungry, hard-bitten man.

Historically, we know how these two types came to be set forth by the Bards of Israel. When the Jews marched north after escaping from slavery in Egypt, they penetrated and passed through the land of Edom; the land that lay between the Dead Sea and Egypt. It was an old center of hunters and nomads, and the Israelites, while they admired the strength and organization of the Edomites, looked down upon them as lesser men; as men who did not have the Great Plan. Now the Great Plan of the Israelites was the building of a strong, concentered state under its own God, Jehovah, devoted to agriculture and household manufacture and trade. It raised its own food by careful planning. It did not wander and depend upon chance wild beasts. It depended upon organization, strict ethics, absolute devotion to the nation through strongly integrated planned life. It looked upon all its neighbors, not simply with suspicion, but with the exclusiveness of a chosen people, who were going to be the leaders of earth.

This called for sacrifice, for obedience, for continued planning. The man whom we call Esau was from the land of Edom, or intermarried with it, for the legend has it that he was twin of Jacob the Jew but the chief fact is that, no matter what his blood relations were, his cultural allegiance lay among the Edomites. He was trained in the free out-of-doors; he chased and faced the wild beasts; he knew vast and imperative appetite after long self-denial, and even pain and suffering; he gloried in food, he traveled afar; he gathered wives and concubines and he represented continuous primitive strife.

The legacy of Esau has come down the ages to us. It has not been dominant, but it has always and continually expressed and re-expressed itself; the joy of human appetites, the quick resentment that leads to fighting, the belief in force, which is war.

As I look back upon my own conception of Esau, he is not nearly as clear and definite a personality as Jacob. There is something rather shadowy about him; and yet he is curiously human and easily conceived. One understands his contemptuous surrender of his birthright; he was hungry after long days of hunting; he wanted rest and food, the stew of meat and vegetables which Jacob had in his possession, and determined to keep unless Esau bargained. "And Esau said, Behold, I am at the point to die: and what profit shall this birthright be to me? And Jacob said, Swear to me this day; and he swore unto him: and he sold his birthright unto Jacob."

On the other hand, the legacy of Jacob which has come down through the years, not simply as a Jewish idea, but more especially as typical of modern Europe, is more complicated and expresses itself something like this: life must be planned for the Other Self, for that personification of the group, the nation, the empire, which has eternal life as contrasted with the ephemeral life of individuals. For this we must plan, and for this there must be timeless and unceasing work. Out of this, the Jews as chosen children of Jehovah would triumph over themselves, over all Edom and in time over the world.

Now it happens that so far as actual history is concerned, this dream and plan failed. The poor little Jewish nation was dispersed to the ends of the earth by the overwhelming power of the great nations that arose East, North, and South and eventually became united in the vast empire of Rome. This was the diaspora, the dispersion of the Jews. But the idea of the Plan with a personality of its own took hold of Europe with relentless grasp and this was the real legacy of Jacob, and of other men of other peoples, whom Jacob represents.

There came the attempt to weld the world into a great unity, first under the Roman Empire, then under the Catholic Church. When this attempt failed, and the empire fell apart, there arose the individual states of Europe and of some other parts of the world; and these states adapted the idea of individual effort to make each of them dominant. The state was *all*, the individual subordinate, but right here came the poison of the Jacobean idea. How could the state get this power? Who was to wield the power within the state? So long as power was achieved, what difference did it make how it was gotten? Here then was war— but not Esau's war of passion, hunger and revenge, but Jacob's war of cold acquisition and power.

Granting to Jacob, as we must, the great idea of the family, the clan, and the state as dominant and superior in its claims, nevertheless, there is the bitter danger in trying to seek these ends without reference to the great standards of right and wrong. When men begin to lie and steal, in order to make the nation to which they belong great, then comes not only disaster, but rational contradiction which in many respects is worse than disaster, because it ruins the leadership of the divine machine, the human reason, by which we chart and guide our actions.

It was thus in the middle age and increasingly in the seventeenth and eighteenth and more especially in the nineteenth century, there arose the astonishing contradiction: that is, the action of men like Jacob who were perfectly willing and eager to lie and steal so long as their action brought profit to themselves and power to their state. And soon identifying themselves and their class with the state they identified their own wealth and power as that of the state. They did not listen to any arguments of right or wrong; might was right; they came to despise and deplore the natural appetites of human beings and their very lives, so long as by their suppression, they themselves got rich and powerful. There arose a great, rich Italy; a fabulously wealthy Spain; a strong and cultured France and, eventually, a British Empire which came near to dominating the world. The Esaus of those centuries were curiously represented by various groups of people: by the slum-dwellers and the criminals who, giving up all hope of profiting by the organized state, sold their birthrights for miserable messes of pottage. But more than that, the great majority of mankind, the peoples who lived in Asia, Africa and America and the islands of the sea, became subordinate tools for the profit-making of the crafty planners of great things, who worked regardless of religion or ethics.

It is almost unbelievable to think what happened in those centuries, when it is put in cold narrative; from whole volumes of tales, let me select only a few examples. The peoples of whole islands and countries were murdered in cold blood for their gold and jewels. The mass of the laboring people of the world were put to work for wages which led them into starvation, ignorance and disease. The right of the majority of mankind to speak and to act; to play and to dance was denied, if it interfered with profit-making work for others, or was ridiculed if it could not be capitalized. Karl Marx writes of Scotland: "As an example of the method of obtaining wealth and power in nineteenth century; the story of the Duchess of Sutherland will suffice here. This Scottish noblewoman resolved, on entering upon the government of her clan of white Scottish people to turn the whole country, whose population had already been, by earlier processes, reduced to 15,000, into a sheep pasture. From 1814 to 1820 these 15,000 inhabitants were systematically hunted and rooted out. All their villages were destroyed and burnt, all their fields turned into pasture. Thus this lady appropriated 794,000 acres of land that had from time immemorial been the property of the people. She assigned to the expelled inhabitants about 6,000 acres on the seashore. The 6,000 acres had until this time lain waste, and brought in no income to their owners. The Duchess, in the nobility of her heart, actually went so far as to let these at an average rent of 50 cents per acre to the clansmen, who for centuries had shed their blood for her family. The whole of the stolen clan-land she divided into 29 great sheep farms, each inhabited by a single imported English family. In the year 1835 the 15,000 Scotsmen were already replaced by 131,000 sheep."

"The discovery of gold and silver in America, the extirpation, enslavement and entombment in mines of the Indian population, the beginning of the conquest and looting of the East Indies, the turning of Africa into a warren for the commercial hunting of black-skins, signalized the rosy dawn of power of those spiritual children of Jacob, who owned the birthright of the masses by fraud and murder. These idyllic proceedings are the chief momenta of primary accumulation of capital in private hands. On their heels tread the commercial wars of the

European nations, with the globe for a theater. It begins with the revolt of the Netherlands from Spain, assumes giant dimensions in England's anti-jacobin war, and continues in the opium wars against China . . . .

"Of the Christian colonial system, Howitt says: 'The barbarities and desperate outrages of the so-called Christians, throughout every region of the world, and upon people they have been able to subdue, are not to be paralleled by those of any other race, in any age of the earth.' This history of the colonial administration of Holland—and Holland was the head capitalistic nation of the seventeenth century—is one of the most extraordinary relations of treachery, bribery, massacre, and meanness.'

"Nothing was more characteristic than the Dutch system of stealing men, to get slaves for Java. The men-stealers were trained for this purpose. The thief, the interpreter, and the seller were the chief agents in this trade; the native princes, the chief sellers. The young people stolen, were thrown into the secret dungeons of Celebes, until they were ready for sending to the slave ships. . . .

"The English East India Company, in the seventeenth and eighteenth centuries, obtained, besides the political rule in India, the exclusive monopoly of the tea trade, as well as of the Chinese trade in general, and of the transport of goods to and from Europe. But the coasting trade of India was the monopoly of the higher employees of the company. The monopolies of salt, opium, betel nuts and other commodities, were inexhaustible mines of wealth. The employees themselves fixed the price and plundered at will the unhappy Hindus. The Governor General took part in this private traffic. His favorites received contracts under conditions whereby they, cleverer than the alchemists, made gold out of nothing. Great English fortunes sprang up like mushrooms in a day; investment profits went on without the advance of a shilling. The trial of Warren Hastings swarms with such cases. Here is an instance: a contract for opium was given to a certain Sullivan at the moment of his departure on an official mission. Sullivan sold his contract to one Binn for $200,000; Binn sold it the same day for $300,000 and the ultimate purchaser who carried out the contract declared that after all he realized an enormous gain. According to one of the lists laid before Parliament, the East India Company and its employees from 1757 to 1766 got $30,000,000 from the Indians as gifts alone. . . .

"The treatment of the aborigines was, naturally, most frightful in plantation colonies destined for export trade only, such as the West Indies, and in rich and well-populated countries, such as Mexico and India, that were given over to plunder. But even in the colonies properly so called, the followers of Jacob outdid him. These sober Protestants, the Puritans of New England, in 1703, by decrees of their assembly set a premium of $200 on every Indian scalp and every captured redskin: in 1720 a premium of $500 on every scalp; In 1744, after

Massachusetts Bay had proclaimed a certain tribe as rebels, the following prices prevailed: for a male scalp of 12 years upward, $500 (new currency); for a male prisoner, $525; for women and children prisoners, $250; for scalps of women and children, $250. Some decades later, the colonial system took its revenge on the descendants of the pious pilgrim fathers, who had grown seditious in the meantime. At English instigation and for English pay they were tomahawked by redskins. The British Parliament, proclaimed bloodhounds and scalping as 'means that God and Nature had given into its hands.'"

"With the development of national industry during the eighteenth century, the public opinion of Europe had lost the last remnant of shame and conscience. The nations bragged cynically of every infamy that served them as a means to accumulating private wealth. Read, e.g., the naive *Annals of Commerce* of Anderson. Here it is trumpeted forth as a triumph of English statecraft that at the Peace of Utrecht, England extorted from the Spaniards by the Asiento Treaty the privilege of being allowed to ply the slave trade, between Africa and Spanish America. England thereby acquired the right of supplying Spanish America until 1743 with 4,800 Negroes yearly. This threw, at the same time, an official cloak over British smuggling. Liverpool waxed fat on the slave trade. . . . Aikin (1795) quotes that spirit of bold adventure which has characterized the trade of Liverpool and rapidly carried it to its present state of prosperity; has occasioned vast employment for shipping and sailors, and greatly augmented the demand for the manufactures of the country; Liverpool employed in the slave trade, in 1730, 15 ships; in 1760, 74; in 1770, 96; and in 1792, 132."

Henry George wrote of *Progress and Poverty* in the 1890s. He says: "At the beginning of this marvelous era it was natural to expect, and it was expected, that labor saving inventions would lighten the toil and improve the condition of the laborer; that the enormous increase in the power of producing wealth would make real poverty a thing of the past. Could a man of the last century [the eighteenth]—a Franklin or a Priestley—have seen, in a vision of the future, the steamship taking the place of the sailing vessel; the railroad train, of the wagon; the reaping machine, of the scythe; the threshing machine, of the flail; could he have heard the throb of the engines that in obedience to human will, and for the satisfaction of the human desire, exert a power greater than that of all the men and all the beasts of burden of the earth combined; could he have seen the forest tree transformed into finished lumber—into doors, sashes, blinds, boxes or barrels, with hardly the touch of a human hand; the great workshops where boots and shoes are turned out by the case with less labor than the old-fashioned cobbler could have put on a sole; the factories where, under the eye of one girl, cotton becomes cloth faster than hundreds of stalwart weavers could have turned it out with their hand-looms; could he have seen steam hammers shaping mammoth shafts and mighty anchors, and delicate machinery making tiny watches; the diamond drill cutting through the heart of the rocks, and coal oil sparing the whale; could he have realized the enormous saving of labor resulting from improved facilities of exchange and communication—sheep killed in Australia eaten fresh in England, and the order given by the London banker in the after-noon executed in San Francisco in the morning of the same day; could he have conceived of the hundred thousand improvements which these only suggest, what would he have inferred as to the social condition of mankind?

"It would not have seemed like an inference; further than the vision went it would have seemed as though he saw; and his heart would have leaped and his nerves would have thrilled, as one who from a height beholds just ahead of the thirst-stricken caravan the living gleam of rustling woods and the glint of laugh-ing waters. Plainly, in the sight of the imagination, he would have beheld these new forces elevating society from its very foundations, lifting the very poorest above the possibility of want, exempting the very lowest from anxiety for the material needs of life; he would have seen these slaves of the lamp of knowledge taking on themselves the traditional curse, these muscles of iron and sinews of steel making the poorest laborer's life a holiday, in which every high quality and noble impulse could have scope to grow."

This was the promise of Jacob's life. This would establish the birthright which Esau despised. But, says George "Now, however, we are coming into collision with facts which there can be no mistaking. From all parts of the civilized world," he says speaking fifty years ago, "come complaints of industrial depression; of labor condemned to involuntary idleness; of capital massed and wasting; of pecu-niary distress among businessmen; of want and suffering and anxiety among the working classes. All the full, deadening pain, all the keen, maddening anguish, that to great masses of men are involved in the words 'hard times,' afflict the world today." What would Henry George have said in 1933 after airplane and radio and mass production, turbine and electricity had come?

Science and art grew and expanded despite all this, but it was warped by the poverty of the artist and the continuous attempt to make science subservient to industry. The latter effort finally succeeded so widely that modern civilization became typified as industrial technique. Education became learning a trade. Men thought of civilization as primarily mechanical and the mechanical means by which they reduced wool and cotton to their purposes, also reduced and bent humankind to their will. Individual initiative remained but it was cramped and distorted and there spread the idea of patriotism to one's country as the highest virtue, by which it became established, that just as in the case of Jacob, a man not only could lie, steal, cheat and murder for his native land, but by doing so, he became a hero whether his cause was just or unjust.

One remembers that old scene between Esau who had thoughtlessly surrendered his birthright and the father who had blessed his lying son; "Jacob came unto his father, and said, My Father: and he said, Here am I; who art thou? And Jacob said unto his father, I am Esau thy firstborn; I have done according as thou badest me: arise, I pray thee, sit and eat of my venison, that thy soul may bless me." In vain did dumsy, careless Esau beg for a blessing—some little blessing. It was denied and Esau hated Jacob because of the blessing: and Esau said in his heart, "The days of mourning for my father are at hand; then I will slay my brother Jacob." So revolution entered—so revolt darkened a dark world.

The same motif was repeated in modern Europe and America in the nineteenth and twentieth centuries, when there grew the superstate called the Empire. The Plan had now regimented the organization of men covering vast territories, dominating immense force and immeasurable wealth and determined to reduce to subserviency as large a part as possible, not only of Europe's own internal world, but of the world at large. Colonial imperialism swept over the earth and initiated the First World War, in envious scramble for division of power and profit.

Hardly a moment of time passed after that war, a moment in the eyes of the eternal forces looking down upon us when again the world, using all of that planning and all of that technical superiority for which its civilization was noted; and all of the accumulated and accumulating wealth which was available, proceeded to commit suicide on so vast a scale that it is almost impossible for us to realize the meaning of the catastrophe. Of course, this sweeps us far beyond anything that the peasant lad Jacob, with his petty lying and thievery had in mind. Whatever was begun there of ethical wrong among the Jews was surpassed in every particular by the white world of Europe and America and carried to such length of universal cheating, lying and killing that no comparisons remain.

We come therefore to the vast impasse of today: to the great question, what was the initial right and wrong of the original Jacobs and Esaus and of their spiritual descendants the world over? We stand convinced today, at least those who remain sane, that lying and cheating and killing will build no world organization worth the building. We have got to stop making income by unholy methods; out of stealing the pittances of the poor and calling it insurance; out of seizing and monopolizing the natural resources of the world and then making the world's poor pay exorbitant prices for aluminum, copper and oil, iron and coal. Not only have we got to stop these practices, but we have got to stop lying about them and seeking to convince human beings that a civilization based upon the enslavement of the majority of men for the income of the smart minority is the highest aim of man.

But as is so usual in these cases, these transgressions of Jacob do not mean that the attitude of Esau was flawless. The conscienceless greed of capital does not excuse the careless sloth of labor. Life cannot be all aimless wandering and indulgence if we are going to constrain human beings to take advantage of their brain and make successive generations stronger and wiser than the previous. There must be reverence for the *birthright* of inherited *culture* and that birthright cannot be sold for a dinner course, a dress suit or a winter in Florida. It must be valued and conserved.

The method of conservation is work, endless and tireless and planned work and this is the legacy which the Esaus of today who condemn the Jacobs of yesterday have got to substitute as their path of life, not vengeful revolution, but building and rebuilding. Curiously enough, it will not be difficult to do this, because the great majority of men, the poverty-stricken and diseased are the *real workers* of the world. They are the ones who have made and are making the *wealth* of this universe, and their future path is clear. It is to accumulate such knowledge and balance of judgment that they can reform the world, so that the workers of the world receive just share of the wealth which they make and that all human beings who are capable of work shall work. Not national glory and empire for the few, but food, shelter and happiness for the many. With the disappearance of systematic lying and killing, we may come into that birthright which so long we have called Freedom: that is, the right to act in a manner that seems to us beautiful; which makes life worth living and joy the only possible end of life. This is the experience which is Art and planning for this is the highest satisfaction of civilized needs. So that looking back upon the allegory and the history, tragedy and promise, we may change our subject and speak in closing of Esau and Jacob, realizing that neither was perfect, but that of the two, Esau had the elements which lead more naturally and directly to the salvation of man; while Jacob with all his crafty planning and cold sacrifice, held in his soul the things that are about to ruin mankind: exaggerated national patriotism, individual profit, the despising of men who are not the darlings of our particular God and the consequent lying and stealing and killing to monopolize power.

May we not hope that in the world after this catastrophe of blood, sweat and fire, we may have a new Esau and Jacob; a new allegory of men who enjoy life for life's sake; who have the Freedom of Art and wish for all men of all sorts the same freedom and enjoyment that they seek themselves and who work for all this and work hard.

Gentlemen and ladies of the class of 1944: in the days of the years of my pilgrimage, I have greeted many thousands of young men and women at the commencement of their careers as citizens of the select commonwealth of culture. In no case have I welcomed them to such a world of darkness and distractions as that into which I usher you. I take joy only in the thought that if work to be done is measure of man's opportunity you inherit a mighty fortune. You have only to remember that the birthright which is today in symbol draped over your shoulders is a heritage which has been preserved all too often by the lying, stealing and murdering of the Jacobs of the world, and if these are the only means by which this birthright can be preserved in the future, it is not worth the price. I do not believe this, and I lay it upon your hearts to prove that this not only need not be true, but is eternally and forever false.

CHAPTER TWENTY-SIX

The Negro and the Warsaw Ghetto

Du Bois offered this address to a 1952 gathering in New York City honoring the Jewish resistance fighters of the Warsaw ghetto. In addition to discussing his recollections of Europe prior to and immediately after World War II, Du Bois acknowledges that his understanding of the persecution of Jews and the tragedy of the Warsaw Ghetto led him to an even greater understanding of inequality and injustice. The problems of the twentieth century were not limited to the color line specifically but included "perverted teaching and human hate and prejudice" in general.

I have been to Poland three times. The first time was fifty-nine years ago, when I was a student at the University of Berlin. I had been talking to my schoolmate, Stanislaus Ritter von Estreicher. I had been telling him of the race problem in America, which seemed to me at the time the only race problem and the greatest social problem of the world. He brushed it aside. He said, "You know nothing, really, about real race problems." Then he began to tell me about the problem of the Poles and particularly of that part of them who were included in the German empire; of their limited education; of the refusal to let them speak their own language; of the few careers that they were allowed to follow; of the continued insult to their culture and family life.

I was astonished; because race problems at the time were to me purely problems of color, and principally of slavery in the United States and near-slavery in Africa. I promised faithfully that when I went on my vacation that summer, I would stop to see him in his home at Krakow, Poland, where his father was librarian of the university.

197

I went down to South Germany through Switzerland to Italy, and then came back by Venice and Vienna and went out through Austria, Czechoslovakia and into German Poland and there, on the way, I had a new experience with a new race problem. I was traveling from Budapest through Hungary to a small town in Galicia, where I planned to spend the night. The cabman looked at me and asked if I wanted to stop "unter die Juden." I was a little puzzled, but told him "Yes." So we went to a little Jewish hotel on a small, out-of-the way street. There I realized another problem of race or religion, I did not know which, which had to do with the treatment and segregation of large numbers of human beings. I went on to Krakow, becoming more and more aware of two problems of human groups, and then came back to the university, not a little puzzled as to my own race problem and its place in the world.

Gradually I became aware of the Jewish problem of the modern world and something of its history. In Poland I learned little because the university and its teachers and students were hardly aware themselves of what this problem was, and how it influenced them, or what its meaning was in their life. In Germany I saw it continually obtruding, but being suppressed and seldom mentioned. I remember once visiting on a social occasion in a small German town. A German student was with me and when I became uneasily aware that all was not going well, he reassured me. He whispered, "They think I may be a Jew. It's not you they object to, it's me." I was astonished. It had never occurred to me until then that any exhibition of race prejudice could be anything but color prejudice. I knew that this young man was pure German, yet his dark hair and handsome face made our friends suspicious. Then I went further to investigate this new phenomenon in my experience.

Thirteen years after that I passed again through Poland and Warsaw. It was in the darkness, both physically and spiritually. Hitler was supreme in Germany where I had been visiting for five months and I sensed the oncoming storm. I passed through Warsaw into the Soviet Union just three years before the horror fell upon that city.

But in Berlin, before I left, I sensed something of the Jewish problem and its growth in the generation since my student days. I went to the Jewish quarter one day and entered a bookstore. It was quiet and empty. After a time a man came into the room and very quietly he asked me what I was looking for. I mentioned certain books and browsed among those he pointed out. He said nothing more nor did I. I felt his suspicion and at last I wandered out. I went that night to a teacher's home. There were a few Americans and several Germans present. The curtains were carefully drawn and then the teacher spoke. He defended the Nazi program in the main—its employment, its housing and roads; but he frankly confessed that he was ashamed of the treatment of the Jews or at least some of them. He blamed some severely but he had friends among them and he was ashamed of their treatment.

Then at midnight I entered Poland. It was dark—dark not only in the smoke, but in the soul of its people, who whispered in the night as we rode slowly through the murk of the railway yards.

Then finally, three years ago I was in Warsaw. I have seen something of human upheaval in this world: the scream and shots of a race riot in Atlanta; the marching of the Ku Klux Klan; the threat of courts and police; the neglect and destruction of human habitation; but nothing in my wildest imagination was equal to what I saw in Warsaw in 1949. I would have said before seeing it that it was impossible for a civilized nation with deep religious convictions and outstanding religious institutions; with literature and art; to treat fellow human beings as Warsaw had been treated. There had been complete, planned and utter destruction. Some streets had been so obliterated that only by using photographs of the past could they tell where the street was. And no one mentioned the total of the dead, the sum of destruction, the story of crippled and insane, the widows and orphans.

The astonishing thing, of course, was the way that in the midst of all these memories of war and destruction, the people were rebuilding the city with an enthusiasm that was simply unbelievable. A city and a nation was literally rising from the dead. Then, one afternoon, I was taken out to the former ghetto. I knew all too little of its story although I had visited ghettos in parts of Europe, particularly in Frankfurt, Germany. Here there was not much to see. There was complete and total waste, and a monument. And the monument brought back again the problem of race and religion, which so long had been my own particular and separate problem. Gradually, from looking and reading, I rebuilt the story of this extraordinary resistance to oppression and wrong in a day of complete frustration, with enemies on every side: a resistance which involved death and destruction for hundreds and hundreds of human beings; a deliberate sacrifice in life for a great ideal in the face of the fact that the sacrifice might be completely in vain.

The result of these three visits, and particularly of my view of the Warsaw ghetto, was not so much clearer understanding of the Jewish problem in the world as it was a real and more complete understanding of the Negro problem. In the first place, the problem of slavery, emancipation, and caste in the United States was no longer in my mind a separate and unique thing as I had so long conceived it. It was not even solely a matter of color and physical and racial characteristics, which was particularly a hard thing for me to learn, since for a lifetime the color line had been a real and efficient cause of misery. It was not merely a matter of religion. I had seen religions of many kinds—I had sat in the

Shinto temples of Japan, in the Baptist churches of Georgia, in the Catholic cathedral of Cologne and in Westminster Abbey.

No, the race problem in which I was interested cut across lines of color and physique and belief and status and was a matter of cultural patterns, perverted teaching and human hate and prejudice, which reached all sorts of people and caused endless evil to all men. So that the ghetto of Warsaw helped me to emerge from a certain social provincialism into a broader conception of what the fight against race segregation, religious discrimination, and the oppression by wealth had to become if civilization was going to triumph and broaden in the world.

I remembered now my schoolmate, Stanislaus. He has long been dead and he died refusing to be a stoolpigeon for the Nazis in conquered Poland. He gave his life for a great cause. How broad it eventually became! How much he realized that behind the Polish problem lay the Jewish problem and that all were one crime against civilization, I do not know.

I remember now one scene in Poland over a half century ago. It was of worship in a Catholic church. The peasants were crowded together and were groveling on their knees. They were in utter subjection to a powerful hierarchy. And out of that, today, they have crawled and fought and struggled. They see the light.

My friend, Gabriel D'Arboussier, an African, recently visited Warsaw and wrote: "At the entrance to the city rises an imposing mausoleum erected to the memory of the 40,000 soldiers of the Red Army who fell for the liberation of Warsaw and who are all buried there. This is no cemetery, cut off from the living, but the last resting place of these glorious dead, near whom the living come to sit and ponder the sacrifice of those to whom they owe life. Had I seen nothing else, that mausoleum alone would have taught me enough to understand the Polish people's will to peace and its attachment to the Soviet Union. But there is more to tell and it cannot be too often told: of Poland's thirty-two million inhabitants six and a half million died. There is also Warsaw, 83 percent destroyed and its population reduced from over a million to 22,000, and the poignant spectacle of the flattened ghetto."

But where are we going—whither are we drifting? We are facing war, taxation, hate and cowardice and particularly increasing division of aim and opinion within our own groups. Negroes are dividing by social classes, and selling their souls to those who want war and colonialism, in order to become part of the ruling plutarchy, and encourage their sons to kill "Gooks." Among Jews there is the same dichotomy and inner strife, which forgets the bravery of the Warsaw ghetto and the bones of the thousands of dead who still lie buried in that dust. All this should lead both these groups and others to reassess and reformulate the problems of our day, whose solution belongs to no one group: the stopping of war and preparation for war; increased expenditure for schools better than we have or are likely to have in our present neglect and suppression of education; the curbing of the freedom of industry for the public welfare; and amid all this, the right to think, talk, study, without fear of starvation or jail. This is a present problem of all Americans and becomes the pressing problem of the civilized world.

Index

abolition: and black religion, 53, 82–83; churches and, 71, 73; Quakers and, 175

Africa: Crummell in, 62; early Christianity in, 110–11; missionaries in, 12, 177–78; religion in, 48–51, 110–11, 163–64

African Methodist Episcopal Church, 9, 30, 36–37, 51, 131–32

African Methodist Episcopal Zion Church, 37–38, 51, 125–26

agnosticism, 4, 7–8

Alexander, Archibald, 76

Allen, Richard, 29–30

amusement, 6–7, 19–28; black churches and, 34; definition of, 22; need for, 22–23

Aptheker, Herbert, 5–8, 10

art, industry and, 193

Asbury, Bishop, 74

athletics, 26–27

Atlanta, black churches in, 127–32

Baltimore, white churches in, 105

baptism, 51; and slavery, 70–71, 114–15

Baptist Church, 51–52, 125; on amusement, 24; in Atlanta, 127, 129–31; black influence on, 49, 165; and black people, 163; history of, 122–23; in Philadelphia, 31, 36, 38–39; and slavery, 71–72, 124, 175

Bennet College, 128

Bethel Church, 30, 49–50; organization of, 32–33

billiards, 23

black churches, 10–11, 47–56; and amusement, 19–28, 34; in Atlanta, 127–32; criticism of, 45–46; differentiation of functions of, 25–26; founding of, 164–65; functions of, 21, 32–36; history of, 29–32, 82–85, 113; hypocrisy of, 24; need for reform in, 22; in Philadelphia, 29–42; recommendations for, 46; recreational function of, 21; social functions of, 15–16, 33–34, 49–50; sociological study of, 109–40; Southern whites and, 137–40; spiritual functions of, 52–53; statistical breakdown of, 31; status of, 36–42, 125–27

203

About the Editor

Phil Zuckerman grew up in Pacific Palisades, California. He received his B.A., M.A., and Ph.D. degrees (1998) from the University of Oregon. He is also the author of *Strife in the Sanctuary: Religious Schism in a Jewish Community* (AltaMira Press, 1999). He is currently a professor of sociology at Pitzer College.